THE BRITISH
INDUSTRIAL CANAL

INTERSECTIONS IN LITERATURE AND SCIENCE

Do we still live in a world of 'two cultures', as C. P. Snow so memorably suggested in the late 1950s? Recent literary scholarship suggests that we don't, though there do continue to be misunderstandings between scientists and humanities practitioners. This series is concerned with the intersections between literary research and scientific and technological advances. It is concerned with the ways in which science as a range of practices and philosophies, and technologies in all their guises, inform literary practice; in how science can also be challenged by literary practices and representations; and in what happens to each of these discourses when they are brought into play with each other. Literature and Science publishes pathfinding research which examines the conjunctions and disjunctions that occur when (possibly) different world views are brought together. It is our mission to bring to readers and scholars at all levels innovative thinking and writing about scientific and literary narratives that concern themselves with the medical humanities, ecocriticism, representations of technology and science fictions.

THE BRITISH INDUSTRIAL CANAL

READING THE WATERWAYS FROM THE EIGHTEENTH CENTURY TO THE ANTHROPOCENE

Jodie Matthews

UNIVERSITY OF WALES PRESS
CARDIFF
2023

www.uwp.co.uk

British Library CIP Data
A catalogue record for this book is available from the British Library.

ISBN: 978-1-83772-003-3
e-ISBN: 978-1-83772-004-0

The right of Jodie Matthews to be identified as author of this work has been
asserted in accordance with sections 77 and 79 of the Copyright, Designs
and Patents Act 1988.

Typeset by Marie Doherty
Printed by CPI Antony Rowe, Melksham

CONTENTS

This book is dedicated to
Roger, Belinda and Xanthe

ACKNOWLEDGEMENTS

I am grateful to have had opportunities to work through some of these ideas with academic and non-academic audiences; those ideas have undoubtedly been sharpened via the keen questions people were generous enough to pose. These occasions include Inland Waterways Association talks in Manchester and York, the Railway and Canal Historical Society conference in Birmingham (2017), the 'Brindley 300' conference at the National Waterways Museum, Ellesmere Port (2016), 'Disrupted Histories, Recovered Pasts' at Bath Spa University (2018), a 'Learning at lunchtime' talk on George Smith of Coalville at the National Waterways Museum in Gloucester (2018), and academic lectures at Portsmouth University, at Leeds Beckett University, for the Institute of Historical Research and for the 'Water Works: The Arts of Water Management' symposium at Northumbria University (2022). The international 'Environment and Culture in Britain, 1688–1851' forum, hosted by the University of Leeds, was an inspiring series to be part of in January 2022. Some thoughts about Sara Jeannette Duncan (Chapter Three) were tested out in *Waterways Journal* 23 (2021), though they are revised and extended here. Conversations with Maarja Kaaristo, Sarah Jasmon and Kerry Hadley-Pryce have poured into my readings. Thank you to the anonymous peer reviewers of my manuscript. Their suggestions were extremely useful; any mistakes and omissions are my own.

This research has been undertaken at, and largely funded by, the University of Huddersfield, on a campus with a canal running right through it. I am grateful for the research resources provided by the institution, including sabbaticals and funding to go to conferences and meetings. I am grateful, too, for the mentorship, support and good humour of my colleagues.

This book has been profoundly informed by my working relationship with the Canal & River Trust, and I thank everyone at the Trust who has been interested in my work and invited me to take part in fascinating canal-related projects. Most of all, this work is indebted to the volunteers who saved the canal network from ruin and who continue to care for it, and its archives and histories, today.

None of my academic work would be possible without the life-giving love of my family and friends, nor the people who allow Roger and me to combine parenting with other labours and pleasures, especially: my parents, Zena and Charlie Matthews, Helen Gildon, Amy Manley, the Solomous and the Stewarts. And, of course, PBC, who have been there for me forever and sustain me every day.

1

INTRODUCTION

Cutting a channel

I am *Industrious*. On board lives a couple in cramped contentment eased by reflections on oily water. When they try to describe their love, it feels sturdy, capacious, able to carry them: like a boat.[1] I am moored at Aspley Basin, near the entrance to a waterway that bore coal, lime, stone, timber, corn, textiles and more beneath England's backbone. The basin was once all warehouses and cranes; horseshoes on stone and the shouts of working men. Today, I float in front of a Premier Inn, observed by businesspeople at the breakfast buffet. The water in which I sit is no longer polluted by the industry the canal originally served, but the air above has been thick with exhaust fumes from the ring road for decades. The motes of coal and black chimney smoke swirl no more over Huddersfield, but those invisible 400 ppm of CO_2 are cause for concern. Across the six lanes of buses, lorries, and cars, a building of glass and neon light leans out, more like the prow of a mammoth cruise ship crashing into the Giudecca Canal of Venice than my own subtle curves. From the perspective of the sixth floor, I appear completely still and picture perfect, only causing ripples large enough to see from up there when I am deliberately swung out from the moorings to traverse the waterway once more. My waters are a marker for those cocooned up there to the season's offerings: glittering sunlight or creeping ice, beads of rain or leaves flopping on the surface. Up there, a figure turns reluctantly away from the view of me and back to her screen.

Canals are often referred to as 'the Cut'. In her live-aboard boater memoir, *Adrift* (2016), Helen Babbs reflects on a stretch of London's Regent's Canal. She interprets Peter Ackroyd's 'liquid history' as one that 'isn't tied to a single moment in time', and suggests that the Cut 'collects around and within it a multitude of buildings, objects, people, memories and ideas'.[2] This sense of liquid history, of the flow of the past into the present, is something this book aims to achieve in relation to the literature of Britain's waterways. Its focus is the industrial canal, with a timeline beginning in 1761 and the opening of the aptly named Bridgewater Canal. Philip Bagwell has called this event 'as dramatic a turning point in the history of British transport' as the opening of the first intercity railway.[3] As Babbs's book demonstrates, the canals do not exist solely as a practical transport network. They are laced through the landscape and have always induced people to think and write about them. A 'gongoozler' is someone who stares idly and at length at activity on a canal. In contrast, I reflect on generations of *active* thought about canals, the connections and implications writers have considered or unconsciously made.

Canals are diverse things to different people: place of work; home; leisure space; heritage; historical architecture; place of meditation; opportunity to encounter flora and fauna. They have had many other meanings, as I explore: symbol of industry, modernity, and the future; contested social space; a place for women to work like men; a landscape to explore and colonise; a place for self-exploration. In the readings I undertake, canals are powerfully metonymic. The book is more than a cultural history of the waterways, and less than a complete literary history of canals. It is an investigation into what this extraordinary human use of water does to our relationship with the industrial past, fractious present and climate-changed future, our sense of self and our place in the world. It involves an intricate and perhaps sometimes unexpected interweaving of ideas, themes, and historical periods in order to read the waterways. This reading takes us from soil to the imagined future, from pottery to the Anthropocene, from canoes to colonialism, from war to sugar, and from mussels to the self – with much more in between.

This introduction sets out some of the existing scholarship and key ideas that flow through my way of reading the waterways. These theories include affect theory, network theory, theorisation of materiality, and ecocriticism, all of which are commonly deployed in literary studies (often having come via other disciplines) but are very rarely used in relation to the history of the waterways. The introduction proceeds by explaining the relevance of *Industrious*, the voice that began this introduction, and moves on to consider what I mean by 'reading'. This includes a consideration of the way in which we 'read' physical spaces with our bodies, in this case extant industrial waterways as a way of being in touch with the past. I also meditate on *when* we are reading, the twenty-first century and the felt effects of climate crisis, a time in which water and fossil-fuelled industry take on new meanings. I think about this period, the Anthropocene, as a particular scene of reading, combined to form the homonymic 'Anthroposcene'. This is a specific context of reception for the texts I discuss that alters *what* and *how* we read. The rest of the introduction also summarises pertinent research about water and about the history of canals after 1761 and, finally, sets out the structure and concerns of the chapters that follow.

Industrious

What is *Industrious*, and why does a 'boat's eye view' introduce sections of the following chapters? Any reader who has walked beside a canal and seen the craft it carries, or looked at pictures of canal boats, will know that boats were – and still are – named for places and people. Some boat owners inherit the name with the boat, others now search for a clever pun. Boat names in art and literature are chosen to be meaningful. For J. M. W. Turner, for instance, the specificity of place to an industrial scene was significant. His *Picturesque Views*, produced between 1826 and 1835, feature a painting of Lancaster from the Aqueduct Bridge. This work has a boat called *Lancaster* in the foreground.[4] An earlier Turner painting of Kirkstall Lock on the River Aire depicts boatmen readying their craft to go through onto the Leeds and Liverpool Canal, constructed in 1770. The artist's Kirkstall Lock sketchbook features drawings of people unloading coals from barges; one is called *Leeds*.[5] The fly-boat featured in an 1858 series, 'On the Canal' in Charles Dickens's *Household Words* is called the *Stourport*.[6] The difficulty of coming up with an appropriate name for the eponymous craft in William Black's 1899 *Strange Adventures of a House-Boat* means it is referred to as the Nameless Barge throughout the text, until the last page sees it christened *Rosalind's Bower*.[7] In Emma Smith's *Maidens' Trip* (1948), a boatman's son is named Leander, after the boat his father captained.[8] Boats are also named for animals and for cultural references. The one that glides through the chapters of this book is named for an idea and a quality. It is *Industrious*, for the coal-fired industry that changed the economy and culture of Britain, for the labour of the people who worked on the waterways and in factories, for the war effort of the 1940s, for the post-industrial landscapes through which the canals largely wend today, and for the work of reading and interpreting.

Industrious (an 'it', not a 'she') focalises the canal, its purpose and its setting in each section. My imaginative descriptions of *Industrious* are entangled in the literary words of others without disruptive quotation marks, but the sources are clearly credited in notes. *Industrious* as a craft outside this book actually features in one of the texts analysed in Chapter Three; here, its existence is expanded and given new incarnations. The book's overarching project is to use literature of the waterways to make imaginative journeys through time and space, putting readers in touch with the past in creative ways in an attempt to newly understand how Britain's industrial history is implicated in its postindustrial, climate-changed present and future. As I walked along part of the Birmingham Canal Navigations in March 2019 with the Black Country author Kerry Hadley-Pryce, whose work features in Chapter Five, we paused regularly to note the layers of time visible from the towpath: converted warehouses and new flats; well-worn stone and cobbles that had seen generations of boots and tow-ropes; decades- or centuries-old signs and bright graffiti; the seasonal changes of submerged flora. Each experience of the canal in Britain is dense with time, and I wanted to find a technique for articulating the simultaneous continuity and change of the waterways. An impossible boat that makes impossible journeys through centuries of canal life, and that criss-crosses the canal network in a way that would never really make sense if you mapped it, seems to me a useful vehicle for exploring both the fictions and realities of time, history, place, culture, and the waters that run through them. *Industrious* is our berth for reading the waterways. *Industrious* also attempts a move away from the anthropocentric, which may seem counter-intuitive in a book about human-engineered water. As Manuel DeLanda has noted, Marxist historical accounts of industry tend to focus *only* on human labour as a source of value: 'not steam engines, coal, industrial organization, et cetera'.[9] *Industrious* is intended as a paradigm that reminds the reader at the outset of each section that human responses to the waterways must also consider the value of water, cargo, craft, horses, stone, and many other non-human entities.

Industrious has two obvious predecessors: one a boat associated with a philosophical problem, the other a human character created by Virginia Woolf. The first is the Ship of Theseus, recounted by Plutarch. Theseus had a wooden ship, on which pieces needed periodically replacing, as with all ships. Eventually, all the components had been replaced at one time or another – was it the same ship? (I also tend to think of this problem as 'Trigger's broom', after an episode of the BBC sitcom *Only Fools and Horses*, and while on a Northern Rail journey to Sheffield shortly before I wrote this Introduction I overheard a railway enthusiast describe our carriage in exactly those terms.) The same phenomenon occurs in William Moens's account of an 1869 voyage by canal through France and Belgium. On the opening in 1810 of a long tunnel at Riqueval in northern France, 'nothing would induce the men working the barges to use it, so great was their dread of it'. However, a reward of toll-free passage in perpetuity was offered by the administration for the first barge through, with one still in use: 'though it has been repaired from time to time that probably little of the old vessel remains'.[10] I am proposing the boat as impossibly continuous, but am also interested in the idea of *Industrious* as a compound object with a transitive identity, shaped by the times and places in which it exists, what and whom it carries, the element on which it is carried, and our twenty-first-century relationships to those things.[11]

The second predecessor I have identified for *Industrious* is Woolf's Orlando. Published in 1928, *Orlando: A Biography* follows the lives and loves of a poet who exists for centuries, sometimes as a man and sometimes as a woman.[12] Inhabiting different times, places and bodies, Orlando offers the reader access inside stories that traditional protagonists may not. Orlando in boat form, as I would like to think of *Industrious*, brings together literary observers, the experience of being almost always in (rather than on or by) the water of the canals, and human lives on board the boat and on the canalside. Rather than anthropomorphism, I propose *Industrious* as anthropo-eccentrism. Writing in this way to introduce the cultural periods and locations of the canal is a gesture towards valuing non-human and diverse experiences and entities as they appear in texts. The book as a whole is an attempt to think creatively about the waterways via literature, and in doing so to think about literature otherwise; to read the waterways affectively, transhistorically, and ecologically.

Reading

This book is open to reading. I mean by this that it explores what and how we read as much as it reads a particular thematic type of literature on the waterways. The reading undertaken is simultaneously impersonal (in that in many cases the texts were written for audiences living long before I was born, and I read texts critically, as an academic); collective (because I read from a cultural and temporal standpoint I share with millions of others); and personal (because we all experience the text and the waterway like no single other person). Here is an example of multiple cultural channels meeting in personal reading practice: in 2018 I was visiting the Worcestershire market town in which I grew up; deciding to browse Coach House Books I alighted on a volume by Tristan Gooley called *How to Read Water*. I am not, at this time, looking to develop the skills for which he advocates, but the title rippled across my consciousness because of the way I had been thinking about *reading* the waterways.[13] Gooley is interested in the little clues that water's behaviour gives us to tides, oncoming weather, local animal habits and the like; one might say he examines the relationships between water and all the other things happening in, on, around, and under it. That way of reading water, I realised, is analogous to the way I read canals and other navigable waterways, examining the human use of water as an inland carrier and the wider processes, cultures and formations that happen in, on and around that usage.

Methodologically, the analysis in this book is open to accidents, coincidence and happenstance that occur because of the wonderfully messy way in which culture operates. The texts in the book are selected a) because they are about waterways; b) because they seem to tell us something about the place of the waterways in British culture; and c) because they are available to me via the accidents, coincidences and happenstance of research. It would be disingenuous to assert that every text to which the book refers has been brought into its bibliography via the neat cataloguing of extant waterways literature. I have, indeed, attempted such bibliographic neatness, but quite often I found out about the texts because I was looking for something else, or because someone mentions them. I imagine the works themselves to be like juicy flies caught in finely-wrought cultural webs stretching across a towpath that I happen to be crashing along. The texts are read roughly chronologically (according to a structure I outline below), and I examine what else is in the web – the political, historical, ecological, scientific, artistic strands. This cobwebby towpath analogy might indicate that it is not just printed texts that the book explores, but the places that produced them. As this introduction goes on to demonstrate, we are lucky to be able to touch, feel, walk beside, and boat along the very canals that played a vital economic role in industrial Britain – and which had a profound cultural impact. The canal space is history we can touch. However, the Canal & River Trust, custodian of two thousand miles of waterways in England and Wales, is not in the business of providing time machines; we can place our hands in the very same grooves that canal workers did two hundred years ago, but as we do so there is an empty crisp packet in the grass, a phone in one's pocket, and vastly more carbon in the atmosphere. We might only interpret the space of the past from the standpoint of the present. Reading literature, with its affective register, is an implicit and persistent movement towards the other (of the past or future, from another place or culture, the non-human) in the twenty-first-century historic canal space.

I have nodded towards the place of affect theory in reading the waterways several times in this introduction already. Mind, body and environment should be considered together when reading affectively.[14] Affective states are hard to pin down, 'fugitive and impersonal', moving 'outside of the individual, irreducible to the more conceptual thoughts or even emotions an individual might have about them'.[15] In authorial responses to the waterways, and in readerly responses to that writing, this work considers the many complicated ways in which we touch, are in touch with, and are touched by, these watery channels to and from the past. As Ben Anderson might put it, the affects of encounters with the waterways happen 'between forms of mediation', between reading, touching, watching, feeling and thinking. Affect may be hard to pin down, but it does not necessarily exceed representation; 'instead representations are themselves active interventions in the world that may carry with them or result in changes in bodily capacity or affective conditions'. In other words, the canal literature encountered in this book has a potential impact on the body's next encounter with the waterways. For instance, no matter that I intellectually understand the political, religious and didactic imperatives of nineteenth-century children's fiction, when encountering the emotive narrative and characterisation of Mark Guy Pearse's *Rob Rat: A Story of Barge Life* I could not stave off a quiet weep in the reading room of the British Library. This affect (and the additional affect of shame that my objective academic research had been punctured by such an emotional response) came with me to the canal the next time I walked the towpath and thought about the childish hands that had reached out for this bridge's low arch, the little feet that had walked those cobbles. The 'spaces and places' of the canal are 'made through affect'.[16]

Patricia Ticineto Clough considers the role of technologies that allow us to 'see' affect and 'to produce affective bodily capacities beyond the body's organic-physiological constraints'. While she does not have canals in mind, these are technologies that, as the texts in this volume demonstrate, reorganise our relationships with water, industry and the past. They are caught in an affective turn that 'expresses a new configuration of bodies, technology, and matter'.[17] These configurations also hint at another of Anderson's statements about affect, one that highlights this book's aim to consider the canals' place in shared cultural memory: 'affects are transpersonal' and collective, 'mediated through encounters'. This means that 'any particular body's "charge of affect" carries traces of other bodies' and that emphasising these encounters 'draws attention to how affective life happens in relation'.[18] The implications for this book are that affective encounters with canal spaces today are always in relation to the uses of those spaces in the past, experiences which pour into the present via shared cultural memory accessible via texts. This is what I refer to as transhistorical reading (Elizabeth Carolyn Miller calls it 'heterotemporal historicism'), and is a product of acknowledging the way in which encounters from different periods open out onto each other, and that our reading present always invades the written past.[19]

There are, already, many cultural and theoretical connections being delineated here: a cultural web of texts rather than a linear survey, links to the past, interdisciplinary strands. An openness to networks of ideas partly explains the catholic interests of each chapter. These rhetorical connections are all articulated in relation to the waterways of Britain: a physical network. This canal network, a system of waterways initially linking materials, industries and markets, is also part of a network of lives, histories, cultures, ideas, animals, natural resources, climate... the list could go on and on. My affective transhistorical reading of the canals is, therefore, inflected (though by no means rigidly defined) by an understanding of the network as a social and cultural form, drawing on a field of study that includes – amongst many others – Simon Prosser, Patrick Joyce, Franco Moretti, Hermione Lee, Manuel Castells and Jonathan Grossman. Ideas are drawn in, too, from Critical Infrastructure Studies, coherently articulated by Alan Liu as the analysis of 'the things, platforms, passageways, containers, and gates – material, mediated, and symbolic – that structure who we are in relation to the world and each other'.[20] Some aspects of Bruno Latour's elucidation of Actor–Network Theory could have been written specifically for reading the historic and extant waterways. For Latour, a good text traces a network, and for me the waterways are a good text. The 'network', then, is not simply the designed, built and operating canal network: it 'does not designate a thing out there that would have roughly the shape of interconnected points, much like a telephone, a freeway, or a sewage "network"'. If we read the waterways as textual (and not simply read the texts of the waterways), then the canals do not merely 'serve as a backdrop or relay for the flows of causal efficacy', but 'make other actors do unexpected things': this book articulates those unexpected things – moving the canal conceptually from network to actor–network, from the cut itself to 'the trace left behind'. The network is 'a tool to help describe something, not what is being described'.[21] It is the *reading* as much as it is the waterways.

In *Network Aesthetics* (2016) Patrick Jagoda similarly sees networks as 'ontologically slippery', simultaneously 'objective things in the world – natural structures or infrastructural technologies' like the canals, and 'metaphors or concepts to capture emergent qualities of interconnection'. However, 'while networks (whether they take the form of metaphors, figures, visualizations, or infrastructures) can help us apprehend various types of complexity', they are, like the canals and their literatures under discussion here, 'grounded in the scientific, political, social, and aesthetic preferences of [their] time'. Jagoda thinks about 'the ordinary affects of networked life-worlds – their promises and failures, their freedoms and constraints'. Networks can be understood as 'immanent opportunities for thinking through human and nonhuman relations'. They might *look* static (after all, the built environment of the waterways has lasted, with care, for centuries), but many representations can 'posit a sense of time, duration, change, and emergence'. Narrative, in particular, 'can zoom in and out of networks to offer both glimpses of macrolevel social networks and experiences of microlevel affective relations'. George Eliot's *Felix Holt: The Radical* (1866) is a good example of this in relation to the waterways, zooming in and out of the social entanglements of a town, the affectively interpersonal, and the networks of industry, global capital and empires. Jagoda asserts that 'literature and art are crucial domains of study in the project of understanding networks' because they politically disrupt 'the experience and configuration of space, time, and social relations' in the 'cultural imaginary'.[22] The chapters of this book consider the politics of space, time and social relations in trying to understand the meanings of the waterways today and in the past.

Caroline Levine's work on the ways that forms, including the network, 'constitute political, cultural, and social experience' asserts that 'patterns and arrangements . . . shape matter, imposing order on stone and flesh, sounds and spaces'. Like scholars of intertextuality before her, Levine connects the etymologies of 'text' and 'network'. Literary texts, she says, might be understood 'as sites, like social situations, where multiple forms cross and collide, inviting us to think in new ways about power'. This book's interest in literary history, cultural memory, heritage, encounters and historically contingent reconceptualisation of the waterways is thus vested in the idea of the canal network and cultural networks as temporal as much as spatial. Ultimately, demonstrates Levine, all beings and objects are 'located at the crossings of multiple unfolding networks that are perpetually linking bodies, ideas, and things through numerous channels at different rates and across different kinds of spaces'.[23] The spaces of this book are the spaces of the waterways, but this literal canal network is read literally and imaginatively as linking bodies, ideas, and things. This, then, is how I read the waterways. But *when* are we reading?

Reading the waterways in the Anthropocene

The answer to the question of *when* we are reading should be obvious: the readings I perform take place now – or, rather, some time before you read these words. But this book insists on making the *when* explicit. I – we – read from a time of climate crisis in the twenty-first-century. What has this to do with the content of what I read? Why think about the Anthropocene when we think about canals? The short answer is: how can one think about anything else? Climate crisis is upon us. The end is nigh. The longer answer is that the acknowledged conditions of the Anthropocene affect how we read about industry, fossil fuels, and power-shifting technological change in the past. Most of the canals flowing through these pages carried coal, or the materials and products of coal-fired processes: industrial Britain ran on coal.[24] As the Duke of Bridgewater opined: 'a good canal should have coal at the heels of it'.[25] Hugh Malet asserts that the Bridgewater Canal 'inaugurated' the age of coal transport.[26] When I note – in the voice of *Industrious* – in Chapter Two that 'this is where it all begins', I refer to the industrial canal in Britain, to a coal-fired, super-charged Industrial Revolution, and the Anthropocene. As Donald Prothero notes, the 'curse of coal' is that burning millions of tons of it has also released millions of tons of carbon once safely trapped in the Earth's crust by the unique conditions of the Carboniferous Period. This creates a 'planetary "super-greenhouse" faster than ever seen in the geological past'.[27] 1761 can be seen as an important marker in the 'boundary period' between the Holocene and the Anthropocene.[28] Canals are uniquely implicated in industrial capitalism in Britain, and today we deal with the catastrophic consequences of that system.

I am not, of course, citing a straightforward cause and effect between British industrial canals and climate crisis. For a start, that would be a Eurocentric perspective. For instance, as Kenneth Pomeranz pointed out, the ubiquity of Chinese canals meant that they had the edge over Europe when it came to waterways until well after 1750, yet China's historic carbon emissions are less than those of the EU (from 1850 to 2012, 12% and 17% respectively).[29] Neither am I suggesting that access to coal was the key or only driver of rapid industrialisation.

This is an ongoing debate amongst economic historians. Philip Hoffman indicates that the connections between coal and the textile industry were initially helpful, and the cutting of transport costs important, but 'coal alone is not the answer' to the question of why Britain's industrial economy raced ahead. What really mattered, he asserts, is institutions – like those that facilitated the transportation of coal. Parliament not only authorised canal building (and toll roads), it assisted by rearranging property rights and 'offering land owners a credible promise of compensation'.[30] Not singular cause and effect, then, but as Andreas Malm outlines in *Fossil Capital* (2016), 'every impact of anthropogenic climate change carries the imprint of every human act with radiative forcing, ... the aftermath and the source – intimately coupled yet strangely disconnected'. For Malm, 'the fossil economy has one incontestable birthplace: Britain'. In the transition from mills powered by falling or moving water to steam, Malm asserts that steam won out because of its 'mobility in space', and the implications of industrial mobility for access to (and exploitation of) human labour.[31] That mobility is due, in part, to the transport network that could bring fossil fuel to industry: the canal. Canals are part of what Miller calls 'the broader complex of extraction-based life and the forms and practices that support it'.[32] In other words, to avoid discussion of the waterways as a *contribution* to the economic and energy system that has changed the climate, and from which we do not seem able to divest ourselves, despite its effects, would be negligent.

The number of critical responses to the Anthropocene in the Humanities alone (let alone in science subjects) is dizzying. Simply put, the Anthropocene is the unit of geological time in which human activities have had an impact on the Earth's ecosystems. Some place the beginning of the Anthropocene as the beginning of the Industrial Revolution, a marker that has profound implications for my study of the waterways. Others suggest that its roots are much deeper in human time, in the rise of agriculture.[33] It might be 'only now' apparent what it meant to burn coal in the eighteenth century, but 'more than half of the carbon exhaled into the atmosphere by the burning of fossil fuels has been emitted in just the past three decades'. The opening of the Bridgewater Canal may have aided the transition from water power to steam by making coal more readily available in Manchester, but it was not inevitable that climate change related to carbon dioxide in the atmosphere would be the result. Indeed, 'we have done as much damage to the fate of the planet and its ability to sustain human life and civilization', says David Wallace-Wells, 'since Al Gore published his first book on climate than in all the centuries – and millennia – that came before'.[34] Malm calls for a return to history, as I am making, 'eyes wide open', to reconsider the place of the waterways 'in the historical totality of the fossil economy'.[35]

The climate crisis clearly affects the operation of the waterways. As Juha Schweighofer has detailed in a European context, flooding results in 'the suspension of navigation and . . . damage to the inland waterway infrastructure as well as the property and health of human beings'.[36] People in West Yorkshire witnessed this dramatically in 2016, for instance, when flooding on the Calder and Hebble Navigation in West Yorkshire caused bridges to collapse, roads to crack, and boats to sink.[37] At the other extreme, 'periods of drought may lead to reduced discharge and low water levels'.[38] This is, of course, not a new problem. When the industrial canal network was in its infancy, it lacked reservoirs to counter long spells of dry weather and this, along with competition for supply, caused canal companies frequently to complain of severe water shortages. The late-eighteenth-century infrastructure responses to drought in the form of reservoirs are, in some cases, still part of Britain's drought preparedness today.[39] The frequency and severity of drought and flooding that we now face is of a different order of magnitude to those experienced as the canal age dawned, partly because of the long-term impact of the industrial canal.[40] The material actuality of this book's focus is therefore different in a time of extreme weather from any other point in the canals' history. But how does the Anthropocene affect our *reading*?

One might ask what a geological period has to do with reading at all. As Celia Deane-Drummond reminds us, geology already makes its meaning through the reading of signs: it is a semiotic practice.[41] Bronislaw Szerszynski explains that what he calls 'natural geological monuments' such as sections of different strata, like those witnessed in the cutting of deep canals, 'can bring together different temporal and spatial registers' because in geology 'vertical *space* corresponds to planetary geological *time*'.[42] This is an idea I first pursue in Chapter Two, as eighteenth-century poets Anna Letitia Barbauld and Erasmus Darwin can be seen imaginatively (and accurately) interpreting geological signs in and through their poetic work. This particular historical instance of semiotic geology reinforces Dean-Drummond's assertion that the way we read such signs differs depending on human historical contingencies. She refers to the 'gaze of the Anthropocene', with a tendency to participate in 'epic reading' of a 'brutally consequentialist' grand narrative, a practice that means pessimism and inaction win the day (while humanity loses).[43] While I have tried to avoid exclusive participation in such reading, preferring to weave between the grand and small scale, exploring ways of being and thinking that move outside pure pessimism, this is no doubt the cultural milieu in which my reading practice exists. The Anthropocene, then, as a geological narrative, entails reading. After all, 'the study of human history was the basis for natural history – not the other way round'. Szerszynski takes the geological reading further, asking 'what happens when we start to see [the Earth] not as being "read" but also being "written"?' He adapts Roland Barthes's semiotic vocabulary to suggest that the Earth 'will pass from being seen as a lisible ("readerly") book of settled meanings to being a scriptible ("writerly")' one.[44] The narrative of the Anthropocene has caused scholars to return to the history of geology and understand the Earth as a text. This goes some way to answering the question of why reading involves the Anthropocene, but it invites another. When the Earth, current home to humanity, is a text, how might this affect our reading of other texts and our relationship to history?

Dipesh Chakrabarty, in what has become a canonical ecocritical work, used the positing of a future Earth without humans to remark that 'our usual historical practices for visualizing times, past and future, times inaccessible to us personally – the exercise of historical understanding – are thrown into a deep contradiction and confusion'.[45] The Anthropocene is not *just* geological, environmental and planetary; it is epistemological. One of the obvious contradictions of writing about (and in) the Anthropocene, especially in this book that focalises the movement of the coal that fuelled industrial Britain, is that I would not wish to live in a pre-industrial civilisation. My life expectancy is, as far as I can tell, satisfactory (though this may alter through the life course from factors such as global heating, pandemics, and antibiotic resistance). I have survived two childbirths, with the luxury of healthcare that was free at the point of use. I chose when to have those children and received paid maternity leave from a professional career. I vote. When I turn on the tap, clean drinking water comes out. I eat delicious foods from around the world. When I am cold, I choose a warmer outfit from a cupboard and press a button to heat my home. I have a weekend and holidays on which to do things other than work. Most of these freedoms are, Chakrabarty reminds me, 'energy-intensive', even at their most basic: the invention of agriculture, cities, and writing. The 'geological agency of humans' is, since 1750, 'the price we pay for the pursuit of freedom' (p. 210). Chakrabarty's third of four theses is especially relevant to this book: the Anthropocene requires that we 'put global histories of capital in conversation with the species history of humans' (p. 212). Outside specialist economic histories of the late-eighteenth and early-nineteenth centuries, the role of canals in British (and imperial) industrial capital is rarely acknowledged. For Chakrabarty, the Anthropocene demands that any critique of capital must go beyond just capital because 'the geologic now of the Anthropocene has become entangled with the now of human history' (p. 212). Conversely, 'the Anthropocene would not have been possible, even as a theory, without the history of industrialization' (p. 219). My reading of the waterways must, then, go beyond just the story of industrial capital because of the entanglement of human and natural history and, conversely, considerations of the Anthropocene ought to include links in the chain of the history of industrialisation such as the industrial canal.

Chris Otter and colleagues advance the idea that 'confronting the Anthropocene does not mean abandoning microhistory and the intimacy of modern novels, but it does involve an appreciation of scaling effects'. For instance, 'the Victorian hearth, the symbol of intimacy, is nonlinearly connected to the amount of carbon dioxide in the atmosphere and the quantity of particulate matter in human lungs'. My readings connect such symbols with the transport network that brought coal to burn and its effects. 'In the Anthropocene', Otter goes on, 'historians need epistemologies, cultural frameworks, and imaginative strategies and policies that allow us to shift back and forth between different scales of analysis'. I suggest that my way of reading the waterways is one such imaginative strategy. I agree that the Anthropocene invites us to complement existing scaling practices 'with new types of scaling techniques, particularly ones extending across long periods of time and linking technologies (steam engines, cars) to vast nonhuman entities (ecologies, climate)'.[46] The technology of the waterways is linked, via reading literature, to such vast nonhuman entities as climate, geological change, water, and evolution.

One of the implications for literary and cultural studies is that recognising the Anthropocene changes the way we read. Focusing on Victorian Studies in particular (which has a direct bearing on Chapter Three of this book), Jesse Oak Taylor notes the 'uncanniness' arising from Victorian artefacts seeming to 'speak to the Anthropocene in ways that belie the historical remove that separates them from our own moment'.[47] In other words, our relation to historicism shifts as the overbearing Anthropocene insists not just on presentism, but on reading in the future perfect tense: what do these artefacts and texts mean today, and when we try to put them back in the context of their production, what *will they have* meant? In this way, they may be considered, in a Derridean way of thinking, 'unconscious texts' because they are 'repositories of a meaning which was never present', a belated meaning. In this book, I self-consciously read the historical waterways, 'producing and following [their own] route', to find meanings that were not lived in the present, nor perceived consciously.[48] This is not because I think I know better than the authors what they were writing about, but because my encounter with their texts takes place in a climactic and cultural context that they had not seen. Cody Marrs has sounded a note of caution that the term 'Anthropocene' risks 'epistemic violence' in relation to texts because it 'risks obscuring the ways in which people previously lived in, conceived of, and represented nature' thus erasing 'the situated practices and knowledges that are indispensable for any literary or cultural historian'. However, these risks must be kept in context of the term's (and the material condition's) power: 'it dissolves – like the Arctic's melting ice – the historical boundaries that previously endowed literary studies with a sense of stability'.[49]

Our relationship to the past changes in the Anthropocene, as does the way we understand and represent our relationship to ourselves in the present, as Robert Marzec has remarked:

> our very senses of identity, of understanding, of storytelling, of culture, of even our existential, Heideggerian attempts to know Being – all of which have been made possible by the climatic stability of the Holocene – lie beyond our customary forms of intelligibility.[50]

We have, as Wallace-Wells concludes, 'already exited the state of environmental conditions that allowed the human animal to evolve in the first place'.[51] For instance, says Marzec – drawing on Amitav Ghosh's immediate classic, *The Great Derangement: Climate Change and the Unthinkable* (2016) – 'realism as a genre is what it is because of its methodical, trustworthy, probable unfolding of events – all in accord with the Holocene's inertia'.[52] Marzec concludes his reflections with the imperative 'to think on all registers of intelligibility the nature and future status of creating narratives in the Anthropocene' (p. 612). How will we know, write and understand our past, present and future selves? Taking these responses to and questions posed by the idea of the Anthropocene together, and informed by Derrida's 'scene of writing' (which, as well as the ideas from his essay that I have already quoted, examines the way that Freud puts different models of writing, representation and interpretation on stage), I suggest the term 'Anthropo*scene*' as the self-conscious perspective from which the texts in this volume are read. The Anthropo*scene* is also dominated by the affects of climate crisis: sweaty dread, cold fear, unhelpful regret, meaningless guilt, overwhelmed confusion and repression of the realities of what faces us in order to get on with our lives, day to day.

Thinking with Water

There have been exciting developments in Humanities research about water, especially in the fields of philosophy and cultural history, but none have yet been particularly concerned with canals. While many have considered our uses and idea of water, the concept of our *literary* relationship to water as technē, as in the canal, has not yet been fully elaborated. This is the way that water is understood throughout this book (though often counterpoised with water as 'natural' as perceived in some of the texts under discussion).

Jamie Linton's *What is Water?*, though around a decade old, is a common reference point in much Humanities scholarship about water. His approach to hydrological discourse necessarily informs my work on the places and relations of water here. We have been taught, via various scientific and engineering principles since the eighteenth century, to think of water as an abstraction, universal and essential, something Linton terms 'modern water'. Now, says Linton, 'the ecological, cultural, and political aspects of water present themselves to us in ways that challenge and defy our abstract understanding of water's nature'. He suggests a 'relational understanding of water' that draws attention 'to the various things and circumstances that, in effect, make water what it is'. We might consider the history of water, 'a story of how people have drawn meanings, ideas, representations, and powers from water', and a story that is 'conditioned at every turn by co-constitutive forces such as climate, season, air pressure, geomorphology, and countless other species that engage with water to make it what it is'.[53] Radhika Seshan confirms: 'water is intrinsically bound with human life and is therefore part of human history and imagination'.[54] Linton uses the term 'hybridity' to capture the sense of everything in our world being both natural and social, categorising water as hybrid because in 'every instance of its involvement with people, it internalizes ideas, material practices, and discourses, as well as the unique properties that emerge from H_2O' (p. 176). It is this hybridity of water *as* water – what we feel when we put our hands under the tap, in a pond, outstretched under rain or dipping in to the canal – and its existence within the canal, understood via people and places and their ideas and practices, that the literature of this book encounters. Linked to mythologies and practicalities of water (including the digging of canals, which Seshan cites) are descriptions of 'water sources, water routes, and life within water'.[55] One of the scholars drawing on Linton's work is Astrida Neimanis. Her extraordinary *Bodies of Water* aims to, as the title suggests, 'rethink embodiment as watery', troubling hegemonic understandings of the body as discrete and coherent with focus on our leakiness: 'drinking, peeing, sweating, sponging, weeping'.[56] Veronica Strang adds that such a 'fluid concept of personhood flowing into (and out of) things, landscapes, other species, and between individual and collective persons' has implications for deposing 'anthropocentric visions of human-environmental relations'.[57] Neimanis proposes that 'water calls on us to give an account of our own (very human) politics of location, even as this situatedness will always swim beyond our masterful grasp, finding confluence with other bodies and times', just as the encounters with the waterways I have so far described, and which flood this book, do. Neimanis finds it important that we 'pay attention to the specific ways in which water travels', and this book answers her call.[58]

Neimanis collaborated with Cecilia Chen and Janine MacLeod to edit *Thinking with Water*. Strang, in a piece on 'flow', asserts that thinking with water not only helps us imagine the spatio-temporal circulation of objects, ideas and persons (and this is hard to avoid when thinking about canals as this was always their stated purpose), but that such thinking 'really comes into its own when we consider it in relation to other material processes of change and transformation'.[59] Each of the chapters that follow is deeply concerned with transformations in culture, society, labour, economy and the self. Chen, MacLeod and Neimanis's introduction asks whether the Humanities is ready to make a hydrological turn. There is a salutary message for those of us thinking about canals: when they are thought about only according to the 'anthropocentric logics of efficiency, profit, and progress', the waters we purport to think about are 'too often made nearly invisible, relegated to a passive role as a "resource," and subjected to containment, commodification, and instrumentalization'.[60] This is a vision of the waterways that I hope to revise, though their existence is necessarily bound up in the logic of capital, and their celebration often framed by the discourse of progress, especially in evidence in Chapters Two and Three of this book. I am also interested in the possibilities of understanding the water of the canals as technē in a way that exceeds mere commodification. Yes, the canal lobbyists and canal carrying companies described the water as a resource that would make money and save time, but the purpose of *reading* the waterways is to show that the many relationships these schemes occasioned (between people, between people and water, between horses and boats, between time periods and places – among many other examples) are much more complicated than those anthropocentric logics allow. Chen, MacLeod and Neimanis propose that 'waters enable lively possibility even as they exceed current understandings', and it is the (sometimes 'disturbing') possibilities of living with the past via affective encounters that I hope the water of the canals may enable. These authors write regularly in the register of the affective, for instance saying that water has an 'undeniable sensual charisma' and that we are 'touched and moved' by the waters we experience (pp. 5–9).

S. E. Wolfe has taken a further step back to examine water discourse, finding that 'emotions must [also] be recognised as playing a central role in water consumption decisions and in water negotiations, governance processes, and policy design and implementation'.[61] It is hard (we might even say impossible) to think, write, and experience water without affect. The aim of Chen, MacLeod and Neimanis's volume is to 'demonstrate how a recognition of water's critical presence in all aspects of our lives can encourage a radically inclusive politics and an invigorated practice of cultural theory' (p. 5). Certainly, the cultural theorising undertaken in this work is invigorated, finds its flow, from the critical presence of water in the texts encountered. Chen, MacLeod and Neimanis remind us that 'all water is situated. Moreover, we are all situated in relation to water', and this comes across clearly in the literary renderings of Britain's industrial waterways (p. 8).

This, then, is the water that runs through this book, as described by water scholars seeming to think about waterways from perspectives that align with my own: historical and social, situated, relational and material, and scaled to encounter vast nonhuman entities. What, though, of scholarship on the network that holds water, the canals themselves? The following section lays out the (waterlogged) field and offers a sense of the history of the waterways in Britain.

Historiography of the Industrial Waterways

Eily 'Kit' Gayford reflected poignantly in the 1970s that the canals could be compared to 'the new edition of a very old book which has been out of print for many years'.[62] The layers of waterways history can be read like a book, but there are also lots of books about those layers of history. As one might expect, many histories of the development of Britain's industrial canals have been told within histories of the Industrial Revolution, often from an economic historical perspective, with authors musing – as indicated above – on the extent of the waterways' role in bringing about or supporting it.[63] In short, canals were better than roads for carrying bulky commodities. In Barrie Trinder's comprehensive *The Making of the Industrial Landscape* (1982), he points out that England was rather behind its continental neighbours in terms of canal developments – by 1700, France already had canals linking major rivers. Once it began, however, 'the construction of the canals had the most wide-ranging effect on the landscape of the period' compared to other industrial landmarks, becoming 'an established feature . . . in most parts of Britain'. He quotes the eighteenth-century topographer William Bray, who called schemes such as the Trent and Mersey Canal 'characteristic of the present age' of enterprise.[64]

What is often termed the 'first canal age' lasted from the opening of the Bridgewater Canal (the subject of Chapter Two) to about 1790, during which time roughly a thousand miles of canal were built, many by 'individual landlords or industrial partnerships for their own purposes' rather than with the foresight of developing a national network. The Bridgewater was not the first canal in Britain, however: the Fossdyke Navigation in Lincolnshire may well take that title – it is regularly cited as a Roman construction (though archaeological scholarship does not confirm this).[65] The Fossdyke is the canalised River Till, with a completely new cut built to link this with another canalised stream flowing into the Trent. Some historians have seen the later canal age as simply a continuation of systems of river improvement like this.[66] Malet points to the important difference between a navigation and a canal in understanding the import of the Bridgewater's innovation: 'a navigation uses a river, with artificial cuts along the shallows, draws its water from it and must therefore follow the fall of the stream'. Canals, meanwhile, can 'go wherever an adequate summit level of water can be obtained'. He notes, too, that the 'idea' of an inland canal network linking up existing ports 'goes back at least as far as Francis Mathew's attempt to interest Cromwell in a London-to-Bristol route via the Isis and the Avon'.[67]

Researching very early canals is inherently complicated by the nature of water: when an artificial waterway is not maintained, water usually returns to the path it followed prior to human intervention, leaving few clues about its channelled incarnation. John Blair, in an imaginative approach to historical sources, uses the etymology of Graveney in Kent ('*grafon eah*' or 'dug river') to suggest that the navigation of salty coastal marshes was already being facilitated by cut channels when Kent was ruled by the Mercian kings in the ninth century. Between the early twelfth and mid thirteenth centuries, there are more documentary references to the opening of Roman canals in Britain and the digging of new ones, but construction tailed off after

1250.[68] In 1539, the city authorities of Exeter wished to make the Exe navigable once more to the city walls, access having been blocked by the closing of a weir channel in 1313. The most expedient route was to cut a new three-mile-long canal to bypass an unnavigable section of the river. Opening in 1567, it was an early example of a pound-lock canal, with six sluices arranged in pairs, allowing lighters to pass each other, overcome the gradient, and allow water to pond up to keep the channel deep enough for barges. Fully loaded boats and barges were still only able to reach Exeter quay at spring tides, and drought made the canal unnavigable: climate has always been a concern with engineered water networks.[69] The Newry Navigation in Ireland is often described as the first inland canal in the British Isles, constructed between 1731 and 1742 to reach the valuable coal deposits of east Tyrone.[70] In 1755, in response to a growing demand for Lancashire coal by salt manufacturers on the Weaver and industries in Liverpool, an Act of Parliament was passed to make the Sankey Brook navigable. In fact, a completely separate canal was built next to the brook despite the scheme having been promoted (and usually remembered) as a river navigation.[71] These examples might be seen as the pre-history of the industrial waterways discussed in more detail throughout this book, beginning with the Bridgewater.

By 1790, England's 'Silver Cross' had been completed, linking four estuary navigations: the Mersey, Humber, Thames and Severn. Between 1791 and 1794 there followed a period of enthusiastic canal building often referred to as 'canal mania'. The resulting network would be significantly improved into the nineteenth century, for instance by the Kennet and Avon Canal, linking London to Bristol (1810), the Worcester and Birmingham Canal (1815) and the Leeds and Liverpool Canal (1816). Canal companies 'made increasing use of railways and tramways', ironically hastening advances in a transport that would become serious competition. To say that the coming of the railways immediately spelled the end of the canals' viability is an oversimplification: Trinder notes that, for instance, the Birmingham canal system 'continued to flourish even after the coming of main line railways'.[72] As Simon Bradley in his 2015 history of the railways reminds us, more miles of canal were built than railways even in the 1830s, and Victorian goods continued to be transported around the country and to ports by navigable waterway.[73] Bagwell records that on some canals maximum tonnages were still being carried into the late 1840s.[74]

I am anxious to point out that much of the historical research into canals takes place beyond universities, and that both non-academic writers and some academic authors produce histories (from the detailed to the sweeping) for the large general readership that exists for canal-related history books. One such researcher is Mike Clarke, who has practical experience of the technologies about which he writes, and decades' of canal research on which to draw when writing, especially about the Leeds and Liverpool Canal and its restoration. Liz McIvor's excellent *Canals: the Making of a Nation* (2015) was written to accompany a BBC television series, and not 'with the academic in mind'.[75] Her introduction to the book describes an approach very similar to mine, a desire to be 'in direct contact with a thing from the past, . . . or being able to stand literally in the footsteps of those who . . . worked in a location every day of their lives' (p. 2). She does, however, suggest that the canals 'interpret themselves' because 'unlike roads and railways, the canals are relatively timeless' (p. 6). While there is certainly continuity, the following chapters actively interpret the very different meanings and the cultures of particular canals in very specific moments.

McIvor's history begins with London's short-lived Fleet Navigation, opened in 1675, which ran from the Thames to the brook at Holburn, and the navigation of the River Lea, and describes early transport schemes as putting the new capitalism to work. 'A new industrial society was being shaped,' she says, 'by the investments of ordinary shareholders' (p. 41). In the 1970s, however, Bagwell noted that 'it was exceedingly rare for capital to be raised in shares of less than £50', all but limiting investment to the wealthy.[76] The Duke of Bridgewater's success (though not ordinary in any sense) in capitalising on his holdings was, in part, McIvor suggests, thanks to his 'willingness to invest' (p. 41). This central role of capital in the building and operation of canals should not be occluded. McIvor's history, like all detailed waterways histories, makes clear that canal routes were always the result of lobbying, disagreement between interested parties, and negotiation. Which industries could benefit from which route? Which existing water courses would suffer? Where could maximum tolls be gathered? How much expense could be spared in minimising the number of locks and tunnels? The documents that describe a canal's passage to parliament, even before a spade has struck the ground, are fascinating records of business and industry. McIvor's book considers the individuals behind these feats of engineering, in particular James Brindley, who makes an appearance in my Chapter Two.

The imagination and innovation that the waterways required, and the new skills and professions they created, means that much historical focus on the waterways has understandably been, almost since their inception and with considerable influence from Samuel Smiles's Victorian *The Lives of the Engineers*, on engineering. It is not the work of this book to spend a great deal of time with this specialist aspect of waterways history, apart from when it directly pertains to the broader cultural understanding and implications of technology. Less attention has traditionally been paid to those who physically built the canals, but McIvor's book is one of the exceptions, along with Anthony Burton's scrupulously detailed *The Canal Builders* (1972). As Burton notes, 'for well over a century the navvy was an important figure in the social and economic history of Britain'.[77] McIvor's chapter on the workers of the Manchester Ship Canal (completed 1894) considers the lives and working conditions (in short: dangerous and unpleasant) of the 17,000 or so workers. John Cassidy literally cast the Ship Canal digger as an heroic-looking figure in a small 1892 sculpture, the dark bronze seeming to make the man glisten with sweat as he wipes his brow, now under the lights of Manchester Art Gallery.[78] McIvor also investigates the lives of those who, on over 25,000 barges, operated the canals, though this is a topic that has received far more scrutiny since the nineteenth century thanks to the philanthropic campaigns of George Smith of Coalville (1831–95) and receives attention in this book in Chapter Three.[79]

There is a genre of academic and general-interest canal histories characterised by an extremely local focus, often in the former case as a product of local history studies, and in the latter because of researchers' deep connections to a particular canal that they have helped to restore or that they boat on. Both types of locally-focused research are indispensable for those of us wishing to write on much broader themes, because their detail and rigour provide historical accuracy. Trevor Hill's 1998 thesis, for instance, examined transport, trade and industry in Shropshire. He situates the county's canals in the context of a navigable river and canal network that had emerged by 1793. As an indication of the *difference* canals could make to the connectivity of trade and industry, the Shropshire network linked

East-Anglian grain producing areas, the pastoral-production areas of north Shropshire and Cheshire, the textile areas of the West Riding and Manchester area, the iron and steel areas of the Shropshire coal-field, Birmingham and Sheffield, the pottery industry of Stoke, and glass production in Stourbridge as well as various coalfields located in Lancashire, North Wales and the Midlands.

Hill is more cautious about the national impact of 'canal mania' in the region than some other accounts, demonstrating that while more than 60% of waterway improvements occurred between 1750 and 1799, by the start of that period nearly 50% of riverside towns were already on navigable waterway systems, and that many towns had been connected by waterways since the 1500s.[80]

Charles Hadfield, one of the most familiar names to canal enthusiasts, took both broad and specialised regional approaches in his prolific historical study of the waterways, from *English Rivers and Canals* with Frank Eyre (1945), *British Canals: An Illustrated History* (1950), *The Canal Age* (1968) and *World Canals: Inland Navigation Past and Present* (1986) to a series that looked at different regions (e.g. the West Midlands and the north of Ireland).

My reference to the role of authors in canal restoration should not be skipped over too quickly; the Inland Waterways Association (IWA), originally a pressure group for the preservation and restoration of canals, has had a profound impact on waterways historiography. Jules Gehrke has done an impressive job of ideologically contextualising the first five years of the IWA. By the First World War, when the canals came under Government supervision, the network was in serious decline. In 1939, Lionel Thomas Caswell Rolt and his wife, Angela, made a now-legendary journey to, as Jules Gehrke describes it, 'embrace the much more simplified engineering and physical labour of the country's nearly forgotten canal system'.[81] The result was *Narrow Boat* (1944), a phenomenally popular elegiac and deeply evocative work of creative nonfiction, which is explored in more detail in Chapter Three. Joseph Boughey accurately refers to Rolt as 'venerated by many enthusiasts for transport in Britain'.[82] By the mid-twentieth century, the canals had undergone an enormous shift in use and cultural meaning, and would see many more. By 1948, *The Times* noted, in relation to holidays, that 'the canals speak at once of leisure and the past'.[83] My revisiting of the literature of the eighteenth, nineteenth and twentieth centuries from the explicit standpoint of the twenty-first is interested in the many things of which the canals speak over seventy years after that *Times* piece.

Rolt's *Narrow Boat* found an immediate fan in a London writer and literary agent, Robert Aikman. Rolt and Aikman corresponded about the priorities of preservation, the future for communities of canal boat people, and potential for ongoing industrial use, and by February 1946 were ready to hold the IWA's inaugural meeting. As Gehrke details, 'between 1946 and 1947, the IWA established a web of cultural and political contacts that helped it reinforce the idea of canals as integral to the countryside' (p. 179). Gehrke makes very clear that Rolt was not involved in the far-right politics of the period, but his particularly nostalgic vision for Britain had significant overlap with those who were (including Harold J. Massingham). Rolt's 1947 preface to the second edition of *Narrow Boat* refers bad-temperedly to the 'left-wing reviewers' of the book who had accused Rolt of 'waxing sentimental and nostalgic over a vanished and largely mythical past'.[84] As an organisation, the IWA could not agree on whether every mile of canal could be saved or whether certain commercially viable sections should be prioritised. Such ideological splits led to Rolt (and others) leaving the IWA in 1950, and their ripples can still be traced in writing about the canals. Gehrke concludes that 'canals moved from being cuts in the landscape that facilitated industry, to becoming corridors of natural beauty and recreation' (p. 185). The following study of representations of canals complicates this single narrative and demonstrates the complex and multiple attitudes to the waterways that exist at any one time. However, it is impossible to approach writing about canals without acknowledging the Rolt monolith in one's field of vision.

Canals and Literary Studies

There are creative writers researching in this area (such as Sarah Jasmon and Kerry Hadley-Pryce), but critical and historical literary studies do not often look to the waterways, beyond a passing mention when discussing industry or mobility. In an example of where canals do get a nod, Charlotte Mathieson notes in a study on mobility that canals 'served an important conceptual function, creating links through which the most isolated of rural regions were both physically and imaginatively connected to the wider world'.[85] Adrienne Gavin and Andrew Humphries posit, in their introduction to *Transport in British Fiction*, 'transport's often unnoticed but integral role in literature'.[86] That collection focuses on technological change between 1840 and 1940 and attendant shifts in cultural perspective, and on optimism about and fear of the new. It does not, therefore, consider the canals, a familiar technology by 1840. Works of philosophical literary criticism (or, rather, blue ecological humanities) such as Steve Mentz's *Shipwreck Modernity* (2015) invigorate approaches to watery literatures and reorientate ways of thinking about scholarly periodisation and thematisation. For instance, trans-shipped commodities were transported into Britain in 'unevenly wet realms'. One might creatively see the Leeds and Liverpool Canal as reconfiguring Britain's place in the blue ecology, conceptually producing an interconnected water space from east to west.[87]

Rivers, of course, are another story. We have very different literary, and indeed epistemological, relationships with rivers and streams, and scholarship reflects this. As Nick Middleton's book on rivers in the Oxford University Press *Very Short Introduction* series reminds us, they have always been 'objects of wonder and practical concern for people everywhere'. They bear not just trade and culture (like canals) but also sediment and conflict: 'they have acted as cradles of civilization and agents of disaster'.[88] They have appeared in literature from the Epic of Gilgamesh to the present. The Cambridge *Dictionary of Literary Symbols* describes rivers marking territorial boundaries, and the significance of crossing them. It offers examples of changes in symbolic states when moving up or down rivers, and the river's relationship to a place and its people. The *Dictionary* also notes that 'if speech or poetry flows like a river, so does the mind', and that the river is often an image of time itself.[89] There is no mention of canals in the *Dictionary*. T. S. McMillin's *The Meaning of Rivers* is a useful reference point, though its focus is American literature. He asserts, as I do above, that 'metaphorically, at least, water is everywhere, figuring prominently in life's flow'. The insistent question of the book is 'what do *rivers* mean?' In 'bringing together different meanings of American rivers and ideas regarding the fluidity of meaning itself', the book attempts to better understand the present. McMillin suggests that 'the systems by which we make meaning are somewhat analogous to river systems', and 'literature presents a special set of conditions in which we can study meaning', making literature involving rivers 'a rich resource for understanding meaning's fluidity'.[90] This is borne out by Katharine Norbury (author of *The Fish Ladder*, 2015), when she collated a list of her top ten books about rivers. Her own work and the list's *Highland River* by Neil M. Gunn use the river to understand the fluidity of meaning about one's self.[91]

The genre of travel writing is swollen with river water, with the *Cambridge History of Travel Writing* devoting a chapter by Rob

Burroughs to rivers. While I suggest that canals have had scant attention compared to rivers in literary studies, Burroughs reminds us that
rivers have themselves been the scholarly poor relation to seas and
oceans.[92] It does not take long to think of a poem featuring a river,
anything from Wordsworth to Kathleen Raine. Challenge someone
to come up with their favourite work of literature featuring a canal,
however, and you might have to wait a little longer.

Apart from the various bodily and metaphorical ways in which
I have asserted we might read the waterways, canals are extremely
textual in their histories. They begin as a human idea, recorded in
letters and meeting minutes. Pamphlets and articles ensue, followed
by Acts of Parliament. Where a boat glides along a canal, a pen always
follows. People have written about the canals in Britain as long as they
have existed; after the navvies have packed up their shovels, authors
construct the industrial canal anew. Nevertheless, they are curiously
absent from fields such as nineteenth-century studies. Works on urban
modernity avoid them, as do books specifically investigating energy
and ecology in the period. Works on representations of Victorian
finance do not consider the waterways – despite, for instance, canal
shares making returns for fictional characters in novels. Though
some pretty dreadful things happen on or are found in canals – particularly Regent's Canal – studies of detective fiction do not tend to
focus on this space. Though there are many Victorian children's books
about the canals, studies of urchins, orphans and the like tend not to
include them.[93] But the waterways are important to the core concerns
of the Victorian period and I hope they will become of increasing
interest to scholars of the long nineteenth century and, as the following chapters make clear, beyond.

As they began to fade away as an industrial reality, the industrial
canal began a new existence in the British cultural imaginary, but
this has yet to be comprehensively explored in literary studies. For
instance, Penelope Fitzgerald's *Offshore* (1979) is set in 1960s London
amongst a marginal community of live-aboard boaters. The boats are
just as present as characters as the humans: *Grace*, *Lord Jim*, *Rochester*,
Dreadnought and *Maurice*. This has yet to be critically paired with Daisy
Johnson's dark and disturbing *Everything Under* (2018), which feels as
if it has foetid canal water dripping through its pages and serves as a
complex companion text to Fitzgerald's *Offshore*. There are numerous
examples of potential textual pairings and thematic corpuses waiting
to be examined for what they might reveal about watery life in Britain.

The twenty-first century canal corpus is dominated by travelogue, canal noir, and romance (see Chapter Five), but there are exceptions. Lee Rourke's *The Canal* (2010) is a philosophical meditation on boredom and the mundanity of cruelty, for instance. A stretch of the canal between Hackney and Islington ('nothing but here. Endless here') becomes the site of unpredictable human and animal interactions.[94] Anthony Cartwright's Brexit novella *The Cut* (2017) explores politics, society and individual lives in the contemporary Black Country, a place I revisit throughout the book. Cairo, 'named for an ancestor who had dug the Netherton Tunnel', makes connections between the working class of the 1830s and workers who have 'lost out' amongst rapacious global capitalism. These people are 'held up for ridicule' by the media, Cairo asserts, encouraged by the same media to vote for the cut with Europe as if 'life's a game'.[95] These literary works are located explicitly in canal settings, and might be productively read together to explore twenty-first-century place and identity.

Flow

The chapters that follow take a broadly chronological voyage with *Industrious*, with a chapter each devoted to, respectively, the eighteenth, nineteenth, twentieth, and twenty-first centuries. To repeat: they should not be considered a survey of canal literature through the ages, but in-depth and connected investigations into particular examples that characterise those centuries, or particular periods within them.

Chapter Two, 'Practical Arts of the Waterways' uses canals to examine the way in which eighteenth-century poetry is threaded into the lacework of scientific, technical, and philosophical culture. It considers the ways in which Anna Letitia Barbauld, Anna Seward, and Erasmus Darwin understood their experience of technological change via poetry, science, and the arts. Barbauld's 'The Invitation' (1773) is put into biographical and cultural context, and read in terms of the way the canal spaces, labour, cargo and connections she describes find meaning today. The poem combines wonder with trepidation, questioning where the technological, industrial, economic, and exploratory advances she witnesses will lead. The poem communicates a sense that industrial capitalism has profound effects on the organisation of labour, on the balance of its benefits, on the immediate landscape and 'Thro' the wide earth' when the British strike out overseas in search of knowledge and new materials. It is a poem of the future as much as our literary past.

Seward's work about the iron industry is also read in terms of ecological damage and imperial exploration. Her ambivalence towards these ideas means that one of her poems produces an intriguing image of a post-collapse landscape haunted by the threat of invasion by the non-white peoples Britain sought to dominate as part of colonisation. It taps into deep cultural anxieties about a post-industrial future.

Darwin's poetry is put in dialogue with his correspondence with his close friend, Josiah Wedgwood, and their mutual (and practical) interest in canals. As with Barbauld and Seward, British industrial developments are closely connected in the poems with colonial expansion. Together, these poets capture the idea that the understanding of physical change (of state, evolutionary, geological, in the landscape, ecological) is part of cultural change, and that allegory and metaphor are required to articulate these processes. Barbauld, Seward and Darwin all articulate lucid links between economy, exploration, experimentation, art, and myth as they make sense of a world featuring new connections via canal.

Even following the dawn of the railway age, the British canal system remained an important transport network for industry in the Victorian period, carrying coal and raw materials to factories and goods around the country and to ports for export. In the second half of the nineteenth century, the waterways also carried an unexpected set of voyagers who are the subject of Chapter Three: adventurers. These upper-class men and women saw the canals as a space for physical and ideological conquest, turning Britain into a newly discoverable land. In their descriptions of what they saw, they echoed colonial travel writing, in particular depicting the working-class people they met as native 'others'. This chapter, 'Colonising Canal-land', thus builds on the questions about colonialism posed in Chapter Two, and the connections between Empire and Anthropocene, and sees colonial discourse turned on the British interior. In this chapter the meaning of the waterways as a feature of national power and industry (as with so much British history) is, as Paul Gilroy puts it, understood within 'a complex pattern of antagonistic relationships with the supra-national and imperial'.[96] The two central nineteenth-century texts for this chapter, Vincent Hughes's 'Through Canal-land in a Canadian Canoe', published in the *Boy's Own Paper* (1899), and Sara Jeannette Duncan's *Two Girls on a Barge* (1891), repeat, replicate, and resituate imperialist discourse in their approach to British working-class people, but in contrasting ways because of the differing perspectives of their authors (a British man and a Canadian woman). They do so against the backdrop of George Smith of Coalville's campaigns to regulate canal boat life, which, from the 1870s, cast the 'floating population' of canal boatmen in particular as savage nomadic tribes. Leisure/sporting journeys along the canals are thus situated in relation to colonial exploration and the lasting effects of a system of industrial capital that demanded expansion and exploitation. The final part of Chapter Three turns to that seminal work in the regeneration of the canals, Rolt's *Narrow Boat* (1944), for transhistorical methodological reasons. It is impossible to read about these nineteenth-century leisure uses of the industrial canal and ignore Rolt's role in *re*introducing the canal as leisure space (though, in fact, his intention was to regenerate commercial, rather than leisure, use). The chapter examines the temporal paradox of *Narrow Boat*, focusing on a textual yearning for an authentic Britishness which is rooted in the past.

Chapter Four, 'Women, War and the Waterways', explores a well-known canon of writing and research in canal enthusiast circles but one that is less often encountered beyond those specialist readers: the autobiographies of 'Idle Women', named for their IW (Inland Waterways) badges, and sometimes thought of as the 'Land Girls of the Canals'; they came to work on the waterways during the Second World War when many boatmen had been conscripted, joined up voluntarily, or left the waterways for other, better paid, work. The Women's Training Scheme began in 1942 and, although only 45 women completed training, and only six women stayed on the canals for the duration of the war, a disproportionate number of those who worked on the waterways wrote about their experiences. These texts are Emma Smith's *Maidens' Trip* (1948) and *As Green as Grass* (2013), Susan Woolfitt's *Idle Women* (1947), Eily Gayford's *The Amateur Boatwomen* (1973), Nancy Ridgway's *Memories of a Wartime Canal Boatwoman* (2014), and Margaret Cornish's *Troubled Waters* (1987).

In a significant departure from previous work on this female history, the chapter also looks at the way the Idle Women legacy has been reimagined in contemporary romance fiction, for instance Milly Adams's *The Waterway Girls* (2017) and its sequels and Rosie Archer's *The Narrowboat Girls* (2018). The contemporary romance genre is seen as 'irresolvably both "conservative" and "progressive" in its form and function', and this chapter underlines and explores the nature of that tension in terms of the history of gendered canal labour and the space of the waterways as a location for exploring the self, drawing also on Lauren Berlant's understanding of femininity and genre.[97] The 'progressive' elements of the novels point to an alternative discourse for exploring women's work, while the conservatism constrains women's power and agency. For Deborah Philips, romance novels share 'an articulation of anxieties about what it means to be a woman, the desires of the feminine, that are inadmissible elsewhere', enabling a different perspective on this history.[98] The chapter looks at the canal space in a time of national crisis, but also what this altered space meant for female identity as constructed via labour and class, and the possibilities of literary genre and form for making sense of those experiences in the twenty-first century. Following previous chapters' preoccupation with Empire, the final part of Chapter Four focuses on the imperial journeys that one of the women's cargos, aluminium, took. Exploring the connections between waterways and Empire across three centuries, I label the industrial canal as 'colonial water'.

Chapter Five, 'Waters of Life and Death', pairs what I term the 'New Nature Writing of the canals' with 'canal noir'. Like the authors Joe Moran reads in an essay on the cultural history of the New Nature Writing (Mark Cocker, Roger Deakin, Kathleen Jamie, Richard Mabey and Robert Macfarlane), New Nature Writing of the canals responds to a 'contemporary eco-political moment', making a 'critical engagement with the rich history of British nature writing and environmental thought'.[99] Unavoidably, they also engage with earlier canal writing such as that of Rolt. The texts on which I focus, Alys Fowler's 2018 *Hidden Nature*, Helen Babbs's *Adrift* (2016) and Danie Couchman's *Afloat* (2019), explore the 'potential for human meaning-making not in the rare or exotic but in our everyday connections with the non-human natural world'.[100] This 'natural' world exists in a post-industrial 'edgeland', a space which harbours diverse flora and fauna in an urban environment.[101] Drawing on the work of Harry Pitt Scott, I argue in this chapter that critical attention to genre writing, both New Nature Writing and noir, brings the text's 'energopolitical unconscious' into readerly ecological consciousness. This consciousness demands a second look: at what the British industrial canal represents in the Anthropocene; at the canal as a space for human experience, action and thought; at the canal as a contact zone with the natural world; and at the canal as a revealing analogue for the politics of contemporary fuel supply. While New Nature Writing focuses on the individual's relationship with nature and the environment, noir, represented here by Kerry Hadley-Pryce's *Gamble* (2018), Andy Griffee's *Canal Pushers* (2020), and Faith Martin's *Murder on the Oxford Canal* (2017), complicates what we can mean by individual responsibility in the Anthropocene, inducing guilt on behalf of a species, economic system, and our past.

Finally, the book's conclusion, 'The Basin', brings together (like boats at the end of a long journey) ideas drawn out by reading the waterways literature of four centuries from the perspective of the Anthropocene. It focuses particularly on energy cultures, Empire, geology, and water. The close examination of literary forms tells us a great deal about the place of waterways in British culture, but *Industrious* takes the reader on a voyage of discovery that is much more than a textual survey. Reading the waterways in the Anthroposcene reveals shifting human – affective – relationships with the natural resources of the planet, and relationships with the touchable traces of the past in the built environment. The scale of our thinking, reading and writing changes with our explicit acknowledgement of climate crisis, its beginnings and impacts. The way we represent human experience, endeavour and success – here in relation to the industrial waterway – is now understood in terms of planetary effects and human extinction at the same time as individual lives and identities. Constantly working across such varying scales takes effort, but that is all right, because we are *Industrious*.

2

PRACTICAL ARTS OF THE WATERWAYS

'Glittering scenes which strike the dazzled sight'[1]

It is 1772 and I am *Industrious*: a vessel; a craft. Water-borne, yet impossibly flying through another element. Far beneath my dropleted timbers are other boats on an old river sprung from the moors rather than the minds and arms of men. The Irwell, with its sisters Irk and Medlock, puts Manchester in place. A long-time trading route, other boats felt a smoother journey along its lower reaches when men laboured to improve the river navigation and join people with people, Manchester with the port of Liverpool, goods with a global market. In time, it will also carry the contamination of the industrial city: ash and cinders, dyes and bleaches, blood and sweat.[2] My journey of liquid ease over the Irwell commences at Worsley-mill. This is where it begins. This is where it *all* begins. In the calm of the basin, thundering waggons delivered to me several tons of the Duke of Bridgewater's coal, mined within infernal shades. Broader boats than I might hold fifty tons, and by the miracle of water are pulled by one horse.[3] The beast burdened with pulling me and my companion boats tied behind will plod nine miles to Manchester, a coal-ravenous town. In decades to come there will be warehouses and wharves to pass; basins at Castlefield, Salford and Piccadilly. Cotton mills will migrate to the banks I edge quietly past, with textile finishers, metalworkers and soap factories filling holds like mine.[4] But for now, there is *Industrious*, a high-flying novelty of the Barton Aqueduct and the start of something. Through the spreading trees, I have a witness. She sees me, each white minute, and she perceives the tensions in what I might mean for her world.[5] She catches a change in the relationship between people and things.[6]

The witness is poet, thinker, and essayist Anna Letitia Barbauld, née Aikin. Her work forms the first case study in this chapter's exploration of the way in which writers understood early canals through a global vision of arts, science and technology – global in the sense of universal and in the sense of looking far beyond England's shores. The chapter moves between the global and two specific English locations: Warrington, historically in Lancashire and now part of Cheshire, and the West Midlands. In this period, Barry Trinder has pointed out, mines and manufactures were seen in multiple new ways, 'as objects of curiosity, as sources of national wealth, as picturesque vistas which could inspire horror in the same way as mountains or rocky seashores'.[7] In terms of representation, Ron Broglio notes that both technology and art work together to transform 'the world out there into inscriptions or intelligible signs on flat surfaces', changing 'the "stuff" found in nature into simple, distinct objects with characteristics that humans can comprehend'.[8] Barbauld's witnessing is the product of a complex set of transformations. Discourses of technology and engineering transformed the Lancashire landscape into a set of plans, which have themselves resulted in a physical transformation of the landscape in the building of a canal.

This chapter argues that Barbauld experienced the change, perceiving it as a harbinger of a greater shift in the working of society, economy and culture. That perception was translated into lines of verse which do not necessarily strive to make all intelligible or comprehensible; they communicate a grasping towards comprehension and intelligibility in the arts and sciences alike. Richard Holmes, in a study of the 'Age of Wonder', asks whether 'discovery and invention brought new dread as well as new hope into the world'.[9] Barbauld recorded and expressed this ambivalence as she explored the interrelation of science, engineering and art. For Lisa Jardine, the 'domain of overlap' between science and art, two 'styles of ingenuity' is 'technological inventiveness'.[10] From an explicitly twenty-first-century perspective, this chapter focuses on poetry that sits in that domain, the specific technology in question being the industrial canal. Visions of a rapidly industrialising Britain from the context of a world altered by anthropogenic climate change and, in particular, images of water from the perspective of a century in which sea-levels are noticeably rising, have different meanings from when the poetry in question was written. Similarly, images of exploration in the age of James Cook are profoundly altered when read in postcolonial terms. In its second and third parts, the chapter moves from the north of England discussed in the first section to the industrialising West Midlands as described by Anna Seward and Erasmus Darwin; while these latter two poets might not be described as friends of Barbauld, they operated within the same intellectual networks and spheres of literary and scientific influence. A key contention here is that what we understand as paradigm-shifting technology of the eighteenth century really felt that way to the poets who explored, celebrated or lamented it at the time. The industrial canal was figured as an important aspect of the changes they witnessed. Poetry expresses far more than the canals' technical or economic actuality – it communicates their cultural and epistemological significance.

Barbauld, witness of the impossible flight of *Industrious*, was born in Leicestershire into a Presbyterian Dissenting family, a happenstance that would shape her 'self-conception and demeanour, and [her] ideas of the citizen and the state'.[11] Her distinctive surname came from the husband she married in 1774, the Revd Rochemont Barbauld, who was descended from French Huguenot refugees. The discourses of Anna Letitia's upbringing made a profound connection between Enlightenment thinking and faith: modernity 'must produce a better religion'.[12] Barbauld's poetry is infused with Enlightenment philosophy, a consideration of what is at stake in the project of modernity, faith in God and in humankind, and with classical images, allusions, and ideas.

In 1758, the year Anna Letitia turned fifteen, the family moved to Warrington, just a few miles from the Bridgewater Canal. Francis Egerton, third duke of Bridgewater, had learnt about canals and engineering on his grand tour and was encouraged by his advisors to commission and promote a new canal, following no existing watercourse, from his collieries at Worsley in Lancashire to the major market for coal in Manchester; he appointed an engineer renowned for his work on water mills and thus created a waterway that would change Britain forever.[13] Hugh Malet calls the engineer, James Brindley, a 'cult figure' whose role in the Bridgewater Canal has been overplayed. Barbauld's heroic rendering of Brindley, discussed later, perhaps contributes to that reputation, and this chapter is concerned more with the canal's existence in literary form than the record Malet carefully corrects.

Malet limits Brindley's engineering role to some surveying of the canal, three years of work during its seventeen years of construction and responsibility for the Barton aqueduct under the general supervision of John Gilbert, Bridgewater's resident engineer.[14] The literary archive, meanwhile, positions Brindley's role as pivotal.

The Aikins' move to Warrington was necessitated by Anna Letitia's father being appointed a tutor at the Warrington Academy; such academic institutions were vital to Dissenters in England at this time as non-Anglicans were barred from entering Oxford and Cambridge, but the academies also offered more up-to-date curricula than the universities, and their high-quality teaching attracted Church of England students as well as Dissenters. Students at the academy were allowed the freedom to 'follow the Dictates of their own Judgements in their Enquiries after Truth, without having any undue Bias imposed on their Understandings'.[15] Such avoidance of bias did not extend to gender, however; Barbauld had some access to the learning that took place under the Academy's roof but it was clearly circumscribed by dint of her sex. Like some of the other radical female intellectuals that formed her social circle as an adult in the early nineteenth century, Barbauld's diminished posthumous reputation was rescued by feminist scholarship of the 1970s and 80s.[16] Another of the tutors at the principled Academy with whom Anna Letitia would become friends was the scientist-philosopher and political thinker Joseph Priestley, who is often remembered today for his discovery of oxygen, and in the 1790s for having to defend himself and his home and laboratory against angry mobs who did not take kindly to his support of the French and American Revolutions. He joined the Academy in 1761, the same year that the Bridgewater Canal opened, and married Mary Wilkinson, another close companion of Barbauld. Despite not being given the full education a young man could expect, Barbauld was surrounded by, read about and contributed to aesthetic, philosophical, political and scientific ideas at the vanguard of eighteenth-century thought. In Warrington Museum, Barbauld and Joseph Priestley today sit serenely side by side, captured in green and blue Wedgwood jasperware cameos.[17]

The sites for Barbauldian literary pilgrimage are unpromising on a wet Wednesday in Warrington: Academy Way and Academy Street are unbeautiful and, of course, little of the landscape she knew remains. Most towns and cities of the north are dominated by the industrial development (and decline) that the canal's moment precipitated.

My own train journey to the town from Manchester was marked by reminders of global twenty-first-century freight shipping: a dizzyingly long train carrying shipping containers, moving slowly enough to catch the names of Chinese and European logistics operations on the sides; glimpses of the Manchester Ship Canal and of the top of a large ship that brought some of the same containers along the Canal from Liverpool. According to Peel Ports, the present owners of the canal, it is a hub for 7.5 million tonnes of bulk liquids and dry bulk cargo and part of a 'carbon-efficient "Green Highway"'.[18] The Peel Group also now owns and operates the Bridgewater Canal, though its waters today carry live-aboard and leisure boaters rather than coal and goods. The lost landscape of Barbauld's Warrington that I failed to recognise was captured, however, some time after she represented it in verse, by her brother, John Aikin, in 1795.

Aikin prefaces his *Description of the Country from Thirty to Forty Miles around Manchester* with an extract from John Dyer's long georgic poem about the textile industry, *The Fleece* (1757). Eighteenth-century georgic poems took inspiration from Virgil's *Georgics* to explore ideas about agricultural improvement, industry, and cultural change – Barbauld, too, drew on Virgil in her work. *The Fleece* contains, in lines about the chimneys of Leeds as seen from Birstall, what is thought to be the earliest poetic description of a manufacturing district. Dyer made notes for an unpublished work, 'Commercial Map of England', and in those described 'how Leeds, Huthersfield, Halifax' lie in a 'homely Northern Countrey, among Steep Hills and Dales' which are 'unfit for Sports and Races' and thus 'undisturbed by the great and Polite' yet are surrounded by navigable Rivers, and Veins of Coal and Pasturage'.[19] Fossil fuels and navigable watercourses drove descriptive interest in the north of England in the second half of the eighteenth century.

Also at the front of Aikin's work is a frontispiece depicting allegorical versions of Agriculture, Industry, Plenty and Commerce – a dense image for the way in which the region saw itself. Later in the *Description*, Aikin described the produce grown around Warrington, consumed locally but also transported to larger markets, including early cabbages and pickling cucumbers. These are today much harder to associate with the town than the wireworks, the industry and commerce, which came later. The rich meadows of the Mersey floodplain produced enviable gooseberries and a kind of damson. Fresh produce was also imported to Manchester by canal from further afield: potatoes from Runcorn, carrots and peas from the Bowden downs, apples from the cider counties (p. 204). Finally in the *Description*'s paratexts, in a visual vignette Aikin allows himself a 'visionary anticipation of the future wonders of canal navigation' with an over-blown version of the Barton bridge featuring merchant ships at full sail passing underneath an impressively arched aqueduct. The Mersey had long been navigable, Aikin explains, from Liverpool to Warrington 'Bank-key' (a name still with us in the twenty-first-century rail network); the Irwell and Mersey Navigation begun in 1720 focused on improving the upper Mersey. Aikin considers Warrington a type of port town, with vessels carrying seventy or eighty tons able to travel up the Mersey with the right tide. In describing a Warrington lost to us, he also points to an ancient town lost to the eighteenth century: water, or rather cross-ing it, had been one of the keys to the town's success because 'there is no bridge over the Mersey between Warrington and the sea, and none for many miles upwards between it and Manchester' (pp. 301–6). Warrington's connection to water is once more emphasised in the manufacture of sail-cloth or poldavy from hemp and flax in the town. These raw materials were brought from Russia to Liverpool, and then by water to Warrington (pp. 302–3).

Aikin saw the development of canal navigations as the obvious extension of improved or canalised rivers. It was the 'original and commanding abilities' of engineer James Brindley that apparently took things up a gear, however. For Brindley, the 'waters of a winding brook' were an inferior mode of conveyance than a bold and imagina-tive industrial canal, including the aqueduct at Barton (p. 112). This, unlike many of the built canal features that appear in these pages, can no longer be seen, lost to the behemoth Manchester Ship Canal in 1893 and replaced with a swing aqueduct to carry the smaller canal over the larger.

Aikin describes how the aqueduct, as it stood for he and his sis-ter to marvel at in the eighteenth century, began 200 yards from the river, over which it was conveyed by a stone bridge 'of great strength and thickness, consisting of three arches'; the largest central arch was tall enough for the biggest barges navigating the Irwell to pass under with masts and sails standing (p. 113). Perhaps the most iconic and continually reproduced image of the eighteenth-century canal is the engraving of the aqueduct that appeared in Aikin's *Description*, a depiction that has left one of the heaviest impressions on archives of the waterways. Aikin recreates the experience of seeing something never before witnessed in England: 'one vessel sailing over the top of another' (pp. 113–14). In 1771, 'Birmingham Navigation: An Ode' by John Freeth (another Dissenting poet) also described 'Astonish'd mortals, from each distant part' coming to the Bridgewater Canal and viewing 'vessels under vessels steer'.[20] Those who had considered the engineering feat 'equivalent', as Aikin remarks, 'to building a castle in the air' (a position one can, perhaps, be sympathetic towards given its ambition at the time) could only admire Brindley's 'creative genius' (p. 114). This epithet was regularly used in relation to Brindley. In his *General History of Inland Navigation* (1792), John Phillips quotes Richard Whitworth's labelling of Brindley a 'great natural genius', and a few pages later 'one of those geniuses which nature sometimes rears by her own force, and brings to maturity without the necessity of cultivation'.[21] One might attempt to revisit the eighteenth-century experience of seeing the aqueduct up close by thinking of the dizzying feeling of looking up from the base of tall buildings, one's gaze travelling up a structure that seems to have no business projecting so high into the sky. That is certainly my experience of, for instance, Manchester's Beetham Tower. It is a more mundane piece of architecture, however, that puts me in mind of the Aikins' observation of the Barton aqueduct.

Striding along the Bridgewater Canal in autumn, from Altrincham towards Manchester (an extension of the 1760s by the Duke of the original canal), the scenery did not alter much with every mile I pounded; trees dropped bright yellow leaves on to the mossy banks and every so often a cluster of boats offered some human variety to the ducks, moorhens, and menacing geese that I met. The markers of eighteenth-century canal commuting remained: a pub called The Old Packet House on Navigation Road, another extant staging post for the packet boats known as the Watch House. With no company but the birds and an occasional cyclist, I spent much of the time imagining the journeys made along the canal in the eighteenth century. When the towpath continued underneath major roads, in particular Manchester's outer ring road, the M60, the noise, speed and height of the vehicles felt alarming and amplified by my dreamy historicising, and I began to doubt the strength of the bridge to hold what seems such a solid road when travelling along it by car. My wandering caught up with Aikin's focus round about this point; his further descriptions of Brindley's designs at Stretford and Corn-brook (familiar now from the Manchester tram map) indicate how well communicated the science of waterways was, as a reading public marvelled at not just the result but the method of making canals and engineering with water. William McCarthy notes that the Bridgewater Canal was 'the only industrial structure [Barbauld] was ever to commemorate in verse' (p. 65).

Barbauld's poem, 'The Invitation', is dedicated to Elizabeth 'Betsy' Belsham, a cousin and friend, and was published in 1773's *Poems*, her first collection. Betsy is joined by, and poetically takes the part of, Delia, virgin goddess of the hunt and the moon, in a scene Barbauld sets via Virgil's *Eclogues* of cool fountains, soft fields and woodlands. Barbauld also wrote an 'Eclogue on Elizabeth Belsham', associating this close friend again with the pastoral and, via Spenser's use of the form in *The Shephearde's Calendar* (1579), with the seasonal passage of time on which the early lines of 'The Invitation' reflect.[22] An opposition is immediately set up between those rural, restorative scenes and crowded, busy cities where smoke 'involve[s] the sky', but the poem as a whole is certainly not a straightforward description of nature versus industry. Delia enjoys the scene with the poet and with Pleasure, whose lyre is in tune with 'the wild warblings of the woodland quire' as she sits on 'daisied turf' amongst 'early primroses', until Barbauld makes a deliberate gesture towards situating herself in the here and now. Delia and the poet hasten away from eternal rural scenes bedecked by Flora, and northern England of the 1770s fills the poet's vision as a suitable poetic subject. She sees the 'labouring plow' on the green slope, helping to produce the fruits and vegetables Barbauld's brother would describe.

Part of this vision, rather than an intrusion into it, are smooth canals reaching over 'th' extended plain' which 'stretch their long arms, to join the distant main' (pp. 14–16). The power of water transport to connect inland territory to the rest of the world is what first comes to mind as the poetic eye lands on the canal. Similarly, in his georgic ode to navigation, Freeth called it 'Liberty's friend' because of the canals' ability to connect Britain with the world: 'Open her sluices and through mountains force,/ To different Lands an easy intercourse' (p. 112). In Barbauld's richer and more complex poetry, the canal's aesthetic contribution to the scene *and* its technological purpose are evoked in the same image. Barbauld reflects on the place of the canal in the landscape with much greater nuance than John Hassell would do in an oft-cited travelogue nearly fifty years later. The title page of *Tour of the Grand Junction* (1819) is adorned with a quotation from William Gilpin, a key figure in the eighteenth-century development of the picturesque as an aesthetic category, determining what to look at in the landscape and how to look at it. In his work, Hassell desperately tries to make the Grand Junction Canal (built to improve the route from Oxford to London) conform to the expectations of the picturesque; this often means ignoring the canal altogether and turning to the countryside through which it passes. Hassell is alive to the industrial purpose of the canals, of course, but the 'hum of men' is muted once his picturesque sensibilities take over.[23]

Having established the place of the canal in the landscape, unlike Hassell, Barbauld's next thought is of the human labour that constructed it:

> The sons of toil with many a weary stroke
> Scoop the hard bosom of the solid rock;
> Resistless thro' the stiff opposing clay
> With steady patience work their gradual way. (p. 17)

The physical cut through the landscape is by no means figured as a large-scale environmental disaster, but as a stroke-by-stroke Herculean effort. Cultural ideas about landscape, the picturesque and the sublime that surrounded the Enlightenment-educated Barbauld should also be brought to bear on Barbauld's representation of the canal in more detail to understand how she poetically responds to this novel artificial waterway without trying to figure it simply as like a river or stream. In his *Observations on Modern Gardening* (1770), Thomas Whately compared smooth and tumultuous courses of water in a landscape, the 'calm expanse to sooth the tranquillity of a peaceful scene' with 'the roar and the rage of a torrent, its force, its violence, its impetuosity' which tends to inspire a terror 'allied to sublimity'.[24] Indeed, though he does not refer to an industrial canal, Whately unconsciously captures an idea with which 'The Invitation' and many other texts in this chapter play: 'the characteristic property of running water is *progress*; of stagnated, is *circuity*' (p. 63). Canals alter such dichotomies of water, because they would be seen to usher in material economic progress by completing circuits of trade and industry. The sons of toil and the canal's designers, engineers and backers have had to 'compel the genius of th' unwilling flood / Thro' the brown horrors of the aged wood'.[25] These are ambivalent lines that I suggest should be read in two contradictory ways at once. First, they draw in the use of the word 'genius' as Aikin uses it later to refer to Brindley. He is a genius of engineering who masters the unwilling water to plot its course where combined economic and geological imperatives prescribe, what Barbauld refers to some lines later as 'the ductile streams obey[ing] the guiding hand' (p. 18). There are disapproving echoes of this mastery in Henry James Pye's river-worshipping 'Faringdon Hill', published the following year. He decries 'channels, form'd by art' to be led 'where no fair current wears a native bed'. In particular, he references Egerton, the landowner and investor rather than the engineer, 'conduct[ing] the swelling sail', hoping that all such schemes will perish.[26]

More strongly than the human genius, however, Barbauld's lines evoke the genius loci, a guardian spirit of an apparently untameable and threatening water compelled to enter the aged wood. The wood is itself understood in two ways. First, it is the delightfully spreading shade turned horrifying. To bring Whately's water to bear on the poem again, in describing the River Derwent he considers the relationship between water and sensation: 'the terrors of a scene in nature' give alarm but in a way that is agreeable 'so long as they are kept to such as are allied only to terror, unmixed with any that are horrible and disgusting' (p. 107). Barbauld similarly directs the reader to such powers of sensation in watery nature. The poem takes the reader's experience of the scene to the brink of 'the brown horrors of the aged wood' but deftly turns to demonstrate art and technology's mastery of the scene; here is an engineering marvel and technical process that tame the flood of water, and a poetic description that tames the sensation of horror (p. 17). Poetry can be understood as analogous to engineering in its ability to manage rising, swelling feeling.

Another way of understanding the 'aged wood' is as formerly standing ancient woodlands, the organic material that breaks down at the surface to mingle with rocks beneath to form soil. Jane Austen writes an idea that comes close to this in a passage about Lyme from her last complete novel, *Persuasion* (1818), also quoted by Noah Heringman in his work on Romantic geology: 'the scattered forest trees and orchards of luxuriant growth declare that many a generation must have passed away since the first partial falling of the cliff prepared the ground for such a state'.[27] The high-quality soil required for such lushness has come about through geological change over aeons, including erosion and organic decomposition. Barbauld has demonstrated an interest in the different materials through which the navvies have wearily dug: clay and rock. Though the term 'geology' was not yet in use, 'The Invitation' is full of it. Dispiritingly, her brother would, in an *Essay on the Application of Natural History to Poetry* four years later, dismiss 'the mineral kingdom' as 'steril, and uncommodated to description'.[28] Nevertheless, Aikin – and Barbauld – had a keen interest in the relationship between natural history and creative cultural forms; their father's colleagues at Warrington published work in this field and it was only via Dissenting academies that natural history entered the secondary school curriculum at all after 1760.[29]

Barbauld's sense of the relationship between aged wood and the soils through which the canal was cut may have been informed by Warrington tutor Johann Reinhold Forster's 1768 *Introduction to Mineralogy*, which promised to identify and classify minerals by, amongst other features, earths and stones. As well as the latest thought in mineralogical science, Barbauld's sense of the soil also echoes that of Renaissance writers who, Hillary Eklund explains, 'considered soil not only as a material resource but also as a site for exploring questions of material and spiritual being, power and belonging, past, present, and future'. Early modern observers knew that 'with its combination of minerals, organic matter, air, and water, soil is animal, vegetable, *and* mineral. It is the living *and* the dead, both flourishing and decaying'.[30] Frances Dolan adds that early modern writers 'addressed the soil not as a given but as a work in progress, and the spur to and beneficiary of creativity'.[31] I suggest that Barbauld's fertile 'aged wood' image, read via historical understandings of soil, is intimately connected to the cut through the earth the newly-dug canal makes, giving access to layers of geological time that were just beginning to be understood as Barbauld composed her poem.

But Barbauld's use of the term 'genius' in the context of the canal also bleeds into Aikin's figuring of Brindley in his *Description*. Brindley becomes, as a genius spirit of water as well as a genius (if rather rough-mannered and semi-literate) engineer, so much less earthy than his biographies would tend to have him.[32] Reading the siblings' work together like this, with Anna Letitia's genius loci and John's genius of engineering, makes the Genius of the Canal that appears in their jointly-authored *Miscellaneous Pieces in Prose* (1773) especially compelling. McCarthy attributes the piece to John, but I suggest that its intimate linguistic connections to 'The Invitation' and the siblings' explicit presentation of joint authorship confound straightforward individual attribution.[33]

In 'The Canal and the Brook: An Apologue' a walk on a pleasant evening after a sultry summer's day brings the speaker to the side of a 'small meandering brook'.[34] The Duke of Bridgewater's canal is invoked by name, and provokes the speaker to throw his/herself onto the bank and envisage a scene 'with the eyes of fancy'. The side of the aqueduct opens to reveal the 'gigantic form' of the Genius of the Canal, clad in 'a close garment of a russet hue' and crowned with a crenelated mark of his mastery. His 'naked feet' are covered in clay and 'on his left shoulder he bore a huge pick-ax; and in his right hand he held certain instruments, used in surveying and levelling' (p. 81). Francis Parsons completed a portrait of James Brindley in 1770. He is far from barefoot and covered in clay in this typical example of eighteenth-century portraiture, but he does, by virtue of monocular perspective, stand as a gigantic form in front of the aqueduct – complete with vessels at full sail – and he leans on a brass theodolite, an instrument 'used in surveying'. There are at least two (poorly) painted copies of this painting, and an accurate engraving by Robert Dunkarton that embellishes the portrait with a large classical urn behind Brindley's shoulder; it is possible that the Aikins saw a copy of the portrait, particularly given the numerous references to urns in the piece, or that it closely enough resembled the image of Brindley in the public mind for it to have informed their Genius of the Canal.[35] The figure compounds the professional engineer and the strength of the army of men who really did get their hands and feet dirty in the enormous undertaking of constructing the canal. This hybridity echoes an earlier piece in the collection, 'The Hill of Science', in which flighty Genius must meet Application, making 'toilsome progress' to ascend the heights of eminence (which are not all they are cracked up to be anyway, according to Virtue).[36] Moving from the allegorical genius of a particular structure, modern and engineered into place, to the very real and recognisable Brindley, propels ancient imagery into the industrial eighteenth century and, simultaneously, like the urn in the background of Dunkarton's engraving, pushes Brindley with a mural crown into an eternally heroic classicism.[37]

The Aikins continue to move images related to the Bridgewater canal backwards and forwards in cultural time. In 'The Canal and the Brook', the Deity of the Stream meets the Genius of the Canal's bombast about its ability to 'pierce the solid rock' and 'connect unknown lands with distant seas' (which, of course, natural watercourses have always done) with haughty disdain. It refers to 'stupendous monuments of Roman grandeur', including 'the aqueducts which poured their waves over mountains and valleys', now 'sunk in oblivion'. In a vision of the future, it declares that 'when the flood of commerce . . . is turned into another course', leaving the canal 'dry and desolate', the river will still 'murmur in song' (p. 86). Depictions of Roman might and ingenuity are thus used to suggest both sempiternity and annihilation, prosperity stretching into the future and the ruins of an hubristic past. Phillips, in *A General History of Inland Navigation* (1792), would go on to predict that the canal 'will be a standing monument of the public spirit and economy of the Duke of Bridgewater *to the end of time*'.[38] From our own perspective, both Phillips and the Deity of the Stream are correct; one can still walk along the Bridgewater Canal and reflect on Brindley's (and others') achievement, but the aqueduct is gone – not because the flood of commerce dried up, but because it swelled and did indeed take another course at the end of the nineteenth century, along the Manchester Ship Canal.

Reading these polysemic lines of Barbauld's industrial poetry in this way, marking out their deliberate contradiction and ambivalence, contributes to the unsettling, as Heringman suggests, of the idea of an incommensurable aesthetic of Nature and 'the dependence of an industrial society on natural resources and depleted landscapes' (p. xv). Indeed, the canal in Barbauld's vision will 'chear the barren heath or sullen moor', sounding almost like Whately's guide to managing the aesthetics of landscape; this is an improvement rather than depletion.[39] As Heringman points out, 'poetry and geology in later eighteenth- and early nineteenth-century Britain are mutually constitutive through the common idiom of landscape aesthetics' (p. 1). The canals' role in making visible the relationship between landscape and geology, occasioning as they do a slice through the earth across a long distance of the English countryside, is in evidence in Barbauld's interest in time, clays, sands and soils and is discussed further when the chapter turns to consider artistic, scientific and technological connections via the canals in the writing of Erasmus Darwin.

Having established the image of the canal in 'The Invitation', Barbauld moves on to emphasise the visual novelty and beauty made possible by technological virtuosity:

> The traveller with pleasing wonder sees
> The white sail gleaming thro' the dusky trees;
> And views the alter'd landscape with surprise,
> And doubts the magic scenes which round him rise.
> Now, like a flock of swans, above his head

Their woven wings the flying vessels spread;
Now meeting streams in artful mazes glide,
While each unmingled pours a separate tide. (p. 17)

McCarthy proposes this as 'the anxious pleasure of a disorientating, fantasylike landscape, something out of science fiction' (p. 65). Certainly it combines the familiar with the surprising: the sails of the vessels long-produced in Warrington (as described by Aikin) are made 'woven wings' as the craft seem to fly at unnatural height. I do not detect, however, the type of anxiety I experienced as the canal passed underneath the M60. In the poem, the familiar image of the watercourse is also made wonderfully strange, as two seem to meet yet retain their independent flow, apparently contradicting the known properties of water. This must have seemed both surprising and half-anticipated in a period of such exciting scientific advance: the mutability of water was under investigation, overturning thousands of years of assumed wisdom about the elements.

Later in 'The Invitation', Barbauld makes explicit reference to such discoveries: 'the hidden cause / Of nature's changes, and her various laws', the 'hunt' for 'her elemental forms' (p. 22). By 1783, just a decade after Barbauld's *Poems*, Antoine Lavoisier was able to describe the synthesis of water with oxygen (isolated as 'dephlogisticated air' by Priestley in the 1770s, whom Lavoisier met in Paris) and hydrogen. As Julia Saunders records, in this age when 'much important scientific work was being done in the home', including Priestley's laboratory at the Academy until 1767, women were much more proximal to these experiments than 'when science disappeared into university laboratories'.[40] Barbauld wrote just before Lavoisier's specific discoveries, but she seems to be tantalisingly close to a conception of the process by which water became, to use Jamie Linton's term, 'modern', the result of an 'epistemological revolution' in which 'ways of knowing and representing water' fundamentally changed.[41] Linton's modern water is an abstraction, with scientifically-understood water being the same everywhere as an essential substance – what would become 'H_2O'. Premodern water is cultural, local, inhabited by spirits, understood as part of the history and myth of a place. Barbauld's 'artful mazes' suggest the interconnection of these attitudes to water, the poem itself acting to bridge the modern and the premodern, the canal and the river, in the way it prefigures conclusions about the chemical composition of water. The 'unmingling' of water in the poem is both natural and unnatural at a time when the definitions of such seemingly eternal objects as rocks, water, and air were being remade. The certainty of where one ends and another begins is clearly at issue in Barbauld's poetic descriptions of water-borne vessels flying through the air, the carrying water resisting what we think we know about its properties as it travels through a channel carved out of the ground and suspended at height. Barbauld's poem not only anticipates the explanation and despiritualisation of water by science, it produces the possibility for modern and premodern relationships with water to co-exist.

Having noted that the canal carries the water 'through the hidden veins of earth' to 'sulphurous mines', Barbauld returns to the river, to consider the 'fame neglected' Mersey as a way of thinking about the Warrington Academy, a 'nursery' for statesmen and poets alike (pp. 17–18). I agree with McCarthy that this section of the poem emphasises Barbauld's exclusion from formal education, though Barbauld was a realist when it came to the tensions between education, class and marriage for women.[42] At the same time as suggesting that the Mersey 'dares to emulate a classic tide', the poet constructs a hybrid classical education from limited teaching and her own reading, unnoticed and uncelebrated (p. 18). McCarthy suggests that Barbauld's 'lines' and 'circles trac'd upon the lettered shore' are something of a sendup of the Academy's students emulating Archimedes by 'figuring their maths problems in the sand' (p. 90). This may be the classical reference Barbauld has in mind, but I think she might also be alluding to Brindley's famously unorthodox methods of communication, and his outsider status in a world of aristocrats and learned men. Samuel Smiles's Victorian writing about Brindley, which produced an enduring mythology of the man, recounts an occasion on which, called to give evidence to the House of Lords for the passing of a canal act (a necessary obstacle speculators had to overcome before they could begin works), Brindley took a chalk from his pocket and drew a diagram of a canal lock on the floor.[43] I suggest that Barbauld is again claiming this genius of the flood for Warrington and an industrialising north. Her reference to his alternative methods of making himself understood also produces the vicinity of the Academy as a place for individuals other than the educated male students to achieve great things. If Brindley can be great, despite having been excluded from formal education, then so can a woman like Barbauld. But she also delights in the opportunity that education, in the form of the Academy, offers for non-Anglicans, whose skills and intellect may now take flight. It is a place in which 'science smiles' and 'gentlest arts' flourish, where the waterways as a product of science may be immortalised in her poetry (p. 20).

The graduates of the Academy will have, in 'distant years' the whole world open to them, to improve Britain's prejudiced legal system, to take their religion through her domain, to travel across the seas – the 'distant mains' evoked early in the poem – and act as ambassadors, discover new medicines, heal the sick. In short, they will make good the promise of modernity to 'produce a better religion' and with their religion produce a better modernity (pp. 19–24). To put the poem's effects in terms outlined by Joseph Drury, Barbauld's combined attention to science and the arts, communication and discovery, demonstrates literature 'not as a reflection' of scientific, technological and engineering knowledge, 'but as a participant in the social and material networks that establish and sustain that knowledge'.[44]

Barbauld's poem is profoundly interested in 'transforming power' (p. 16). This is not just the natural power of Flora to transform an icicle to a flower described in the early section of the poem, but the power of engineers and a human labour force to transform the landscape in the service of an industrial, coal-fuelled economy, in science to transform the epistemology of elements, in the transformative power of education, and a transformed society in which women and minority groups might achieve greatness. Saunders points out that both Barbauld's poem and Priestley's *Experiments and Observations on Different Kinds of Air* (1774) 'capture a moment in history when a scientific and political culture is poised on the brink of change'.[45] Hofkosh suggests that, in this moment, Barbauld's poetry uses the affective 'as a form of knowledge'. She explains this as 'a medium of the senses, a mode of apprehending the material world' that 'thinks through feeling but is not reducible to it' as a way of moving 'towards understanding the implication of the personal or individual in a complex ecology of material conditions and social formations'.[46] In 'The Invitation' that 'complex ecology' features landscape as depth beneath the surface as well as what is in view, geology, chemistry and other sciences, technology and engineering, industry, education, religion and labour. Using classical conceits and female friendship as a framework and store of rich imagery and allusion, the poem is an exercise in apprehending the new material world that the Bridgewater Canal brings into existence, and should be understood as a pivotal literary text in bringing that 'complex ecology' of later eighteenth-century Britain into focus. To read the poem as a simple celebration of engineering advancement would, then, be to underestimate the ambivalent complexity of Barbauld's work.

White suggests that, in 'The Canal and the Brook, the Aikins ask their readers to participate in both the rational aesthetic claims of the Canal and the affective aesthetic claims of the Brook'.[47] Readers are required to grapple with the cases made by two dissonant voices. The Genius of the Canal is disagreeably dismissive of the brook's unpredictable flow, especially as the canal is so impressively buoyed by 'exalting commerce'. It is hard to argue with 'banks crowned with airy bridges, and huge warehouses', a hinterland 'echoing with the busy sounds of industry'.[48] This is the 'social plenty [circling] round the land' that 'The Invitation' predicts. The 'weary stroke[s]' of the 'sons of toil' who built the canal resonate throughout the poem's proceeding lines, however, undermining the obviousness of that social plenty: to whom is it available and how is it distributed? Unlike John Dyer's over-optimistic poetic speculation about the factory-style organisation of labour following industrialisation in *The Fleece* – an idealism that seems horribly misplaced with the benefit of hindsight – Barbauld has reservations about the changes she perceives happening around her.[49] John Phillips, in 1792, may laud the labour-efficient canal compared to 'seven or eight stout fellows labouring like slaves, to drag a boat slowly up the river Irwell', presenting the waterways as an enlightened product of modern industrialised Britain (while Britain continued to get rich from transatlantic slavery), but Barbauld's poem is always looking to reach beyond the ostensible benefits of a new system or structure to understand its implications.[50] When she uses repetition in her direction to 'this, this little group' of Warrington students, in whom she has a great deal of hope, she draws the reader's attention to those who are outside the 'this, this'. The canal will move people and produce quickly to and from the 'distant main', and there are opportunities aplenty 'o'er seas and rocks', but when they get there, how will they treat what they find? The 'spoils' of foreign harvests will be brought as tribute back to Britain, but in lines reminiscent of an emphasis in James Thomson's patriotic *Castle of Indolence* (1748), the sense of these spoils as plunder also sullies the aspiration. Thomson's Industry sees a Britain 'quicken'd by mechanic arts', 'glow[ing] with toil', and social Commerce joins 'land to land', marrying 'soil to soil'. However, '*without* bloody spoil' the 'gorgeous stores' of other lands are brought home; bloody spoil appears as a present absence, reminding the reader that spilt blood is often the companion of exploration, conquest and appropriation.[51] Barbauld is hopeful about an era of exploration and discovery that the arching aqueduct symbolises, but she also has reservations – and these extend to the scientific method and its unintended consequences. Like Priestley, some of the Warrington graduates will 'trace with curious search the hidden cause/ Of nature's changes and her various laws'. Such a search risks 'untwist[ing Nature's] beauteous web' and 'disrob[ing] her charms', the curious search becoming a 'hunt' to find 'her elemental forms'. Saunders reads this as changing 'the initial imagery of a search into the rape of Nature by the scientist' (p. 511). Barbauld, then, projects the changes in the physical world around her into the future, considering the epistemological and ethical shifts that accompany a well-connected, easily transported, scientifically educated cohort of ambitious young men.

A meditation on the industrial canal, stretching its long arms to join the distant main, provokes an unsettling future image of pillaged overseas lands and nature unravelled. This is not the only darkly poetic image of the future that Barbauld would construct. As she composed 'Eighteen Hundred and Eleven', Britain had been engaged in an expensive war with France almost continuously since 1793. That long poem, like 'The Invitation' before it, reveals what Francesco Crocco terms 'the contradictory nature of Barbauldian counter-patriotism', though it was received at the time of its publication, and is largely remembered, as unpatriotically anti-war in political sentiment. Crocco suggests that, despite this reputation, the poem still reifies British imperialism, figuring it as 'an innocuous instrument that spreads civilization'.[52] Nonetheless, the poem is best known for the apocalyptic statement that 'Arts, arms and wealth destroy the fruits they bring'.[53] This 'trinity of arts/science, arms/techne, and wealth/capital', says Crocco, 'both sustains and destroys civilizations by spurring them on to the dead end of empire' (p. 91). The line seems to revisit, in its ambivalent relationship to the later lines of the poem, the combination of powers that converge on the Barton aqueduct as Barbauld witnesses and feels what it seems to mean for the future. 'The Invitation' anticipates both the exultant and problematic explorations and voyages that an industrial future (symbolised by flying vessels) will bring, and also the future vision Barbauld crafts later in her career. This doubled projection enables, I suggest, her industrial reservations to speak to the post-industrial, Anthropocene present, for she was a poet profoundly interested in what the changes of her century would mean for later ones she could barely imagine.

Near the beginning of 'The Invitation', Pleasure, like a migratory bird, flies to warmer climes to escape 'winter's hand'. There is foreboding in the winter that Pleasure escapes, however: 'hollow winds foretell approaching storms'. Storm season in the twenty-first century is something to dread in many parts of the world, as storms and hurricanes become deadlier and more frightening as a result of climate change.[54] The Intergovernmental Panel on Climate Change measures global warming in degrees above pre-industrial levels. The industrialising moment that Barbauld captures in her meditation on the aqueduct, clearly sensing humanity to be on the cusp of monumental change, feels, here and now, to be a hollow wind foretelling the storm that would approach centuries later, that batters us today and in years to come. Even a rise of 1.5°C – a global temperature increase that seems wildly optimistic given the speed of policy and behavioural change – results in extreme heatwaves, heavy precipitation events, flooding, sea-level rise, ocean acidification, risks to food, energy, and freshwater availability (and consequent political and civil unrest).[55] Approaching storms. I do not claim that the Duke of Bridgewater's canal is the root cause of climate change. However, I follow Andreas Malm's transhistorical suggestion in *Fossil Capital* that 'every impact of anthropogenic climate change carries the imprint of every human act with a radiative forcing', the 'aftermath and the source intimately coupled yet strangely disconnected'. I have already described Barbauld's poem as bridging the modern and the premodern, but I also understand it, as a text written in and about the industrial past read today, as coupling the twenty-first-century aftermath and the eighteenth-century source of anthropogenic climate change. Malm points to a number of events and processes, from the building of the railway networks to the American invasion of Iraq 'as a series of moments in the historical totality of the fossil economy', events like the opening of the Bridgewater Canal that are 'retroactively suffused with a new significance, calling for a return to history, eyes wide open'.[56] My contention is that 'The Invitation' has always been making this call.

One example of this is the poem's reference to the 'sons of toil' who constructed the canal, intimately connected to the miners in the 'sulphurous mines and caves' (who are not explicitly mentioned but who haunt the image of 'social plenty circl[ing] round the land'). One of the general hypotheses of Malm's *Fossil Capital* is about labour and industry, namely that 'the power derived from fossil fuels was dual in meaning and nature from the very first', organising human praxis as well as harnessing energy (p. 18). 'The Invitation' has been signalling this duality since 1773. It is a poem of wonder mingled with trepidation, questioning where these technological, industrial, economic, and exploratory advances will lead. The poet senses that industrial capitalism has profound effects on the organisation of labour, on the balance of its benefits, on the immediate landscape and 'Thro' the wide earth'. Barbauld leaves the reader with the knowledge that the next generation, in its ambition and propelled by scientific and technological learning, will 'launch our souls into the bright unknown'. The brightness of this horizonicity is dulled, and the hopefulness of the unknown compromised, by the last stanza. These lines are poetically formulaic as a device for the departure of the Muse, but they see this figure 'fold up her fluttering wing' and turn away from the canal and thoughts of the Academy's sons to take refuge in 'the green lap of spring' (p. 24). The poet gazes keenly into the future, but what she sees there (perhaps the drought and hunger, flood and strife that are and will be climate change's effects), causes her Muse to droop and hide her head in the green of nature.

'Where the Cyclops usurp the dwellings of the Naiads and Dryads'[57]

It is 1787 and I am *Industrious*. The wood of my previous incarnation is gone and I have travelled south to Shropshire; I am forged from the ore of the earth: a nineteen-by-six-foot tub of riveted wrought-iron plates. I make my watery way, miraculous once more, up and down steep gradients to Brierley Hill above Coalbrookdale Iron Works. I am still loaded with coal, that black-magical ingredient in the industrial wonder of this haphazard gorge. The discovery here that blast furnaces might use coke to smelt iron is the origin story of my laden back and forth, and now there are more than twenty such furnaces in the little dale.[58] Coal travels down to the fiery works via tunnel and shaft. Away from this branch, the canal wends a far-from-straight way to meet the Severn about three miles distant, descending two hundred feet to unpoetic Coalport, but my metallic sides will never feel the unpredictable currents of ancient Sabrina, nor are her sailed trows destined to ascend angelically the inclined planes of the gorge. The arching Ironbridge spans the Severn, and the trows sail proudly beneath. For perhaps two hundred years craft have carried metal frying pans and plates from the forges here along the Severn to

Gloucester and from there to. . . everywhere. Coalbrookdale is where iron weighed in to this industrial story, affecting every other major industry, but not all who observe it welcome its power.[59] Another woman witnesses, and this one is sure that what she sees she does not like; a swan happier far on the Severn than the canal.

This time, our witness is 'the Swan of Lichfield', Anna Seward. Trinder has described the landscape of the Ironbridge Gorge, Coalbrookdale's locale, as 'horrendous and, at the same time, compulsively fascinating' to Seward's contemporaries (p. 89). It is a far cry, though not a great geographical distance, from Seward's home on the cathedral close of Lichfield in Staffordshire. Seward's life, loves and attitudes have been wrangled over by scholars, largely because of the role Sir Walter Scott played in constructing her posthumous literary reputation. Born in Eyam in Derbyshire (a name recognisable to many as the village that sealed itself off in the seventeenth century to prevent the spread of plague), Seward's father, Thomas, was made canon residentiary of Lichfield in Staffordshire; when Anna was thirteen the family moved to the bishop's palace in the shadow of the imposing three-spired cathedral, drawn skywards out of the red Staffordshire soil in the fourteenth century as a monument to faith, glory and Almighty power.

Inside the cathedral, the snowy purity of white marble memorialises Seward with verses by Scott. The memorial was originally raised by Seward herself for her father, the 'simple tablet' marking 'a father's bier'. Above (and completely overbearing) the tablet sits a classical Grace beneath a willow whose branches bear the 'silent and unstrung' minstrel harp. The poet's voice 'lies smothered here in dust', though readers of the tablet are urged to 'seek her genius in her living lay'. Scott's elegiac inscription is traditional in its tropes, but it also chimes with my approach to poetry in this chapter, understanding the poets in their own historical context, but making the most of the way that their lines speak so clearly to later centuries; the living lay. Scott might further be indicating a watery architectural legacy of Seward's in his use of 'lay'; it is also an old word for a lake or pool, and after a visit to the Serpentine in London in 1772, Seward was instrumental in landscaping the city's Minster Pool, emulating the shape of the Serpentine and developing New Walk around it.[60] In doing so, she created a use and understanding of still water that conforms to Whately's expectations in *Observations on Modern Gardening*, a use of water that is still admired as picturesque and restful in contemporary Lichfield. In adulthood,

Seward would see herself as a hybrid product of her rural early youth and the genteel refinement of this cultured city.[61] Soon after the move to Lichfield, her parents adopted five-year-old Honora Sneyd; after the death of Anna's sister the friendship between Seward and Sneyd intensified, and this would become one of the key relationships of Anna's life and a continually revisited theme of her poetry, continuing after Sneyd's death from consumption in 1780.[62] Interpretations of this relationship, and of her thirty-seven-year companionship with the married John Saville, have been characterised, suggests Seward's biographer Teresa Barnard, by attempts to 'pigeonhole' her feelings and practices 'by twenty-first-century values' or based on 'half-formed truths found in the information in letters which have been heavily edited and censored'.[63] Barnard privileges Seward's created self-image, of 'the independent, self-sufficient writer, an intellectual who constantly searches and challenges, exploring numerous and varied aspects of culture and society' (p. 3). While I value Seward's textual self-creation here, I also insist on reading her works with an eye to twenty-first-century values because they have important things to tell us today about the paradoxes of ecological discourse in a culture that still values financial growth apparently above all else, about scientific and technological advancement, and about Britain's relationship with the world.

Seward came to national public artistic attention with her 'Elegy on Captain Cook' (1780) and 'Monody on Major André' (1781). Throughout this chapter, I want to re-emphasise that a focus on the industrial waterways of Britain is absolutely not an inward turn to the purely national; all three key poets under discussion here saw the industrialisation of the nation as implicated in the fact and meaning of global relationships. I turn to Seward's images of industry below, but wish to pause briefly at the first of her most famous poems in order to demonstrate her attitude to Empire. In her 'Elegy on Captain Cook', she is much less equivocal about British exploration than was Barbauld. For the greater good of humanity, Seward asserts, Cook 'quit imperial London's gorgeous plains' to voyage into unknown seas. Like Barbauld's image of the good the Warrington graduates might achieve, Cook would 'Plant the rich seeds of [Humanity's] exhaust-less store;/ Unite the savage hearts, and hostile hands' bringing peace and comfort to all.[64] Seward presents an archetypal stiff-upper-lipped Englishman, as he stands resolute on deck in the midst of stormy seas. 'This dove of humankind' finds his imperial beneficence checked on first reaching Aotearoa/New Zealand, however, as the 'frowning natives . . . scowl with savage thirst of human blood!' (ll. 87; 91–4). This unhappy contact between Cook and his men and the native Māori is detailed in (amongst other records) Peter Moore's object biography of Cook's ship, *Endeavour*.

After coming ashore at seemingly the same landing site as one of the early Polynesian migrations, Cook's party separated and the boys left guarding the yawl were surprised by men understandably perturbed by the arrival of these strangers. The ensuing confrontation resulted in the death of Te Maro of the Ngati Rakai hapu. This is not detailed in Seward's poem, of course, but is postcolonially redeployed by Māori poet Robert Sullivan in his *Captain Cook in the Underworld*, activating 'analogies between making poetry and travelling on bloody journeys of exploration', seeing Cook not as 'first discoverer' of New Zealand, but as 'a belated and brutal voyager following in the wake of the great Polynesian explorers'.[65] The blood and thunder of Seward's poem reads, from a postcolonial position, not as savagery meted out on peaceful European civilisation, but the savage death of Te Maro and many more.

As well as becoming a hugely successful poet by honouring colonial heroes and construction of heroic national mythologies, Seward was, says Barnard, a proficient businesswoman, managing her father's portfolio of stocks, shares, bonds and monies as well as her own property and copyright negotiations and publishing contracts. This is no naïve and dutiful daughter 'contentedly embroidering or mending lace', but a woman of the world whom other writers, scholars, scientists, and theologians endeavoured to meet in Lichfield or sent letters by wagon and canal. Her will hints at business interests in the industrial canals: ten shares held in trust in the Trent and Mersey Navigation, six shares plus bonds in the Staffordshire and Worcestershire Canal, £100 bond in the Chesterfield Canal and a share in the Birmingham and Fazeley Canal.[66] She did not put her mouth where her money was: her poetic reaction to industry is no uncomplicated celebration of industry.

Seward devoted a sonnet to John Sargent's dramatic poem, *The Mine* (1785), in her 1799 *Original Sonnets*, and in this attention to another poet we find a textual connection to the Aikins, for Sargent cites John's essay on the poetic use of natural history in his preface to *The Mine* – and he is, understandably, as disappointed as me in Aikin's dismissal of the poetic potential of minerals. Sargent asserts the right of the poet to 'avail himself of [scientific] discoveries, and by deriving new images and similitudes from them, to confer on his work a greater degree of utility and embellishment' as part of a move to 'unite poetry and science'.[67] In her sonnet, Seward allies the image of Orpheus with that of exploration, as she would in her 'Elegy to Captain Cook'; a brave bard voyages symbolically to the underworld, taking the mine as a bold new poetic subject. Seward explains Sargent's personifications in a footnote and explicitly compares this device to Erasmus Darwin's Sylphs, Gnomes and Salamanders in *The Botanic Garden* (1791), to which this chapter turns later. Seward's sonnet celebrates not only Sargent's poetic craft by suggesting that Petra and Fossilia praise poetic attention to them, but also the 'charm that mineral scenes display'.[68] The horror of mining and the working of ores is entirely absent from that poem, but finds its description in her sonnet 'To Colebrook Dale' and longer poem 'Colebrook Dale'. In the former, Seward, like Barbauld, invokes a genius loci, this time of Colebrook.[69] Colebrook's genius, however, has failed to act sufficiently in the role of guardian, has been 'faithless to his charge'. The woods and vales, rocks and streams of this place, once inhabited by Naiads and Nymphs, now echo to the din of the 'ever-clanging forge', rendered in line with poetic tradition as a 'swart Cyclops', and 'hears the toiling Barge' – water transport, both river and connecting canal, is central to the destruction. The faithless genius has permitted 'dark-red gleams' from fires on all Colebrook's hills, meaning that the beams of sunlight that ought to reach the dale are shrouded with large columns of 'black sulphureous smoke, spreading like veils of 'funeral crape upon the sylvan robe/ Of thy romantic rocks', polluting the very winds and staining its 'glassy floods'.[70] Ultimately, the environmental degradation is so complete that even the poet's spell is broken and her descriptions cease; the catastrophe is unrepresentable. A failure of ecological stewardship, noise, air and water pollution, ecodeath: such images are frighteningly relevant to the twenty-first century.

The year that Seward published her famous 'Monody on Major André' (1781) saw the region of what is now called Coalbrookdale (one word) become an industrial tourist attraction as Abraham Darby III drove the great Ironbridge project, the first ever cast-iron bridge, to completion. This structure, as iconic and wonderful as the Barton aqueduct, was 'vigorously promoted as a spectacle', with artists commissioned to paint it, and Thomas Jefferson famously purchasing an engraving of it to hang in the White House.[71] As Donna Coffey remarks: 'visitors came to Coalbrookdale not in spite of the industrialization, but *because* of it' and, she says, they came 'for the same reason that they rubberneck at a traffic accident today'. In Coalbrookdale, 'the collision they were looking at was the collision of the past and the future' (p. 153).

Ironworks were not, of course, new in the eighteenth century – an earlier form of forge, a bloomery, was recorded at Coalbrookdale in 1536 and there was a blast furnace there from 1658, with the availability of water power, 'glassy floods', being a key factor in the location of forges.[72] Seward's imagination must thus travel a considerable distance back in time to envisage an unpolluted Coalbrookdale. Ironworks' damning association with noise, flame and smoke can be traced throughout the history of English literature and, anthropologically, much earlier in meaning-making social practices in Britain. For instance, Melanie Giles has shown that the violence of ironworking in the Iron Age, pounding, crushing, heating and hammering, meant that symbols of the craft were used to 'negotiate moments of social crises', but that the productive process of ironworking may also have been used as a metaphor for other transformations including procreation.[73] Jumping forward in time, Shakespeare and Drayton inherited attitudes from classical literature, the type explicitly referenced by Sargent in *The Mine*.[74] When Seward hammers out an idea of what industrial ironworking means to place, poet and environment, it has been forged in the literary crucible of Roman poets, Renaissance writers, John Milton's *Comus*, and her own contemporaries.

In 1787, Seward visited Ludlow Castle in Shropshire, where Milton's masque had been performed to John Egerton, 1st Earl of Bridgewater (the Canal Duke's great-great-grandfather) in 1634. Malcolm McKinnon Dick has suggested that this literary pilgrimage provided Seward with 'a language to criticise the industrial landscape of the Midlands', featuring as it does an attendant spirit and Sabrina the nymph, Fairies, Elves, Naiads and numerous mythical figures.[75] Todd Borlik argues that Shakespeare's contemporaries envisioned themselves 'as inhabitants of a sordid neo-Iron Age', and Seward's sonnet similarly evokes a hellish past and frightening future cloaked in mythology.[76] From the perspective of the Anthropocene and amidst dire warnings about the survival of human life on this planet, her stance seems well-grounded; Trinder reminds us that without the growth in iron production such as that seen at Coalbrookdale, and the spread of foundry skills, the steam engine could not have been manufactured in great numbers, a key trigger in the modes of production that see us experiencing climate catastrophe.[77] Indeed, the Museum of Iron today boasts that 'Coalbrookdale iron changed the course of the world'.[78]

Seward returns to and elaborates on the images she has so densely poeticised in the sonnet in her longer poem, 'Colebrook Dale'. Penny Fielding places Seward's poem within a 'new kind of self-consciousness' emerging during the eighteenth-century industrialisation of Britain, a self-consciousness that understands the 'natural' via 'the threat of pollution or industrial manipulation'. While Seward and Barbauld's depiction of the canal is very different, they both use poetry to make sense of what these waterways mean and represent, how they *feel* different to rivers and hold a different cultural place. The link between Genius and genius loci is, Fielding claims, here disrupted, marking a rupture 'between national industry and native stream, and between nature as continuous, abstract process and as felt, singular spot'.[79] That spot is the 'scene of superfluous grace' immediately marked out in Seward's poem as 'wasted bloom', 'violated'. Here, the Genius, bribed by Plutus – the god of wealth – sleeps while 'tribes fuliginous invade', chasing away wood-nymphs and Naiads.[80] Clearly, Seward's primary meaning is of a people embodying the noxious smoke and particulate of industrial pollution, but the image interestingly answers the imperial discourse of her 'Elegy for Captain Cook', imagining a dark invading force, 'dusk artificers', swarming over England's mossy dales and glens, as Cook and his men appeared in negative to the inhabitants of Aotearoa/New Zealand.[81] It brings to mind a jarring passage in Emily Eden's account of her travels in British India between 1837 and 1840. Eden imagines a time when 'the art of steam is forgotten and . . . some black Governor-General of England will be marching through its southern provinces'.[82] Eden's association of this apocalyptic reverse colonialism with a retreat from the age of steam is particularly relevant for a transhistorical reading of Seward's fuliginous invaders, pointing to the image as a signifier of what mining and other industries as part of British colonisation would do to the environments of Australia, New Zealand and other colonised lands (which I discuss further in Chapter Four).[83]

In contrast to the fuliginous tribes, the nymphs and naiads of unpolluted Coalbrook were fresh, fragrant and silent but are now 'usurpt by Cyclops'. Once more, the 'throng'd barge' shouts down the natural world. Seward comments on the global export of iron, traded for spice in Ceylon and gold in Brazil; like Barbauld's poem, Seward's literary treatment of industry demonstrates the canals' role in connecting Britain to the trading world, products finally 'wafted o'er our subject seas/ To every port'. Seward's nationally possessive attitude to 'our subject seas' is in contrast to Barbauld's tentative gestures towards the watery horizon.[84] Coffey sees Seward linking, 'with almost prescient clarity . . . the destruction of the dale to the demands of capitalism and imperialism', but I think this underplays Seward's enthusiasm for Empire.[85] Instead, this global vision hints at an unsettling feature of Seward's poem: it does not complain about industry and imperial trade *per se*, but suggests that there are better places for the industry that supplies trade than Coalbrookdale, more 'unpoetic scenes', such as the drizzly moors above Sheffield or the 'barren wold' of Ketley to the north of Coalbrookdale.[86] Dick labels this attitude 'environmental apartheid'.[87] Should the industry of Coalbookdale relocate, Seward imagines a restoration of verdant nature. While this dream shares much with hopeful twenty-first-century discourses of 'rewilding', the deliberate large-scale reinstatement of damaged ecosystems, it also evokes the kind of creeping return of nature that later cultural forms tend to associate with postapocalyptic or post-collapse narratives of human evacuation or crisis.[88] Seward calls for 'sylvan Colebrook's winding vales [to be restored] / To beauty and to song'. While her hopes for restoration entail beauty as perceived by the human eye and the renewal of poetic song in that vale as well as the 'wild woodland choir', I emphasise the non-human orientation of the idealised vision of the place, the 'Dryads, fair-hair'd Naiades', even the 'venal Genius' who has been asleep at his post.[89] It is a fantasy future for Colebrookdale that bears no resemblance to its human habitation, and behind its mythic language resides, I suggest, a fear that there can be no straightforward return to a pre-industrial utopia. If Coalbrookdale becomes once more fresh and fragrant, there will be no humans around to enjoy it.

This doubt about what is to come can also be read in Seward's contradictory attitude to the wonders of one of Britain's great industrial centres. Her lauding of Birmingham as a powerhouse of industry and export are the central example of her general appreciation of industry at the same time as a specific objection to its location. In Birmingham, 'the growing London of the Mercian realm', Seward proposes that science 'leads her enlighten'd sons' to invention and innovation.[90] Historian Peter Jones advises caution when 'linking transport improvements to urbanisation and industrialisation' but the waterways were certainly part of this second city's story of industrial success. The third section of this chapter looks more closely at the Grand Trunk Canal, but by the time Seward decried the iron manufacturing in Coalbrookdale whilst hailing the manufacturing might of Birmingham, the landlocked city was well connected by water. As Jones records, the 1768 passing of the Birmingham Canal Bill enabled the construction of a waterway through the Black Country and with a view to joining up with the Staffordshire and Worcestershire Canal, bringing in raw materials and eventually connecting Birmingham's products to the Severn or taking them north via the Trent and Mersey Canal to Hull or Liverpool – and from there, the world.[91] The route to Hull was shortened further with the Birmingham and Fazeley Canal in the 1780s.

James Keir, industrial chemist and geologist, is heralded in the poem as one of Birmingham's 'fam'd Triumvirate'.[92] He chose a site for his chemical (and later soap) works, Tipton Green, with ready access to the Birmingham Canal in 1781, and Matthew Boulton and James Watt used the same logic to locate the Soho Foundry at Smethwick in 1795. Other industrialists saw the benefit of opening manufactories near the canal in order to access cheaply transported coal and water for steam engines. Seward finds a modern kind of genius in Birmingham, and those men facilitated and relied on the transport potential of the waterways to realise their industrial scientific ambition. While living with Richard Lovell Edgeworth in Ireland, Keir translated Pierre-Joseph Macquer's *Dictionnaire de chymie* (1766).[93] He moved to the West Midlands in the 1770s and via Erasmus Darwin began friendships with various members of the famous Lunar Society – 'a small but influential cluster within the wider, pan-European community of late-eighteenth-century natural philosophers'.[94] In fact, Darwin quotes Keir's chemical dictionary in the copious notes to *The Botanic Garden*. Keir began experiments in glassmaking and further experiments in chemistry, and while developing his glassmaking business at Amblecote (a product that obviously benefits from smooth transport via water) he became one of the original shareholders in the Stourbridge Canal Company, designed to link Amblecote with the Staffordshire and Worcestershire Canal.[95] We return to postindustrial Stourbridge in Chapter Five, but as an eighteenth-century figure, Keir brings together all the experimentation, aesthetic appreciation, entrepreneurialism, industrial nous, innovation and practical sense for which the Lunar Society is famed, and his interests are tightly bound with the development of the waterways.

The biographies and successes of Boulton and Watt are exhaustively catalogued in the annals of British industrial history. Watt first specialised in making precision instruments, and would eventually improve surveying equipment necessary for the planning of new canals. In October 1766 he began a survey for a projected canal between the Firth of Forth and the Firth of Clyde, attending parliament in connection with the Canal Bill, and would go on to survey and act as engineer to a number of navigations, including the ambitious Caledonian Canal. In 1763–4 he famously was asked to repair the Newcomen engine of the natural philosophy class at Glasgow University and identified several problems with the design, beginning a series of experiments on the design of steam engines that would, through collaboration and patience, bring the world the Boulton and Watt steam engine, efficiently harness steam for manufacturing, and power the Industrial Revolution.[96] In the 1760s, Boulton commissioned his Soho Manufactory, where, prior to Watt's involvement, he manufactured a wide range of products including cut-steel mountings for cameos and mountings and flutings for vases. Watt's engine would not have been nearly so successful without Boulton's flair for marketing. The early market for the engine was mines in Cornwall, one of the earliest orders was placed by the Birmingham Canal Company, and the Coalbrookdale Company was to become an important customer and supplier of engine parts to Boulton and Watt.[97] The people, places and processes of late eighteenth-century industry in Shropshire and the West Midlands are so intimately connected that to mention Birmingham's 'fam'd Triumvirate' is to invoke the very notion of steam power and all it could and would change, scientific experimentation and the pursuit of knowledge, manufacture as an art and industry, and objects that travelled by water inland and across the sea.

Seward labels the industrial inventor an artist, one who produces the means by which industry flourishes; the men she wrote about certainly did not separate art and science: Uglow confirms that at this time and in this place 'you could be an inventor and designer, an experimenter and a poet, a dreamer and an entrepreneur'.[98] One of the contentions of this chapter is that, whatever their differing views on the effects of industry, poets who depicted the new industrial waterways did not see the process of producing a poem as entirely different to the making of canals, machines and wrought iron. The poem itself, especially the sonnet, with its technical reproduction of metre and rhyme, is analogous to factory production. The waterways were an integral part of the modern world the poets navigated, be it with trepidation, confusion, celebration or distrust. The speaker of 'Coalbrook Dale' praises the 'vast' and personified Boulton and Watt engine with its huge 'extended arms' and 'soft-seeming breath/ Of the hot steam'; Barbauld saw the canals stretching 'their long arms, to join the distant main'.[99] This is industrial modernity, and the poets are wrapped in its embrace. Seward imagines the steam to be like a soft breath, but also exclaims over violated Coalbrook. The wary ambivalence of Barbauld's attitude to a changing world becomes in Seward's work outright paradox.

As well as Birmingham's 'fam'd Triumvirate' of inventors, Boulton, Watt and Keir, the poem celebrates Joseph Priestley, whose experiments with oxygen are described as tracing 'the viewless Aura's subtle breath / Through all its various powers', connecting Priestley's science to Watt's. What name does Seward give to the 'arch-chemist', the spirit of drawing 'from Nature's stores' all that is latent or revealed? Genius. Rather than understanding the link between the genius loci and Genius as severed, as does Fielding, I suggest that reading Seward's repeated usage in the light of Barbauld's doubled genius is to interpret an unavoidable and creative tension in the poetics of industry. Birmingham is a city devoted to art and knowledge, and its striving spirit means that every passing month its buildings 'creep on the circling plains', uprooting 'hedges, thickets, trees'.[100] There is both celebration and lamentation in these lines. Peter Jones posits 'industrial enlightenment', an open-minded and experimental scientific culture in Birmingham and the West Midlands, as the 'midwife to Industrial Revolution'.[101] Seward clearly understands this deep relationship between scientific knowledge and manufacturing but is not, to continue Jones's maternal analogy, prepared to endure the child with all its faults. What Seward's poem produces, rather than a wistful depiction of Coalbrookdale without the coal and iron, is a post-collapse landscape haunted by the threat (to a white poet) of black colonial invaders. Seward's vain hope that Birmingham will one day draw its 'massy ore' from somewhere less poetic than Colebrook both ignores the contingencies of geology and raises the spectre of Birmingham's manufacturing prowess waning; its success is impermanent just as all its vivacious genius sons will one day die.[102] Reading in the Anthroposcene makes particular interpretations of these apocalyptic visions legible; there is no possibility of a return to a prelapsarian Edenic vale.

'Winding in lucid lines'[103]

Back to 1774, back to timbered sides; I am *Industrious* and you follow me back and forth through time and space. I come and go, reformed, refilled, re-placed, and the possibilities of this particular journey send the minds of great thinkers much further back in time; aeons, epochs. No coal in my hold as I float along the Trent and Mersey Canal. This time, I carry with me the Barton Aqueduct and the Coalbrookdale forge. Not as memory, not as idea, but as delicate green and black images painted on a packed-in-straw creamware dinner service, topped by a green frog in an escutcheon. They are bound first for London, where the good and the great will admire the hundreds of pieces at Greek Street, then to the Frog Palace of a Russian Empress. The fluid motion of the canal seems designed to carry such eminently breakable pottery, and here it really was. Josiah Wedgwood cut the first section of sod; Brindley's expertise was brought to bear on the plan, but now he is no more: the water flows longer in the canal than does life flow in the designer. As I make my horse-pulled way from the manufactory, I may not yet proceed all the way to the mighty Mersey; stone defeats the passage of water at Harecastle yet. As the Empress's cargo raises the waterline on my sides, an approving friend looks on from Etruria Hall on the hill. This accelerating evolution in the economy of decorative art, industry and invention finds a ready champion.[104]

Whether Erasmus Darwin really did see any of the famous Frog Service loaded on to barges at Etruria, or even whether those particular scenes made their way on to the plates in Staffordshire or in Chelsea is a matter of conjecture and poetic licence of the type taken by A. N. Wilson in his neo-eighteenth-century novel, *The Potter's Hand* (2012). It has received surprisingly scant scholarly attention but brilliantly captures the spirit of the Wedgwoods, Darwins and their historical moment. Darwin's enthusiasm for invention and ideas is no exaggeration at all, however. One might even call it an incurable enthusiasm, for he was at least once the victim of his own inventiveness. In 1768, he attempted to improve on the design of his carriage, fell from it and broke his patella. Wilson's literary project is to reimagine, for a twenty-first-century readership, the sense of individuals striving and collaborating to produce a new world of art, invention, and exploration, one glimpsed by Barbauld and explored by Seward, and to try to articulate what that horizonicity might have felt like for writers and experimenters pushing towards it.

In terms of more contemporaneous representation of Erasmus Darwin – if not necessarily less invented – Anna Seward's *Memoirs of Darwin* cover the period until his move to Derby in 1781. She devoted as much attention to his fascinating network of collaborators and friends – including Keir, Watt and Boulton – as do much later commentators.[105] Darwin and Seward met when Darwin arrived in Lichfield as the local physician in 1756, and Darwin first met Wedgwood in 1765. Darwin, if not beautiful, was certainly 'agreeable', with ready good humour and wit in spite of a serious stammer, and 'a sunny smile'. Despite 'a highly poetic imagination', he resisted the urge to publish his poetry for many years, afraid of the damage it would do to his serious scientific reputation. In this, we see this chapter's first recognition of any kind of discursive division between poetry and science, but it was only to be a temporary one as he eventually published his poetry having first made his name as the author of bold scientific works. In 1770–1, after the death of his first wife, Darwin began work on the enormous *Zoonomia*, which is remembered for being the work in which he advanced an early theory of evolution, and which would eventually be published in 1794 after he solicited feedback from James Keir.[106] In this work, the whole of nature 'is one family of one parent', albeit made by 'the great Creator'.[107] So committed to this idea was Darwin that he added a controversial Latin motto to his family coat-of-arms of three scallop shells: *E conchis omnia*, 'everything from shells'.[108] Seward called the work 'ingenious, beyond all precedent, in its conjectures, and embracing, with giant-grasp, almost every branch of philosophic science'. She was particularly impressed by the ways in which Darwin traced 'those subtle, . . . concealed links' between these branches of knowledge.[109] This attitude to learning and investigation epitomises the minds of the authors and other figures in this chapter, men and women who saw the ways in which poetry, botany, engineering, decorative art, exploration, biology and chemistry were co-implicated, and how producing something in one field could potentially open new possibilities in one or more of the others. To read Darwin's work is to witness someone revelling in knowledge.

Zoonomia points to the changes in the life of an individual animal (such as the frog adorning Wedgwood's imperial dinner service, from tadpole with gills to 'aerial animal with lungs'), to the breeding of animals, to inherited 'monstrosities' or mutations, and to the 'similarity of structure' of various animals. All animals, Darwin concludes, 'have alike been produced from a single living filament' and have changed in the course of 'lust, hunger and security'. The time period over which biological diversity has evolved in Darwin's reckoning is a pretty accurate 'hundreds of millions of years', a timescale he settled on thanks to his interest in geology.[110]

He shared this interest with his friend Josiah Wedgwood, who, as a potter, was profoundly concerned with where particular kinds of clay and minerals could be found. In the trenches through geological time that the cutting of a canal necessitated, Wedgwood and Darwin heard of and discussed finds that served as evidence for Darwin's evolutionary theories. Wondering how the remains of shellfish could be found miles inland, and considering strata of limestone, Darwin turned these evolutionary-geological investigations into poetry several times, one example being in *The Temple of Nature* (written 1798–9). Comparing the finitude of human life to geological ages with reference to tombstones, the poem asserts that the spiral shells of long-gone creatures are crushed over aeons to form 'the marble mountain, and the sparry steep' underwater, until those 'primeval islands' were raised 'into day'. Thus 'huge isles of rock, and continents of sands' are, in their formation over millions of years, 'mighty monuments of past delight'.[111] King-Hele estimates that as early as 1770 Darwin believed that all life had developed from primitive sea creatures, possibly thinking of the tiny shell-like fossils found in limestone.[112]

Remarkably, such associations between canals, geology and fossilised evidence of natural history can still be made today; in late 2018, work on restoring lock fourteen of the Grantham Canal turned up 200-million-year-old ammonites from the Blue Lias geological formation.[113] A nineteenth-century description of the cutting of the Union Canal described similar finds: 'many *Ammonites*, or *Cornu-Ammonis*, which appeared as if formed of brass; ... besides these, petrified cockles, muscles [*sic*], and oysters, were in abundance, and the earth appeared to contain much mineral substance'.[114] What is notable about Darwin's poetic pondering about inland seashells is that it occurred just as the waterways were opening up passages from the Midlands to the sea; each new discovery in science and engineering inspired novel connections in an intellectual mapping of knowledge, often using one discovery as an analogue or metaphor to light the way towards another. As he would later assert: 'since natural objects are allied to each other by many affinities, every kind of theoretic distribution of them adds to our knowledge by developing some of their analogies'.[115] From the Midlands to the sea via canal, from sea creatures to the diversity of animal life on planet earth, from the cutting of a canal to the layers of geological time: Darwin witnessed, reasoned, suggested and articulated slow natural historical and rapid industrial change at once.

How did Darwin come to discuss the geology of canals with Josiah Wedgwood? The success of the Duke of Bridgewater's canal had, of course, led many industrialists and speculators to consider what canals might do for them, and one early suggestion was for a canal joining the Trent to the Mersey, and thus the port of Hull to that of Liverpool. This initial design proved too expensive even in the planning, but in 1760 the Genius Brindley and another civil engineer, John Smeaton, proposed a revised plan of a section from the pottery industries in Burslem to Wilden Ferry, south of Derby, with a branch connecting to Lichfield.[116] Darwin had planned an iron-rolling and slitting mill to the north-east of Lichfield where the turnpike road crossed the Trent and where Brindley's canal would join the river. They planned to dig part of the route in advance, capitalising on the drop in gradient from the canal to the river to power their iron mill, and then sell that part of the route back to the canal company. The canal was a success, though Darwin expended much energy (and money) negotiating land, engineering problems and expenses. Here, Darwin had got directly involved in canal business, but for Wedgwood's Trent-Mersey plan he was more of an enthusiastic consultant and engaged shareholder than architect.[117] Wedgwood revived the Trent-Mersey canal idea as the 'Grand Trunk Canal' with the support of fellow potters in the region. As Brian Dolan notes, 'given the state of the roads around Burslem it was amazing that any of the potters' goods survived more than the first few miles of the adventure'.[118] Wedgwood had support from a number of other interested parties, from iron and flax dealers to salt manufacturers and landowners, though he had to fight off opposition from rival schemes, those whose water supply would be affected, and other landowners. He managed to prove to the 'Gentlemen of Birmingham' that they would save £10,000 in land carriage in a year once the canal reached their town, especially advantageous to import/exporters; as ever, local canal concerns are intimately connected to global trade.[119]

The proposed plan was to join the river Trent near Wilsden in Derbyshire with the river Weaver in Cheshire, the Bridgewater Canal or the Tide-way in the river Mersey, whichever proved most expedient, with a tunnel at Harecastle. Wedgwood considered that 'this scheme of

Navigation is undoubtedly the best thing that could possibly be plan'd for this country'.[120] As with most canal schemes requiring support in this period, a pamphlet was called for to convince others of its benefits. Darwin authored this, but, to his chagrin, it was heavily edited by Wedgwood's business partner and friend, Thomas Bentley. In describing the general advantages of inland navigation, the pamphlet points out that 'whatever facilitates our trade, and has a tendency to increase it, deserves universal encouragement, as it is essentially beneficial to the public'. Again, the key benefit cited is that canals provide 'easy communications between the distant parts of a country, and from each of those parts to the sea'. The pamphlet promises that canals will enliven and enrich the areas they pass through. If these and attendant benefits may seem to advantage only 'the mechanic, the manufacturer, or the merchant', the aristocratic reader is encouraged to think again, for a canal will apparently bring many advantages to the 'landed gentleman' – whose support is, of course, vital to the success of any canal bill.[121] The digging of the Trent and Mersey, Bentley's pamphlet insisted, might also 'occasion the discovery of mines or useful minerals . . . which were never apprehended to be in the places where they are found, and which, but for these public works, would have been for ever buried in the earth'. In other words, who knows what we might learn about the layers hidden beneath the surface? The canals are an opportunity to dig a line through time. In laying out the advantages of this particular route, the pamphlet mentions a 'vast bed of rocksalt' from Northwich to Lawton which might be useful 'in Metalurgy, and several of the mechanic arts'. Canals, like pottery, are always a question of geology and this one could furnish landowners with geological finds from coal to alabaster.[122] The Staffordshire Wedgwoods were successful potters precisely because high quality coal and clay could be found in the vicinity and salt and lead needed for glazing in nearby Cheshire and Derbyshire.[123] Josiah had samples of clay sent to him from around the world, analysing them in his laboratory at Etruria; with his Lunar Society friends he travelled around the Midlands studying rocks and fossils, always interested in land stratification and types of clay.

Late 1765 saw Wedgwood charging around, as Darwin had done, meeting and placating landowners, ensuring supplies of the pamphlet, and drumming up subscriptions to raise the necessary funds. Wedgwood and Bentley were writing to each other so frequently about the canals in this period that it began to inform their very metaphors. For instance, in January 1766, Wedgwood appealed to Bentley to 'put your business into such a Channel as it will move along with the assistance of your good partner for a few months'. In September of the following year, Wedgwood chided Bentley about coming to Burslem: 'leave off trimming your old skiff, come & assist in puting a new one upon the stocks. Her name shall be SPEEDWELL – we will make a NEW RIVER for her and COMMAND SUCCESS.'[124]

Work began on the canal in 1766 with Brindley the chief engineer once more, and digging at Harecastle for the great – if not strictly necessary – tunnel began a year later. Workers unearthed unrecognisable fossilised bones and Wedgwood sent them to Darwin in what King-Hele calls a 'potent parcel from the past'. King-Hele surmises from Darwin's correspondence that 'when Darwin thought more about it, he came to the conclusion that species must have changed over the long periods of time needed to bury the Harecastle fossils'. Weeks later, Darwin visited mines in Derbyshire; the bones sent to him from Harecastle and the fossilised remains of ancient animals in the mines set him 'on his evolutionary path'.[125] Wedgwood yearned to be making such visits; in a letter to Bentley he reports that Brindley had told him of the same mines at Matlock: the miners 'throw all the spars, &c &c into a brook wch washes away all the Dirty & light parts & leaves a great variety of ponderous bodys behind – I long to be Fossilizing amongst them'.[126] Wedgwood's desire to touch the mysterious bones of the past washed clean of time speaks through the ages in his energetic letter writing; this is a haptic yearning that we might experience today when faced not only with natural historical objects, but the now antique pottery fashioned by Wedgwood himself. While Darwin used the fossils to understand evolution, Wedgwood was constantly on the lookout for new materials for his fashionable product. In January 1768 he informed Bentley, in a letter that discussed the branch of the canal to go to Etruria, that he had 'try'd all the Fossils you sent me which had the appearance, or distinguishing quality of S:P'; this was probably saltpetre, or potassium nitrate used in glazing, and Wedgwood uses the term 'Fossil' here more generally than we use it today to mean 'mineral', a use that became obsolete in the early nineteenth century apart from our ongoing use of 'fossil fuels'.[127]

A February 1768 letter from Wedgwood to Bentley in Liverpool tells him of the 'wonderfull and surprising curiositys we find in our Navigation!', another potent parcel from the past. Under a bed of clay workers discovered 'a prodigious rib, with the vertebre of the back bone of a monstrous sized Fish, thought by some connisieurs to belong to the identical Whale that was so long ago swallowed by Jonah!' Under a stratum of gravel was found another bone that confounded the anatomists Wedgwood consulted: 'they cannot decide whether it is the *first*, or *last* of the vertebre of some monstrous animal, nor whether that animal was an inhabitant of the *Sea*, or *Land*'. Wedgwood good naturedly, and with an apt metaphor, cannot account for these finds nor the strata of fossilised plants and says that he is 'got beyond [his] depth', turning instead to 'what better suits [his] Capacity, the forming of a Jug or Teapot'.[128] Time and again natural history, geology, pottery and the canals are combined in activity, metaphor, theory, and making. As Tristram Hunt notes, canals, 'great agents of modernity', led Wedgwood and his peers 'to understand themselves in the deeper slipstreams of time'.[129]

Wedgwood's voice echoes through the centuries in his letters to Bentley, so lively and idiosyncratic is his correspondence. In November 1779 Wedgwood announced to Bentley that he had 'begun upon a great undertaking – The arrangement of my fossils & making a catalogue for them.' By 'fossil', Wedgwood again refers not just to the ammonites and prodigious ribs of organisms preserved in the ground, but of any mineral substances dug from the earth. His priorities for geology and natural history are made clear: 'as a potter, I make *clays* my first article, after which *stones vitrifiable* will follow'. He lists steatites (varieties of talc), including his beloved jasper, sagar, clay, shale and coal. As Wedgwood's letters speak to us today of a past historical age, so Wedgwood's fossils clearly speak to him and his fellow scientists of past geological ages and the uses to which those remnants might be put, yet he refers to them as 'silent and innocent'.[130] The samples themselves are a calming escape from the world of industrial espionage, thieving labourers, and the pressures of trade.

It was not just clay as a material that intrigued Wedgwood, but the shells that also inspired Darwin, in particular the shape of shells and how they might be used in pottery. On display in the Wedgwood museum when I visited were examples of Wedgwood's 'conchology', with Queen's ware and Pearlware pieces from the 1780s taking the shape of nautillis and pectern shells, featuring seahorse filials, and decorated with shell images. These forms draw not only on Wedgwood's own knowledge of shells but the work of his contemporaries, such as the English naturalist Emanuel Mendes da Costa's illustrated *Elements of Conchology* (1776) and *British Conchology* (1778).[131] In Wedgwood's collection there are even pectern shell-shaped tea-caddy spoons in different coloured jasper. Wedgwood's geological and natural historical interests informed not just his choice of materials and enamel experiments, but brought the *shapes* of those scientific inquiries into eighteenth-century homes as a fashionable fossil. Like the swirl of an ammonite, means and process are folded into each Wedgwood product so that the finished artefact contains the time, ideas, materials and methods that brought it about, every piece referencing its journey to existence. This is evident in tea-caddy spoons that are made *from* jasper 'fossils' on which Wedgwood performed countless experiments, and in their form point to the fossilised sea creatures about which Darwin hypothesised as he composed *Zoonomia* and having seen the evidence as the Trent and Mersey Canal was dug. It can be seen also in the inclusion of canals on the Frog Service; that a thousand-piece dinner service could be commissioned from Russia and safely transferred from the Midlands to London for trans-shipment is possible because of the waterways depicted on the surface of its plates. Wedgwood's intricate spirals of means, process, product and consumption speak eloquently of the Enlightenment concerns of his social circle and of the historical moment captured similarly by Barbauld and Seward, showing the canals not simply as a practical contingency but as integral to the web of scientific and artistic production which ushered in a new episteme.

These intricacies find poetic expression in Darwin's great (and famously well-footnoted) work, *The Botanic Garden*. It consists of two parts, 'The Economy of Vegetation' and 'The Loves of the Plants'. Like Sargent, Darwin aims to 'inlist [*sic*] Imagination under the banner of Science'.[132] Structurally, 'The Economy of Vegetation', which has more relevance to the concerns of this chapter than does Part II, is in four cantos devoted to the elements, with the Goddess of Botany addressing in turn: the Nymphs of Fire, the Gnomes of Earth, the Nymphs of Water, and the Sylphs of Air. As in Barbauld's and Seward's poems examined here, the First Canto of 'The Economy of Vegetation' introduces 'the Genius of the place', but this genius loci is not in conflict with the human intellectual geniuses of Darwin's work including, as does Barbauld's poem, James Brindley. The Nymphs of Water smiled on Brindley's cradle, says the Goddess, nursing 'with fairy-love the unletter'd child'. They spread their secret spells around his pillow, revealing hydrological mysteries, 'pierced all your springs, and open'd all your wells'. The result is the 'bright serpent' of the canal, wending its way through the countryside: 'Far shine the scales, that gild his sinuous back, / And lucid undulations mark his track'. Effacing the labour of the men who dug the canals, it is 'with strong arm immortal BRINDLEY' who leads 'His long canals, and parts the velvet meads'. This section of the poem praises the 'lucid lines' and the 'rising locks', refusing to privilege the natural lines of rivers and streams. Not only does Darwin's poem make sense of the new geographical connections forged by industrial waterways, it suggests that the canals newly make anthropocentric sense of geography, bringing together materials, industry, markets and ports. Thus, 'Plenty, Arts, and Commerce freight the waves'. On Brindley's imagined tomb, suggests Darwin, 'MECHANIC GENIUS stands', counting 'the fleet waves, and balance[ing] the lands'.[133]

Wedgwood, too, is lauded in 'The Economy of Vegetation' and, once more, geology, natural history, canals, and art are seen as interconnected fields of inquiry. Darwin begins his celebration of the potter with a meditation on clay, 'Soft as the Cygnet's down', a material that will 'change obedient to the whirling wheel'. The stanza points to Chinese advances in pottery, then to the original Etruria, before suggesting that the Gnomes of the Earth and the Fire-Nymphs must collaborate in the success of a 'new Etruria' on 'Britannia's isle'. Wedgwood's continuity with, improvement on, and depiction of ancient Greek arts could not be more fitting for this genre of eighteenth-century poetry, emphasising as it does the connections between mythology and scientific investigation, and the way in which both discourses attempt to make sense of and narrativise the apparently inexplicable, responding to human 'hows' and 'whys' with theories of forces, events, relationships, properties and causes. Darwin's literary innovation was to see that these radically different yet complementary ways of making sense of the natural world in an age of rapid discovery could in turn be expressed via poetry as a way of exploring this classical and modern scientific complementarity.

Wedgwood's clays and cobalt are just one example among many of geological investigations in *The Botanic Garden* – and Darwin uses this very term in one of his notes. He even includes a cross-section of the earth as he understands it at this point in the history of the development of the discipline of geology.[134] Several of these references once more make the connection between geological finds and evolution (as it would become known). For instance, in the Third Canto, the Goddess addresses the nymphs' adornment of conch shells with 'glossy volumes roll'd' of 'azure, green, and gold'. The note to these lines muses that 'some of the most common fossil shells are not now known in their recent state' and that more common seashells are not found fossilised. Darwin asks 'Were all the ammoniae destroyed when the continents were raised? Or do some genera of animals perish by the increasing power of their enemies? Or do they still reside at inaccessible depths in the sea?' Eventually, he asks 'do some animals change their forms gradually and become new genera?'.[135] There *is* an explanation for the seemingly incalculable variety of soils, stones and minerals, for the layers of the earth, for the shells found buried inland and the mysterious bones dug out with the canals; readers might grasp the complex action of time, forces, gases and liquids via evidenced description and conjecture, using mythological figures as discursive placeholders and explanatory allegory. Like Barbauld, for instance, Darwin considers the 'time-fall'n woods', compacted as Gnomes teach 'transuding dews' to pass through them. In his note, Darwin suggests that this process, followed by the washing away of soluble parts of the morass, was 'productive of many fossil bodies, as flint, sea-sand, selenite, with the precious stones, and perhaps the diamond'. The poem reinforces over and over again that there are hidden layers of previous natural formations in the ground; as these are uncovered – by mining, canal cutting, and geological investigation – the uses to which new materials might be put, and the explanations for those layers, are waiting to be written by scientists and inventors.

Darwin and Wedgwood's letters and *The Botanic Garden* demonstrate that the cutting of canals revealed fossils that provided evidence for the changing of animal forms and the role of fossils in soil and rock formation. They enabled Wedgwood's works of art to make it safely to market. As previously noted, they pushed 'Plenty, Arts, and Commerce' to 'freight the waves'. This sense of the waterways connecting the whole of the nation, including the landlocked industrial Midlands, to the globe, finds an ambitious extension in Wedgwood and Darwin's mutual interest in Sydney Cove. This interest reflects what Hunt calls Wedgwood's 'instinctive belief in the righteousness of British imperial actions abroad'.[136] Darwin briefly mentions Wedgwood's Sydney Cove medallion in *The Botanic Garden*, trusting that its 'brightening scenes' of Hope attended by Peace, Art, and Labour will 'cheer the dreary wastes at Sydney-cove'.[137] The subject is dealt with in much greater detail, however, in Darwin's 'Visit of "Hope" to Sydney Cove, Near Botany Bay', subtitled 'designed to accompany the medallions on that subject which Mr Wedgwood intends to transmit thither'. It was written in 1789 after Wedgwood sent Darwin the engraving of the proposed medallions, which would be made from Botany Bay clay.

The design for the medallions was drawn by Henry Webber, brother of John Webber who had sailed as draughtsman with Captain James Cook on the *Resolution* and whose images appeared in *A Voyage to the Pacific* (1784). The clay had been sent by Captain Arthur Phillip, settler of the Sydney Cove colony with 850 convicts and 200 naval officers, the beginnings of white Australia, to Sir Joseph Banks – then president of the Royal Society and previously Captain Cook's naturalist on board *Endeavour*. Phillip had arrived in Australia with the 'First Fleet' on 18 January 1788, shortly before two French ships made it to Botany Bay.[138] Before the French party left in March, the expedition's naturalist, Abbé Jean-André Mongez, a mineralogist, ornithologist, entomologist and chemist, told Phillip that the Sydney Cove clay from which the settlers had made failed attempts to construct shelters could be used to produce excellent pottery. When Banks sent the clay, via the HMS *Fishburn*, to Britain, he mentioned this recommendation, and the fact that Aboriginal peoples used the clay to decorate their bodies. The finished medallions were sent to Phillip, the clay returning symbolically whence it came, with the 'Second Fleet' in January 1790.[139]

An image of the medallion's design and Darwin's poem preface Phillip's *Voyage to Botany Bay* (1789), with the detail that 'the clay proves to be of a fine texture, and will be found very useful for the manufactory of earthen ware'. The design itself 'represents Hope encouraging Art and Labour, under the influence of Peace, to pursue the employments necessary to give security and happiness to an infant settlement'. The *Voyage* text anthologises a number of 'authentic papers' to construct its account, including a journal entry from 22 January 1788 which describes a meeting between the white settlers and Aboriginal people. One man had 'a kind of white clay rubbed upon the upper part of his face, so as to have the appearance of a mask' and a woman had this clay decoration on her face, neck and breasts.[140]

Aboriginal performers today continue to emphasise the significance of clay body painting; Djakapurra Munyarryun of the Bangarra Dance Theatre, for instance, insists that 'we never dance without ochre on . . . because that's what we have been doing for . . . a thousand years. Body paint for us is really important for our culture'. Matthew Doyle of the Tharawal community has recreated a style of body design that relates to, and uses clays from, the Sydney area. Luuli Grayson explains that 'if you see someone with the same body painting, you know they are part of your family'.[141] There was a similar effect on the 'First Fleet' – but the woman's body paint marked her out for them as not-family, as other. I do not intend to suggest that Captain Phillips and his crew should be expected to have interpreted Aboriginal practices from the perspective of Aboriginal people; they were fashioned by the ideologies of their time and place. A transhistorical reading of Phillips's *Voyage* account and its intertexts (including Darwin's poem and Wedgwood's medallion) can insist that as consumers of the texts – voyage account, poem, and medallion – in the twenty-first century we recognise the colonial significance of their attitudes and actions. The settlement which was the cause of such celebration also meant the dispossession of Aboriginal peoples.[142] We have the benefit of hindsight to recognise these British celebratory works for what they would come to represent, and rather than simply laud Phillips, Darwin and Wedgwood as uncomplicated heroes of an age of discovery, we can consider the echoes of the words and deeds in our own century, a time of reckoning.

Wedgwood is often remembered for his anti-slavery campaigning – referenced by Darwin in *The Botanic Garden* – and for his support of American independence. However, in the production of the medallions he colluded in the imperialist intention to remove raw materials from Australia, stripping it of natural resources, those already used by indigenous peoples, for the benefit of Europeans. Bruce Pascoe's careful rereading of early white European settler accounts of Australia records the clay being used in the rendering of wood and bark-constructed homes, basaltic clay soils being terraced for agriculture, the construction of irrigation channels using clay in a similar way to Brindley's 'puddling' in Britain, clay weights attached to fishing nets to keep them beneath the water, the building of metre-high dykes along rivers, and the making of storage vessels and mourning caps – practical and symbolic pottery. Darwin's celebration of the medallions and the colony is nothing short of imperial propaganda – propaganda in which the canals are implicated. There is no doubt that Darwin's work reflects the conviction that Europe's apparent 'superiority in science, economy and religion directed its destiny'. In particular, says Pascoe, British industrial success seemed to lend its colonial ambition 'a natural authority', a belief that it was Britons' 'duty to spread their version of civilisation . . . In return they would capture the wealth of the colonised lands'. Most of the early explorers were not in Australia 'to marvel at a new civilisation; they were here to replace it. Most were simply describing a landscape from which settlers could profit'.[143]

Hope, in Darwin's poem to accompany the Sydney Cove medallions, is clearly a white European figure: she has a 'rosy smile', 'golden hair' and 'snowy hand'.[144] She has travelled on, and therefore with, Wedgwood's medallions to this 'new' land. She speaks to the 'wild plain', addressing an apparently empty, uncultivated and uncared-for land – precisely the rhetoric that Pascoe has attempted to overwrite in the twenty-first century. She imagines the future: broad, built streets and a crescent like that completed in Bath in 1775 (ll. 11–12). Radiating out from new cities across 'cultured land' of wheat and orchards will be 'bright canals, and solid roads' (l. 14). Darwin did not, one can be fairly sure, know of the Aboriginal canals that existed before the Europeans had even laid eyes on Australia. In this European-modelled civilisation will 'Peace, and Art, and Labour' flourish – as if they had not existed on the continent before the arrival of Europeans? This poem of Darwin's is no literary masterpiece, but it is an important marker of the way in which canals were envisaged by some as integral to the model of British modernity, here destined for forcible export. The section of this chapter that has focused on Darwin has repeatedly emphasised the creative interconnections in his work of geology, natural history, canals, and art; to this list must be added, with the Sydney Cove poem, colonialism.

Across diverse methods of articulating physical change in Britain in the eighteenth century (be that the plan, the geological investigation, letters and journals, classical mythology, scientific methodology, lobbying pamphlet, or poem), the industrial canal is no practical afterthought but deeply implicated in these various modes of explaining the present, wondering about the distant past, and imagining the future. What the poems under scrutiny also capture is the sense of how physical change itself, and the understanding of physical change, is part of cultural change, and that allegory and metaphor are required to articulate these processes. Barbauld's witness of the change in the landscape wrought by the Bridgewater Canal is rendered as a harbinger of a social and economic shift, a stretching towards the horizon – literally and figuratively – that ought to be approached cautiously. Barbauld's concern is with the beneficiaries and victims of industrial and overseas ambition. Seward's objections are to the *mis*placement of industry alongside its inevitable pollution of the natural landscape. Only Darwin's work is an uncomplicated hymn to industry.

His scientific understanding lends his writing incredible prescience, but he is reluctant to consider the as-yet-unimagined consequences of industrialisation. Wilson provides Wedgwood with a kind of epistemological exceptionalism, calling him a 'very different man from all these other industrialists' involved in the construction of canals and roads because he combined the sensibilities of an artist, 'commercial skill' and a keen scientific mind.[145] However, I suggest that Barbauld, Seward and Darwin similarly articulate lucid connections between economy, technology, exploration, experimentation, art, and myth as they make sense of their newly canalised world.

> It is 1799 and I am *Industrious*. A distant clock tower resounds to twelve chimes of the bell and the water flows on. A century turns, and the water flows on.

3

COLONISING CANAL-LAND

I am *Industrious* at the fag end of a glistening British century defined by Empire. 100 years has passed since Seward's sonnets. I am heavy with salt from Stoke Prior: another cargo scooped from the earth since the Iron Age. All has changed in this century; nothing has changed for millennia. I am steered along the Grand Junction Canal, completed to connect London with the rest of the watery lacework in 1805. It was once the aorta *ascendens et descendens*, and the life, blood, and circulation of the articles of inland trade, until a fire-breathing monster roared along the tracks of progress with a shriek, and a roar, and a rattle, boiling its blood.[1] The startling novelty of the canal has been surpassed; steam is the thing. Craft built in the era of railways and of ocean-going steamships hardly realise the vast change the country has seen, nor how great and fundamental that change is.[2] I pass now through the great parks of noblemen who granted per-mission for this cut through their land in a different time, a different world. At Cassiobury, the windows of a pretty fisherman's cottage are suspicious eyes on the woman whose capable hands are at my tiller. The sporting pleasures of the park seem to have infected the canal, for I now share these waters with those who travel on them not for work but leisure.[3] Some of them unwittingly replicate the rapacious acquisitiveness of their countrymen abroad, tearing up all the world to keep the wheels of industry turning.

The two core nineteenth-century texts of this chapter, Vincent Hughes's 'Through Canal-land in a Canadian Canoe' (1899) and *Two Girls on a Barge* (1891) by Sara Jeannette Duncan, turn our atten-tion to the last decade of that century and new leisure uses of the

canal. The chapter also re-examines a seminal work in the regeneration of the canals, *Narrow Boat* (1944) by L. T. C. Rolt, in the light of
these nineteenth-century works. In the nineteenth century, the canal
network was extensive: by 1835 'only upland communities in Wales,
Northern England, the South-West and some other rural areas lay five
miles beyond of a navigable waterway'.[4] By the 1890s, water had been
overtaken by rail; the industrial canal age has reached its carrying
zenith and begun to decline between the journeys of *Industrious* in
Chapters Two and Three. There was still enough commercial interest in 1888 to warrant the formation of the International Congress
on Inland Navigation, with representations from across Europe. In
May of that year, a conference at the Royal Society of Arts (initially
called the Society for the Encouragement of Arts, Manufactures and
Commerce) heard that of the roughly 4,000 miles of inland navigation
across the country, canal companies still owned 1,445 miles, public
trusts owned 930, the railways owned 1,333 miles and 188 miles lay
derelict. The canals continued to be understood as a means of making
Britain commercially competitive in the global marketplace, but one
that was underperforming. Calls came from various quarters in the
later nineteenth century to nationalise the waterways. The town of
Northwich was offered at the conference as an example of the ongoing
use and value of the canals: 'though 35 miles from Liverpool' its salt
industry had been able to make use of the Trent and Mersey Canal
'and commanded the trade of the world'. (The salt industry is particularly pertinent to the third section of this chapter, about *Two Girls
on a Barge*.) The canal itself had 'increased 20 times in value', and
others could have seen similar dividends had the railway monopoly
not broken up the continuity of the network. Another speaker pointed
out the false economy of rail's relative speed in transporting goods
and materials: 'the fourfold speed on the railways being attained at a
fourfold cost'.[5] Nevertheless, by 1894 the water traffic between London
and Manchester was said by one newspaper correspondent to have
'vanished into thin air', the waterways 'choked by the greed of the great
railway interest', becoming 'mere mud-banks or puddles' where once
they were vibrant transport links.[6]

In terms of leisure use, the author of the humorous yet informa-
tive series, 'On the Canal' in *Household Words*, is an 'extraordinary
tourist' to travel by canal in 1858, having 'nearly exhausted' England
for novel sights and stories. He joins the *Stourport*, 'a fair specimen of
the fly-boats which are now employed in the carrying trade upon the

canals that intersect England in every direction'. The author asserts that the canals will always maintain their position as conveyors of non-urgent heavy goods, failing to predict the railway companies' deliberate neglect of waterways in their ownership.[7]

Canal water is sprinkled surprisingly sparsely through the pages of Victorian literature, considering the ubiquity of waterways in industry, urban environments and the wider national landscape. In one example where it does appear, Charlotte Elizabeth Tonna's *Helen Fleetwood* (1841), Helen's adopted family must navigate their way from a rural, agricultural existence to an industrial urban one in Manchester, from the past to the future, and they do so by canal. In Anthony Trollope's *The Kellys and the O'Kellys* (1848), Martin Kelly travels, with great fortitude and an appetite for the 'leg of mutton, floating in a bloody sea of grease and gravy, which always comes on the table three hours after the departure from Porto Bello', on the Ballinasloe canal boat on Dublin's Grand Canal. Passengers on such a journey are 'doomed to a twenty hours' sojourn in one of these floating prisons'.[8] Dickens refers to canals in comparison with railways in both *Hard Times* (1854) and *Dombey and Son* (1848). George Eliot's *Felix Holt* (1866) looks to forms of transport as a way of characterising the past, in this case the days of coach travel. Eliot compares the sights and sounds of that long, slow journey to a future where travel will more likely resemble a 'bullet' being 'shot . . . through a tube'.[9] The canal is part of that older way of life, but it is also what marks the opening of change; not just a passage for water, but a passage to the future. It becomes, in this literary example, a way of signalling the navigation of religious, political, and cultural transition in England.

In the last months of the nineteenth century, *The Boy's Own Paper* published Vincent Hughes's account of voyaging with a friend named Jacky 'through canal-land in a Canadian Canoe'. The narrative embeds the canal in sedimented layers of idealised English history (the Civil War, Edward V), as L. T. C. Rolt would do in the mid twentieth century. Like two of the authors discussed in Chapter Two, Hughes's narrative takes in a view of Lichfield cathedral, in this instance in the distance from Fradley. The men had acquired a 'light and well-built' canoe from a friend in France and, thanks to another friend at the Grand Junction Canal Company, obtained the requisite passes to travel from the Thames at Brentford to Kendal in Westmorland. Commentary on such passes are a commonplace throughout boating travelogues on canals in the nineteenth century, signifying not only the advanced bureaucracy of the nineteenth-century canal network, but also that this bureaucracy did not quite know what to do with leisure travel on the canal: are passes required or may canoeists be waved through? What rights do these travellers have in this space? Are they privileged or persecuted as users of the industrial waterway? Travelogues raise but do not satisfactorily answer such questions, indicating the contestation of canal space that will persist for centuries. The passes are also regularly a textual signifier of class in the nineteenth-century, as gentlemen sportsmen express their amusement or annoyance when petty officials demand that they play by the rules set for those who labour on the waterways. Such figures expect to be able to pass with impunity through any space in which they choose to travel. To deploy a term much in use in the 2020s, they feel 'entitled'. Hughes and Jacky were delayed at their very first lock 'by a string of canal barges coming through to catch the morning tide', and this rather sets the tone for the short travelogue: the actual work of the canals is often seen as a slightly annoying disturbance to their canoe adventure – unless they want a lift.[10]

This third chapter looks, then, at Hughes's narrative in intertextual canal-cultural context, especially the writing of other canoeists, and in dialogue with the fictionalised travelogue *Two Girls on a Barge*, in order to understand how aspects of British imperial ideology of the nineteenth century can be traced in the cultural picture of the canals a century on from their inspiring industrial ascendance. In this chapter's final section, my reading reaches beyond the boundaries of the nineteenth century to consider Rolt's *Narrow Boat* because it is impossible to read today about leisure uses of the industrial canal in the past and ignore the fact that this is now the predominant use of the waterways. Rolt helped *re*introduce the canal as leisure space (though, in fact, his intention was to regenerate commercial, rather than leisure, use), and his work is caught between the sense of intrepid adventure voiced by Hughes and Duncan, and the complex questions of authenticity on the waterways explored further in Chapter Five.

Other articles published alongside 'Through Canal-land in a Canadian Canoe' in the collected annual volume of *The Boy's Own Paper* in 1899 give a sense of its publishing context. The annual opens with the imagined daring exploits of a young Robert Clive – not yet 'of India'.[11] There are interviews with Victorian cricketing heroes.[12] There is an illustration of alligator shooting in Florida and accounts of one thousand days in the arctic, an Indian conjurer on the Mediterranean Station in Malta, and the longest bicycle ride ever attempted.[13] There is advice on things like 'tenting as a holiday for boys'.[14] 'Through Canal-land in a Canadian Canoe' thus finds itself at the confluence of sport, exploration and Empire. Explicitly, an article by Henry C. Devine about 'Roughing it on the Thames' asserts that 'British boys anxious to "rough it"' have no need to wait until they trek 'the South African veldt, shoot elephant in Burma, or bivouac on the Andes' because all these experiences 'can be got in their own country'. Indeed, 'adventures, hardships, and hairbreadth escapes galore may be picked up like blackberries' if the boy in question has 'the pluck and grit associated with the name of Englishman'.[15] In other words, in the later nineteenth century the narratives of colonial adventure were self-consciously turned geographically inwards to the British Isles. Here, I look at the way this inward turn applies specifically to the industrial canal.

The first section's key contention is that Hughes's work (and that of his contemporaries and antecedents) transforms the canals into a space for physical and ideological conquest. In the second section, I examine how the Canadian Sara Jeannette Duncan (writing as V. Cecil Cotes) fashions a slightly different script. Duncan's use of irony and self-conscious intertextuality in *Two Girls on a Barge* presents a refracted version of the muscular, masculine urge to dominate the canal space, but ideologically finds much in common with the micro-genre of nineteenth-century British canal travelogues in its assumptions about class and Empire. The chapter thus blends factual accounts with fiction and, as Justin Livingstone points out, there was already a tendency among the 'celebrated explorers of Africa' in this period to 'publish novels alongside the authoritative expeditionary narrative'.[16] Hughes and writers like him depict the British working-class people they meet on and near the waterways as native 'others', repeating, replicating, and resituating imperialist discourse. As Bernard Porter notes, Britain itself 'was made up of imperialists and subjects', and the power of class at home was an analogue for the power of the imperialist abroad.[17] Duncan's representation of the people of the British waterways also uses the language and discourse of Empire, but as someone with outsider status in relation to male imperial hegemony she presents this in more nuanced ways than do the other writers I discuss. In *Narrow Boat*, Rolt continues the tradition of an authoritative and didactic travelogue tone, measuring the life and pleasures of the 'townsman' against pre-industrial tradition.

Reading the waterways and their textual imperial connections in the late nineteenth century and into the twentieth century not only enables a postcolonial interpretation of the British canal, it shines a light on the way the pervasive ideology of Empire inflected attitudes towards class and gender on the waterways in Britain. One reason to think carefully about Empire and the canal is because the economics of British imperial possession required a transport infrastructure to carry raw materials and consumables from the Empire to the home country's inland manufacturing centres and markets, and goods back out to imperial markets: cotton in to Manchester and textiles out; sugar in from the Caribbean; guns out from Birmingham; tea in from India; Australian wool; Canadian wood. However, the period on which most of the chapter focuses – the 1890s – lies between the end of the Navigation Acts in 1849 and the system of Imperial Preference from 1932, meaning imperial markets faced stiff competition at this time. More than the logistics of imperial commodities transport, however (which is taken up in Chapter Four), I am interested here in the way that a kind of 'Empire thinking' permeated so many areas of cultural life for those who had other forms of privilege (in particular class privilege), including the nascent leisure use of the waterways.

A Boy's Own Canal Adventure

I am *Industrious*, one of a string of barges pulled by a tug through the intense darkness of the Blisworth tunnel on the Grand Junction Canal, caressed by reverberations and echoes. The tug has an unusual cargo today of two confident young men and their canoe. Their confidence wanes, though, as the captain tells a thirty-year-old boggart tale I have overheard many times before. He tells them of the steamer *Wasp*, which unexpectedly met a boat being legged through the tunnel in the opposite direction. Steam is the thing. So much steam and smoke from a newly-stoked fire. The vessels collided, and the unholy darkness became a smoking, choking hell.[18] 'Do you feel the suffocation?' leers the captain now. 'Can you hear the cries of drowning men?' Whether they do or not, the men are quieter the deeper we go, and keep ducking their heads as if the roof will take them off for them to join the boggart chorus of Blisworth. They take their time to compose themselves once we are through, so I pass them slowly, only to see them further along. The wind buffets me and their small craft, offering a challenge to one as if he hopes to prove he is still a man, no phantom yet. He believes he can conquer the water, the darkness, the wind. He turns broadside on to the full force of a gust. Over he goes, a mouthful of the water that people do not wish to drink. He makes his way to shore and ducks behind a tree to change his wet clothes.[19]

Hughes and Jacky are somewhere between adventurers, explorers and sportsmen, though there is a clear difference between Hughes's travels in Britain and what imperial canoeist explorers such as the ill-fortuned C. H. Coulthurst undertook: exploration was, Dane Kennedy reminds us, 'a distinct and rigorous enterprise with its own epistemological logic and codes of conduct'.[20] Nevertheless, this is how Hughes *wishes* to be seen. The opening of the narrative describes wanting to look for a new experience, positing variety as the spice of existence, but also wanting to 'explore . . . comparatively un-known canals' – unknown, of course, to men of their class and experience but not to the men and women who worked on them every day. Hughes consistently points out where they have achieved exploratory 'firsts', such as being the first canoe to paddle across the swivel bridge by which the Bridgewater Canal is carried over the Manchester Ship Canal – an engineering development which takes us back to the awe-inspiring aqueduct that had carried the Bridgewater in the last century. Hughes knew he would have a ready audience if his canal narrative was framed as exploration into unknown territory. David Livingstone's *Missionary Travels and Researches in South Africa* (1857), for instance, sold more than 70,000 copies.[21] The clear textual predecessors of Hughes's canoe travelogue are, however, the works of John MacGregor. Some detail from and context of these is examined here, in order to set up the imperial adventure mould in which Hughes wrote, and to make literary linkages between the British industrial canal and the Suez Canal.

Though rarely remembered outside canoeing enthusiast circles, MacGregor was as famous as Livingstone in his day – indeed, he met the explorer at his father's house in Dublin.[22] At this time, Livingstone was propounding 'his views on the question of African civilisation by recommending the growth of cotton upon an extensive scale', with trade between Britain and South Africa 'a means of abolishing the slave trade and advancing the interests of European civilisation'. He wrote to MacGregor in February 1858 to explain that he intended making 'the Zambesi a path of lawful commerce by stimulating the tribes inhabiting its banks to engage in collecting and cultivating the raw materials of English manufactures'. MacGregor promised to place his pen 'at the disposal of Dr. Livingstone' and illustrated his bestselling travelogue. Livingstone's exploration of an African river can thus be understood, via the raw materials of manufacture, as connected by water to the British manufacturing districts through which Hughes would paddle, inspired by the canoeing exploits of Livingstone's correspondent and textual collaborator, MacGregor. MacGregor's biographer, Edwin Hodder, asserted that his 'character may be summed up in one word: manliness, in the fullest, freest sense – physical, moral and spiritual'. He stood for 'muscular Christianity'.[23]

There would be several iterations of the *Rob Roy* canoe – named for MacGregor's famous ancestor and modelled on craft from North America and Kamchatka – but the first was fifteen feet long and made of oak.[24] His early boating took place on the Grand Junction Canal at Weedon in Northamptonshire, but MacGregor was no lover of canals until he reached the Suez late in his career. For instance, he compared the exploration of a new river with the 'voyage of life': 'our minds would only vegetate if all life were like a straight canal'.[25] Canals were unadventurous almost to the point of moral neglect, it seems. While planning a route through France he insisted that 'I would not leave the pleasant current for a slow canal, until the last possible opportunity' (p. 163). Later, he notes that, even at its best, canal scenery has 'scant liveliness, the whole thing is so prosaic and artificial, and in fact stupid'. The difference between 'a glorious river encircling you with lofty rocks' and the 'confining' canal 'was something like that between walking among high mountains and being shut up by mistake in Bloomsbury-square' (p. 167). Rivers are glorious; canals stupid. The reader is left in little doubt which kind of waterways to select for manly adventure. In the Middle East, however, via canoe, 'the canal thus examined becomes well worth investigation'. 'Have I not', he said, 'invented a new mode of seeing old lands?'[26] It seems that the visible engineering venturesomeness of Suez in the nineteenth century made the canal more interesting, and travel along it more congruent with an ideology of muscular imperial Christianity.

The French held European cultural pre-eminence in Egypt, and Britain had clear ambitions in the region – though as MacGregor paddled down the Suez the British government was officially opposed to the Canal because of the commercial competition it promised to the routes Britain controlled; the landing of British troops in Alexandria in 1882 would be a more definite push towards its 'informal empire' in the Middle East.[27] It is also near-impossible to hear the name 'Suez' without thinking of the end of Empire and the Crisis of 1956. Its importance to Britain coincides with the peaking and decline of its Empire more broadly, serving as a synecdoche for trade, ambition, power and crisis. This change of setting for MacGregor, beyond Europe, and the imperialist attitudes with which it is charged, alters the meaning of the canal as a location for adventure.

It was, Hodder tells us, MacGregor's 'great ambition' to see a boys' newspaper established to counter the 'current literature' (p. 387). *The Boy's Own Paper*, published by the Religious Tract Society from 1879, was 'the nearest approach to his ideal' (p. 357). The paper was, Penner says, 'an identifiably masculine publication', promoting 'a brand of British masculinity that was modelled on the core values of chivalry, sportsmanship, self-help, and philanthropy' (pp. 147; 20). It is thus no surprise that MacGregor's biography was published therein as 'A Stirring Life-Story'.[28] Not only was the paper popular with colonial and missionary readers, tying them closely to British culture and identity, but sport, including canoeing, was expressly linked with 'a British imperialist agenda that reinforced patriotic sentiment and responsibility'. Further, Empire was depicted as 'an exhilarating product of industrialism, capitalism and scientific advancement'.[29] Empire in *The Boy's Own Paper* seems, then, to collect up the themes of Barbauld's poetic vision in 'The Invitation' and see them brought to triumphant fruition. However, those enjoying its fruits are a limited constituency: white middle- and upper-class Victorian authors in *The Boy's Own Paper*, and the readers they hoped to produce. Penner shows that 'travel writing, adventure fiction, and missionary reports' in the paper 'transformed the foreign landscape into a recognisable part of the British Empire' (p. 185). Hughes's narrative, in the same newspaper, turns Britain's waterways into a recognisable part of imperial ideology.

There are a surprising number of canoe travelogues from the later nineteenth century, partly due to MacGregor's popularising of the sport. By the 1890s there were three magazines which appealed to canoeist readers. Famously, Robert Louis Stevenson recounted his *Inland Voyage* via canoe with Sir Walter Grindlay Simpson in 1876 from Antwerp, through Belgium and into France towards Paris. Stevenson painted a very romantic picture of the experience, in spite of being spat on by children from a bridge at one point (a regular occurrence for the women on boats in the next chapter). Stevenson and Simpson met kindred canoeing spirits in the *Royal Sport Nautique*, finding the waterways to be an international homosocial space: 'we were English boating-men, and the Belgian boating-men fell upon our necks'. The tone of Stevenson's narrative meanders from sporting interest to the anthropological, as he asserts – echoing closely the sentiments of many writers at this time about the Romani people: 'these *canaletti* are only gypsies semi-domesticated'.[30] This attitude also appears in *Two Girls on a Barge*, and is discussed further in the second part of the chapter.

Two years after the publication of MacGregor's travelogue, three anonymous adventurers travelled by canoe and skiff as recounted in *The Waterway to London* (1869 – also the year that the Suez Canal opened). There are clear nods in the preface to MacGregor: 'Get a canoe of your own, and if you can't reach the Red Sea, Nile, or Jordan, or even the Danube, Rhine, and Seine, paddle about on your own native rivers'. There is explicit mention of the 'Rob Roy' and 'our friend MacGregor' later on.[31] Richard Fairhurst has used signed copies of the book to identify the voyagers as Alfred Taylor Schofield (the author), his brother R. Harold A. Schofield and Will, a friend of theirs from Rochdale.[32] As the title suggests, these sportsmen make their way through England in the opposite direction to Hughes, beginning at the basin of the Bridgewater Canal in Manchester – then informally known as Cottonopolis. They even make a (mistaken) visit to Coalbrookdale and a (deliberate) tour of the chinaworks at Coalport, making a cut back in time to the earlier industrial concerns of the canal. Like Hughes, these voyagers find their patience 'sorely tried' by the 'endless succession of canal-boats' they meet; it is not clear what else they expected to find *on a working canal*. They remark on the 'famous aqueduct over the Mersey', referring the reader to Smiles's *Lives of the Engineers*, and thus drawing attention to textual relationships with the canal: reading this waterway to London calls on other readings (p. 12). The 'bargees' from whom the adventurers receive a significant lift along the Shropshire Union Canal are described as 'the most obliging, civil, and kind people', treating them with 'unusual respect, differing considerably in manner from the free and enlightened operatives in Cottonopolis' (p. 30). The workers of the waterway are, for this author, a cut above the factory workers located where they began their journey. Operatives in Lancashire mills had worked with slave-produced cotton from the United States, which was brought along the canals from Liverpool, until just three years before his canoe voyage – and if Livingstone had his way it would be colonised Africa which supplied cotton for the north's textile trade as part of a process of civilisation. The adjectives, 'free and enlightened', seem to be intentionally ironic given the unfavourable comparison between those in factories and the amiable bargees. Reading that phrasing in the broader context of global industrialised and imperial capital, however, draws attention to the enslaved and the colonised, those who have and might supply the workers' raw materials. The connection between Britain's bloodied global relations, its industry and waterways are momentarily brought to the surface by Schofield's comparison.

By the time Hughes and Duncan were writing, the canals were ripe for rediscovery – they held, of course, a very different place in the nation's industrial systems than they had at the beginning of the century and, as the examples above demonstrate, there was an existing readership for narratives of waterway discovery. James Stephen Jeans noted in 1890 that the rapid extension of the railways led to the canals being largely regarded as 'obsolete and useless'. Canals, Jeans opined, 'as they were built a century ago have no longer any function to fulfil that is worthy of serious consideration. Their mission is ended; their use is an anachronism'.[33] Duncan and Hughes certainly paint those engaged in the carrying trade as quaint anachronisms, but they also show that the canals need not only be thought about in relation to their original use, and my reading of them is indeed a serious consideration. These are no 'journeys without maps' in late-nineteenth-century canal travelogues, but an exercise in ideologically *re*mapping the dark industrial interior of the country; as MacGregor would have it, a new mode of seeing old lands.[34]

An example of doing just this comes at the challenging 18-mile Blisworth Tunnel, hand-dug between 1793 and 1802, where Hughes and Jacky make use of a steam tug, in use there since the 1870s. 'The journey through this subterranean passage was a most novel one to us who had never been through a tunnel of this description before', recounts Hughes. 'The intense darkness, only illuminated by the light from the boiler fire, was most uncanny, while the wonderful reverberations and echoes occurring in the tunnel quite startled us until we became used to the situation'. The skipper of the tug 'in the manner of his kind . . . accentuated the eerie feeling of the place by spinning all sorts of creepy yarns about canal boatmen who had mysteriously gone overboard in the pitch dark, and never been seen again'.[35] The canal is a home territory deliberately made strange to highlight adventure. Kennedy notes: 'it became possible in the nineteenth century to . . .

discover the known anew' (p. 6). However, in exploring Blisworth, Hughes fails to recount the experience in a new way at all: *Two Girls on a Barge* included a very similar narrative eight years earlier. In that work, the train of barges pulled by a steam tug contributed to the eeriness, for the 'black water is always hungry', and if one slips and falls in 'the tug goes forging on, and the barges cannot stop, and the darkness is intense'. In this version of the tunnel crossing, 'Mrs Bargee', the professional boatwoman, also conforms to the 'manner' of her 'kind'. The passage is 'deathly still' but 'an indefinable Presence moved with [them] in the blackness'. That darkness, and the proximity of damp stones 'played fantastic tricks with the imagination', every sense becoming 'distorted, unnaturally acute'. The same story is told here as in Hughes's narrative, about what happens if 'the black water swallows ye'. In the depths of the tunnel, the water becomes phosphorescent, and water drips from the 'glistening spire' of a stalactite.[36] The tunnel is presented in both travelogues as unnatural, uncanny, and truly frightening; the atmosphere is accentuated for the narrators by what they paint as the almost hysterical credulity of the waterways natives, which is easy for them to shake off and condemn once the boats emerge into the sunlight.

Classically racist imperialist fictions, such as H. Rider Haggard's *King Solomon's Mines* (1885) and *She* (1887), and narratives such as Livingstone's *Missionary Travels*, tend to treat 'native' superstition as both the reason for conquering and means by which to conquer non-Christian peoples, but the uncanny darkness of caves and subterranean passages is nonetheless heightened for their Western characters by native myths and beliefs. White adventurers must call on their apparently innate reason and moral strength to resist the influence of strange territories. In attempting a new mode of seeing old lands, Hughes also conforms to the generic expectations of imperialist narratives.

The towed journey through Blisworth indicates another echo from imperial travel and adventure narratives, and that is the canoeists' reliance on those people who work on and near the canal; this assistance is never properly credited, simply constituting the nuts and bolts of the adventurers' story rather than offering full acknowledgement to the unnamed workers of the waterways. At Hanwell, still known for its flight of locks today, Hughes and Jacky 'had a brief chat with an old bargee, from whom we got some useful advice', patronisingly described as 'not wholly free from chaff'.[37] These incidental conversations can be read collectively to understand the tourists' relationship with the people of the waterways on whom their journey relies. A 'rus-tic' advises the use of canal clay on a wasp sting, the pair get a tow to Stone in Staffordshire from a monkey-barge (a narrowboat with living space), and avoid having to go dangerously through another tunnel in their canoes with the aid of a man, a boy and a wheelbarrow. We never learn the names of these helpers, and it seems doubtful that Hughes and Jacky do either. Regularly 'taking advantage' of 'the good-nature of the bargees and their wives', the men 'found them a most interest-ing and sociable lot of people', and are often treated like 'honoured guests' on board (p. 10). At Harecastle, a locked-out miner is given two shillings to 'cheerfully [trot] on ahead' to open locks for them: the use of such an equine verb indicates a supercilious attitude. The next paragraph begins 'after getting through the locks. . .': the miner has been forgotten by the end of the sentence in which he appears. At Stoke-on-Trent, they are given shelter in a 'wayside cottage', but it is as if the cottage is empty for all the detail of its owners. On the Lancaster Canal all barges are cleared out of their way to offer them a smooth journey. At Kendal they obtain the assistance of a man with a horse and cart to take the canoe and their luggage to Kendal Station.[38]

Postcolonial research on imperial travel narratives, such as that of Felix Driver and Lowri Jones, has drawn attention to previously 'hidden histories' of exploration, emphasising the contributions of indigenous peoples that made European expeditions possible: these floating domestic travelogues contribute nuance to our understand-ing of hidden histories set in more exotic climes. In other words, even when the explorers in question are paddling along British canals, they take advantage of good-natured workers for transport, information and accommodation. The adventure, however, is still wholly theirs as they tell it. To pay too much textual attention to the way in which their journey floats not just on water but on the labour of the working class is to get dangerously close to the dirty realities of the author's power and privilege. Konish, Nugent and Shellam explain that the focus on mediators in the story of exploration works 'against a conventional emphasis on the exploits and achievements of the singular heroic explorer' – figures like MacGregor and Livingstone.[39] In MacGregor's case, he is reliant during his Middle East voyage on people selling bread and coffee from boats on the Suez, his dragoman, muleteers, men to pitch tents, a cook, and individuals offering directions and accommodation.[40] These cross-cultural encounters and opportun-ities for exchange are rarely seen as such – in Hughes's narrative the privileged white males are not exactly open to what they might learn from their waterway mediators, even when they directly bene-fit. 'Indigenous' waterways knowledge is undervalued here, as it was within global exploration narratives, but is similarly vital to the success of exploration. The working 'others' of the journey are depicted like a lock, or the wind, or a current in the water.

Having enjoyed rural scenes for much of the journey, on the North Staffordshire Canal, 160 miles into the voyage, the canoeists notice that 'the scenery for some distance assumed the aspect peculiar to manu-facturing centres'.[41] They come face-to-face with the fact that coal and industry were still the *raison d'être* of the canal, not pastoral paddling. Coal was still central to industry. Georges-Louis Leclerc, in *Epochs of Nature* (1778), had earlier identified a seventh planetary epoch, 'the time of man', defined by the advancement of civilisation 'prom-ised by abundant fossil fuels'.[42] Such human advancement, as it was understood by the late nineteenth century in high imperialist terms, required energy, infrastructure and expansion. Elizabeth Carolyn Miller has framed the roughly 100 years from the shift to steam in British manufacturing in the 1830s as 'a period when Britain came to understand itself as an empire thoroughly dependent on extraction'.[43] Leclerc's 'time of man' is posited in the century before the narratives I focus on here, and a different vision was advanced in the century after by W. E. B. DuBois: 'a civilization without coal' to come.[44] The white British middle-class understanding of the fossil-fuelled time of civilised man, sandwiched between Leclerc and DuBois, relied on: the domination of territories and workers at home and across the world; on digging resources out of the ground at ever faster rates (and with ever larger profits); and, in order to enjoy their leisure at the apex of civilisation, on forgetting the whole distasteful business.

The manufacturing context into which the canoeists float offers a startling depiction of a working-class crowd depicted like colonised natives as the canoeists reach the industrial north. In its context, genre and language, the narrative inadvertently connects the waterways to the imperial Anthropocene I have just described: coal, canal, labour, and the travel narratives of Empire come together in this scene:

> During the rest of the day's paddle we were in the very heart of the coal-mining district, and our progress caused no little comment and wonder to the crowds of "locked-out" miners and their families. So embarrassing became their attentions at length that we had to

abandon our original intention of landing at Wigan, owing to the numerous crowd awaiting our approach at that place.

Twice we essayed to get ashore, but finally, not appreciating the appearance of the motley crowd, we pushed on until we reached Plank Lane, where, the crowd of idlers being a little less dense, we summoned up pluck enough to venture shore.

Even here we found ourselves the centre of attraction to the people; rough miners crowding around as we lifted our canoe from the water, to stare in amazement at our appearance, some even going so far in their admiration of our little craft as to pass their hands along its polished sides, all the while expressing their opinions in such a broad vernacular as to be almost unintelligible to our Southern ears. They thought it was a joke upon our part when we told them that we had paddled all the way from London in the canoe. The way they nudged each other and winked solemnly was most expressive.

Their attentions at last became so overwhelming that we were compelled to give the craft into the care of the friendly lock-keeper and beat a hasty retreat.[45]

Hughes's reference to the 'very heart' of the coal-mining district echoes explorer travelogues. Intriguingly, on an occasion when Livingstone uses such language in *Missionary Travels* it is to describe Mambari tradesmen at the 'crossing of the confluence of the Leeba and Makondo', bringing English manufactured goods 'into the heart of Africa'. The Mambari tell the Makololo with whom they trade that the cotton products 'came out of the sea' because 'to Africans our cotton-mills are fairy dreams'.[46] Hughes represents the English miners producing the fuel for these very mills in a very similar way to Livingstone presenting naïve Africans, as the miners stare in amazement at the canoe and touch its sides in wonder, communicating in a bewildering native tongue foreign to the explorers' ears. Miller notes that 'mining communities were thought of as a race apart' in the nineteenth century, something that is 'well established in the primary and secondary literature of the period'.[47] Natives in the heart of Africa and workers in the heart of the coal-mining district are, in this ideologically imperialist writing, off-kilter analogues of each other. On a waterway connecting the 'heart of Africa' with British imports from the coast canoes are commonplace but advanced manufacturing is unbelievable; on a waterway taking coal directly to the mills, the manufactured goods are quotidian and the canoe an amazing sight.[48]

The Leeds and Liverpool Canal, on the banks of which this incident occurred, gave large 72ft boats from Wigan easy access to a major port, though by the time Hughes and Jacky visited there were three railway stations in the town, and people had begun to refer to the place as 'Coalopolis'.[49] Toll roads were used to improve the ruinous existing roads from the early part of the eighteenth century. These were followed by a scheme to make the River Douglas navigable in the 1740s, a waterway which reached its cargo-carrying capacity within thirty years of opening. Factories and mills were built alongside the canal, changing Wigan into a manufacturing centre, with horse-drawn boats covering the distance to Liverpool in twelve hours or so. Most local collieries already had horse-drawn tramways to move coal from the pit heads, which were extended fairly easily to the canalside.[50] The canal was used for coal transport until the 1970s.[51]

In order to reorientate the scene described by Hughes to the miners' perspective, some further detail about Wigan coal is necessary. Coal was the essential fuel for a range of local industries from brass-workers to glass-makers, as well as being lucrative in export to larger cities, and the cleaner-burning cannel was used to heat homes. By 1861, ten per cent of the male population of Wigan, some 90,000 people, were employed as miners.[52] Industrial relations in the town were acrimonious throughout the second half of the nineteenth century, and the sight of 'locked out' miners as in the extract was not particularly unusual. Miners were not treated as employees, but closer to what we recognise as zero-hours contractors today, receiving a small amount per ton of coal mined. This was, of course, dangerous work: explosions at Arley pit in the 1850s killed tens of men and boys at a time. When the miners' requests to increase the amount paid per ton was turned down, they withdrew their labour. When the demands were met, as in 1890, the price of coal was ramped up for the consumer and the mine owners made even bigger profits.[53] A collier in Wigan in 1891 could earn 7 shillings a day, around £30 in twenty-first century money.[54] 1893's coal strike saw the *Hull Daily Mail* riff on the saying about sending coals to Newcastle; Scottish coal was being imported to Liverpool and sent on to Wigan.[55] This strike lasted sixteen weeks and resulted from coal owners demanding a 25% *reduction* in wages. Strikes were not only about wages and the price per ton; in 1895 the Garswood Hall Colliery Company tried to impose a more difficult method for extracting coal, which was tantamount to a reduction in wages as the miners insisted tonnage would be lower.[56] In such strikes, hundreds, if not thousands, of miners would be locked out at a time (up to 5,000 during a strike in 1894), so the crowd that the canoeists witnessed would certainly have been large and, perhaps, not a little intimidating. Newspapers give detailed accounts of the industrial disputes. Indeed readers of 'Canal-land' may have been familiar with industrial Wigan landscapes as the *Illustrated London News* featured pictures of strikes and disasters.

There is no attempt in Hughes's narrative to humanise the striking miners, let alone understand their predicament. The canoers' 'embarrassment' in the face of the crowds highlights their difference from them, their inability (or, rather, unwillingness) to meaningfully communicate with the miners, and effaces the labour relations that lead to the miners underemployment – they are simply 'idlers'. Indeed, Hughes and Jacky consume the strike as yet another form of privileged adventure, as they are given a tour of the deserted mine. The very worst that the miners do to the canoeists is touch the boat and show wonder at the adventure, yet Hughes and Jacky are too frightened to come ashore. But perhaps, as adventurers, they also have in mind the 1886 death of Austrian Karl Hinkelmann in present-day Mozambique at the hands of a 'native chief' – Hinkelmann's young English companion escaped to tell the tale.[57] Maybe they read of the Revd George Grenfall of Birmingham who, in the course of his exploration of African waterways, 'met with not a few difficulties from the hostility of the natives'.[58] Perhaps the news reported in the newspapers in the 1880s of the territories Stanley was heroically claiming were at the forefront of their imagination, and the tales of dangerous German and Spanish encounters with natives from the river. In all likelihood, they remembered MacGregor's exploits on the River Jordan. Near the village of Salhyeh (Al-Salihiyya), he came face-to-face with hundreds of screaming 'Arabs'. A 'black giant' swam furiously towards him, 'brandishing the white shank-bone of a buffalo'.[59] This incident is illustrated in the work, and the implication of savagery could not be clearer.

For the canoeist fashioning himself as an explorer, a bank of curious natives *was* probably something to be nervous about, requiring 'pluck' to face it. It was also a generic convention of the explorer tale. Hughes translates that nervousness into narrative, and his countrymen become inarticulate, strange, incredulous, motley. While this last adjective is a depreciative reference to a diverse or varied group, the etymology of the word is from the particoloured coat of a fool in the sixteenth and seventeenth centuries: Hughes makes fools of these striking workers in his attempt to position himself as the brave adventurer. More than this, the connections the text makes between striking miners and colonised others, via its generic predecessors and use of language, takes on greater significance when read from a postcolonial perspective. Adventurer explorers like Livingstone and MacGregor saw territory in Africa, the Middle East and Australia as theirs to explore and Britain's to claim in order to supply its mills and factories – with civilising side effects. The 'Philosopher of the Factory', Andrew Ure, declared: 'it is to our coal, iron, rivers, seaports, canals, highways, capital . . . that our large share in the trade of the world is to be ascribed'.[60] Empire fed British industrial capitalism, and the waterways were an integral part of industrial development, even at the end of the century. Hughes's narrative stakes a claim on the space of the industrial waterways as an exciting if privileged tourist destination, and his attitude to their working people echoes the treatment of colonised peoples exploited in the service of industry's great machine, especially those textually captured in travelogues. This is not to say that the work of a bargee was akin to that of the factory worker, miner, or certainly the plantation cotton picker. What I want to emphasise is the correspondence between a sense of middle-class entitlement to leisure on the waterways (and the mediation the journey required), and the inescapable nexus of Empire and industry whose logic governed production and consumption in nineteenth-century Britain. Hughes's attitudes resituate foreign colonialism on the English waterways, and in doing so draw attention both to the implication of the canals in Britain's exploitative interests abroad and the imperialist treatment of workers in Britain.

Hughes's work finds the perfect riposte in the 1972 BBC film, *The Black Safari*, narrated by and starring the renowned director Horace Ové. The film begins with European explorers 'discovering' Africa and sending their logs home, then presents itself as the reverse, 'an account of a Black Man's expedition along the Upper Reaches of the Leeds and Liverpool Canal to find the Centre of Britain', risking their lives in 'savage Lancashire' with a naturalist and anthropologist aboard.[61] They enter a lock, their 'gateway to the maze of watery channels on which the British tribes rely for all their communication'. Naturalist Bloke Modisane is sent ashore to investigate new plants that might be developed as cash crops back home – recalling Livingstone's enthusiasm for developing an African cotton industry. The common daisy is renamed in Modisane's honour, echoing the practices of naturalist-explorers. The group makes its way to the 'famous, forbidden city of Wigan', as if responding directly to Hughes's account. In this region, Ové intones, 'those who do not serve the gods of work or industry do not hold up their heads as free men', but the observation is about the decline of industry. The film is a well-observed parody of the assumptions and claims of nineteenth-century explorers, but it also visually and literally revisits 'canal-land' with the effect of making even clearer the imperial ideological subtext of Hughes's account.

The chapter now turns to consider a voyage conceived by women, in contrast to the other nineteenth-century narratives so-far discussed, involving a writer who considered herself colonial rather than metropolitan, an outsider to the discourses of white male power ostentatiously performed by the Victorian adventurer-explorers featured in this section.

New Women on the Canal

I am *Industrious*, built by the Farrins in the 'Salt King' John Corbett's Stoke Works. Corbett's father was a canal carrier, and *his* father was on the land. Such is the story of Midlands industry. Other boats at Stoke once carried salt for the British Alkali and Imperial Salt and Alkali Companies, iron for the foundry and slack coal: tons and tons of coal.[62] Corbett later owned those companies, and their boats, while the railway took care of the coal. This century, a furiously steaming engine overtakes me on many journeys, but still the waterways perpetually ripple with trade. Corbett is just turning his attention away from salt and towards philanthropy. With that turn the dream of the Droitwich Ship Canal dies, just as Manchester's nears completion; salt water might have flowed into, rather than out of, ancient Salinae had the ambition been delivered. There is no salt now on board. A strange cargo instead. 'Looks like a tea party!' shouts a boy from the bank.[63] There are steamer chairs, a Japanese paper umbrella and Liberty curtains, as I make my way from London to Coventry in search of Maggie Tulliver and Lady Godiva.

One of Hughes and Jacky's stops in 1899 was at Nuneaton, to explore the birthplace of George Eliot.[64] This, as well as other overlaps in their route and points of interest on the way, closely connects that narrative with the journey of Sara Jeannette Duncan's *Two Girls on a Barge*, for the latter was a literary pilgrimage in its genesis; Maggie Tulliver of *The Mill on the Floss* (1860) inspires the women (not, in fact, girls) to seek out the exact location of George Eliot's schooling in the Midlands.[65] These two travelogues are, though, different, for reasons of tone, gender and imperial identity.

Duncan was born 'Sarah Janet' in Brantford, Canada in December 1860. Her Presbyterian father was originally from Fifeshire, Scotland; her mother was from New Brunswick and of Irish heritage. Like many women of her time and class, Duncan initially trained as a teacher.[66] Around twenty years before Duncan was born, Brantford saw a commercial boom thanks to the Grand River Navigation Canal, offering cheap water transport and access to world markets, so she grew up with a waterway as industrial backdrop.[67] Duncan became an assertive career woman, choosing journalism as her profession and marching into newspaper editors' offices and demanding to be hired – even if that meant working from home if women were barred from the newsrooms, and wrangling invitations around the globe. Her first sea voyage as a journalist was to British Honduras, for instance, at the invitation of the governor.[68] She was a seemingly fearless traveller, and this attitude permeated her lightly fictionalised early narratives. Following her engagement to Everard Charles Cotes, whom she met at the Viceroy of India's residence, the author went to stay with her prospective in-laws at Newington Rectory in Oxfordshire, and spent a lot of her marriage shuttling between India and Britain for the sake of her career. It was, it seems, during this Newington stay that she embarked on the barge voyage described and embellished in *Two Girls on a Barge*. First published in the *Lady's Pictorial*, *Two Girls* shares formal and thematic similarities with Duncan's earlier *A Social Departure*.[69]

There are four in this party, not just 'two girls': the narrator, Edna, Talbot ('the Cadet') and 'the artist'. Ironically, their floating holiday home has the name *Industrious*, also giving its name to the boat propelled through this book. *Industrious*, as the introduction notes, was a real boat owned by the famous salt manufacturer John Corbett mentioned in the novella. The boat was associated with the salt works from the 1870s, carrying salt from Stoke Prior near Droitwich to London, returning with silver sand from Linslade or chalk from Harefield, both required for glassmaking in Smethwick.[70] It seems that the boat was sold to one of Corbett's former steerers in 1893, and it would be satisfying to think that this was the 'Mr and Mrs Bargee' of the novel.[71] In addition to verisimilitude, the name of the boat is a clear indication of the view the reader is intended to take of its leisured temporary residents: with a pinch of salt. *Industrious* departs from Moore's Wharf, Paddington, and along the Paddington Arm of the Grand Junction Canal. They spend their first night at Willesden, then on to Uxbridge, Rickmansworth, and Cassiobury Park. On they travel to Berkhamsted then Tring, then Blisworth and Braunston Tunnels, both represented in the floridly gothic terms described earlier in the chapter. They pass Rugby, and then arrive in Coventry, where they track down the school that inspired the journey in the first place.

Misao Dean has undertaken a thorough study of irony and politics in Duncan's novels and journalism and some of this pertains to *Two Girls on a Barge* and its relationship to class and Empire. Duncan's fiction, says Dean, 'calls for a new kind of heroine,. . . an independent, thinking woman who is aware of the social conventions that limit her actions' and able to challenge them.[72] Duncan's heroines fit comfortably if not exactly into the *fin-de-siècle* cultural silhouette of the New Woman, a 'cultural archetype of early feminism'.[73] The term 'New Woman' first emerged around 1889, and indicated characters who upset traditional ideas about gender, sexuality and social space. The most stereotypical manifestation was 'the emancipated, smoking and bicycling Girton Girl', named for Cambridge's Girton College opened in 1873 – and Edna is nicknamed Girton in *Two Girls*.[74] The illustrations show the female protagonists in dresses and skirts rather than trousers, they do not smoke, and there is no clear depiction of female sexual desire beyond Edna's moderate appreciation of Talbot.[75] They might not be the caricatured New Women striding through the pages of *Punch*, but they acknowledge that stereotype and represent Dean's 'new kind of heroine'. In terms of tone, Dean suggests, Duncan 'wrote within a tradition that regarded irony not as a world view but as a device to enhance meaning' (p. 22). Dean asserts that Duncan's work is fully engaged with the politics of Empire, her ironic tone entertaining while also making the reader ask some serious questions about narration, characters and context. The reader, Dean says, 'must attempt to assume the ironist's point of view, to find the positive values, as [Henry] James puts it, that lie behind the ironic ones' (p. 39). The narrator, in fact, refers to 'Mr. James' in *Two Girls*, as she does in *A Social Departure* and *An American Girl in London*.

Politically, Dean characterises Duncan as a 'red tory', believing in a 'natural social hierarchy', progress, and social reform. Her oeuvre presents a 'critique of the dominant ideologies of imperialism, unrestrained capitalism, bourgeois democracy, and patriarchy'. She hoped to redefine 'women's role in the public and private spheres' and 'argued for the goal of women's financial and moral independence'. She believed in British heritage and the cohesiveness of an English-speaking 'Anglo-Saxon race' across Empire at the same time as supporting practical, white-governed independence for colonial countries (pp. 16–18; 101). Having been born and brought up in Canada and having lived in India, she thought carefully about the relations between colony and metropole. She felt a cultural affinity with Britain, then, and believed in the Empire as a civilising force for good while being critical of its authority in practice. It is important to make absolutely clear that Duncan was no anti-racist nor anti-imperialist in her writings. A quotation from *The Imperialist* makes this explicit: 'The Empire is summed up in the race, and the flag flies for its ideals'.[76] I am not setting Duncan up in opposition to Hughes, but using her work to show that the waterways' connection with Empire at the end of the nineteenth century is not a singular nor straightforward one, and the connection looks different from Duncan's position than it does from Hughes's.

Two Girls on a Barge sets out its irony first in terms of representation itself, in a very similar way to Duncan's *A Social Departure* and *An American Girl in London*. As 'the Cadet' (Talbot Bernard Gove) plans the cabins, the reader is told that 'rectilinear lines were the fashioning of life to the Cadet, he was drawn in them himself' (p. 6). Characters become caricatures as they take on the qualities of exaggerated behaviour: they are drawn along those lines. Later, an aesthetic description of the water is undercut by an aside: 'the Cadet could not refrain from the expression of a sentiment' (p. 45). The narrative voice has expressed sentiment about the attractiveness of the canal, but to do so (especially as a logical man) is reframed as excessive. The text has a subtle way of putting its own assertions under erasure. The discursive effects of this ironic erasure can be seen in a further example from the novel; the artist who joins the party is 'an embryo R.A. [Royal Academician]', who will come along if the women ask 'very prettily and could persuade the gentleman of the advantages of a canal as an artistic field' (p. 6). The 'prettiness' of both femininity and the canal are wryly placed in the same sentence – clearly Edna's Uncle, making the request, does not intend the same type of prettiness to apply to both, making a mockery of artistic snobbery and expectations of female behaviour. The bridges over the canal are, it turns out, 'such self-conscious pictures – they even framed themselves', just as the novel is self-conscious, drawing back to frame itself in its cultural context (p. 45). With picturesque brick and tile barges in their shadows, the bridges cause the artist both 'happiness and pain', an overwrought state in the face of the desire to represent (p. 15). Meanwhile, the mathematically-minded Cadet ignores 'the dusky tints of the old stones and the subdued tone of the mosses' in favour of the 'weight of the cubic feet of water' (pp. 49–51).

The party's attitudes to the canal, its workers and culture cast a lightly comedic and pseudo-anthropological eye over everything. For instance, they observe an instance of waterways vocabulary: 'to mash your tea is colloquial canal' (p. 36). At the same time, the narrative draws back to cast it as a humorous observation. An earnest declaration about the 'independent mould of thinking' amongst canal dwellers is undercut (again) by a wry statement about not having to pay land tax (p. 39). Like other nineteenth-century writing, *Two Girls* casts individuals as 'types', but with characteristic irony. Reading the politics of this typology today, few of the wry jokes still land, while other instances are crudely racist or patronising. The tourists have more respect for the working wisdom of Mr and Mrs Bargee than does Hughes (with his comment about 'chaff'), perhaps because they are obviously and wholly reliant on them for their transport. Like the journalist who travelled 'On the Canal' for *Household Words*, the narrator is intrigued by the fact that the Bargees' knowledge does not extend further than the canal to the towns and countryside through which they pass: it is rectilinear.[77] Duncan's depiction of waterways labour is, then, respectful in places, while also allowing the tourists to poke fun at the bargees' accents and dialect. I am most interested here, however, in the way that bargees (as they are referred to in the text) are racialised via the racist-imperialist language that dominated much late-nineteenth-century writing, and via their comparison with another ethnic group in Britain: Romani people, otherwise known as Gypsies.

Romani people had for centuries been regarded as an 'other within', and in the nineteenth century they were regularly depicted in ways that drew explicitly and implicitly on colonial discourse.[78] One of the most famous writers from earlier in the century who inspired many of those publishing fiction and non-fiction in the 1880s and 1890s on this topic (such as Charles Godfrey Leland, F. H. Groome and Theodore Watts-Dunton) was George Borrow (1803–81), author of *Lavengro* (1851) and *The Romany Rye* (1857). Duncan refers to Borrow in *The*

Imperialist, and while there is no evidence that she knew Borrow's work as early as the writing of *Two Girls,* it is likely that she was aware of the literary figure of the gipsy in nineteenth-century Britain.[79] The connection between bargees, Romani people and colonised natives is made most clearly in the novel via the figure of Mr Gershom – a thinly disguised version of the Victorian philanthropist George Smith of Coalville. I want to position one of Smith's works as an important intertext to *Two Girls,* and considering Duncan and Smith together helps to make sense of the imperial politics of reading the waterways.[80]

The party initially have no idea who Gershom/Smith is, until his identity is revealed as the author of *Canal Adventures by Moonlight,* on a copy of which someone has negligently balanced a blacking jar. Smith, a vigorous campaigner who was instrumental in the passing of the 1877 Canal Boats Act (requiring the registration of boats and limitations on how many people might live aboard) published *Canal Adventures* in 1881. The work was intended to show how poorly the Act was being observed, allowing conditions on board boats that did not belong 'in Christian England in this the nineteenth century', and lobbying for amendments to the legislation to give it more regulatory teeth. The work describes what Smith saw as he walked along the canal between Rugby and London in the frozen December of 1878, as well as recollections of other 'adventures'. Smith had previously campaigned successfully for the rights of children working in the brickfields – where he himself had laboured as a child – and continued to campaign vociferously for the education of gipsy children. He tended to see the problems facing gipsy and canal children as one and the same: their residences needed to be registered so that their schooling could be enforced, and their parents needed religion and temperance.

It is a Bohemian aesthetic that first allows the comparison between bargees and Romani people in *Two Girls:*

> One barge in particular struck this note in us as we crossed lines with it. It was being drawn by a gipsy girl. Rather, a bargee girl with a gipsy face, and a red kerchief on her head . . . It had a Neapolitan effect that we envied her. In fact, we attempted it ourselves, but our disadvantages outbalanced the effect.

The description of a 'bargee girl with a gipsy face' directly echoes a description of a ten-year-old girl in an 1888 book for children, Amos Reade's *Life in the Cut.* That work is dedicated to George Smith (the model for Gershom in *Two Girls*): 'the man who has done most for the Canal people of old England, living amongst us, but still outside the pale of law and civilization'.[81] 'Pale' in this sense has been used to mean an English territorial possession with legal jurisdiction since the fourteenth century (OED), so its use in relation to George Smith directly links missions to 'uncivilised' groups within Britain with the civilising mission of Empire. The narrator and Edna's 'disadvantages' are, of course, ironic: she speaks from a position of enormous privilege when she and her friend play at being 'gipsy bargees', and she knows it. The value that lies behind the ironic one is a belief in social and racial hierarchy, meaning that their envy is affectation and the adoption of costume a playful performance. The playfulness relies on the understanding that bargees and gipsies are different to Girton girls and authors. This exoticising observation is of a piece with the rest of the novel, but the introduction of Mr Gershom feels like a section pasted in from a different work. He is even introduced as having 'something sincere' about him – sincerity being hard to come by elsewhere in the novel; he is the ironic text's moral anchor, where the semiotic slippage of irony is finally tied down. For instance, he thoughtfully points out the inappropriateness of the group's playfulness when he invites them with him to visit a gipsy camp: 'I don't know about its being awf'ly *neat!*' (p. 103). Even his religious Band of Brothers is dismissed as cultish, though, when it seems it might prevent Edna from attending dances with the narrator: passing through the Braunston tunnel seems to break Gershom's spell of sincerity.

Where *Two Girls on a Barge* makes much of its luxury, *Canal Adventures by Moonlight* did the opposite, going into detail about the physical and financial hardships Smith was prepared to face for the children and boatwomen of the canals. The fact that he goes unrecognised in *Two Girls on a Barge* would surely be much to his chagrin, as he is noticed wherever he goes in *Canal Adventures by Moonlight*, recognition often accompanied either by much-needed funds or threats to tip him in the canal. As well as seeing canal children and gipsy children as essentially interchangeable, he depicted their lives as those of native savages. He notes 'heathenish brutality', 'savage despair', boat-children like 'half-starved water rats', and boatwomen with children 'whose language was so disjointed that I could with great difficulty understand what they were talking about'. He sarcastically refers to this as a 'specimen of English civilization', meaning, of course, that they make a mockery of the notion. He distinguishes between these sorry examples and healthy men and horses accompanying boats which do not house women and children and rest on the Sabbath. Smith spends a week on a boat laden with rice, leather, paraffin, hemp-seed and oil, travelling 'up country' from London to Leicester. He is appalled to witness two women not quite dressed having washed their clothes in the canal, a 'disgraceful proceeding' happening 'in broad daylight, within the sound of the church-bells of the capital of Christendom'. One wonders what he would have made of the respectable Hughes getting changed behind a tree after his dunking. He describes 'lots of swearing women and children, as ignorant as Hottentots'. He witnesses the 'sorrowful spectacle of some two hundred men, women, and children living in a state little better than the Zulus of Africa'.[82] Smith's work is itself intertextually woven, with frequent references to his earlier *Our Canal Population* (1878), newspaper articles, tracts, letters, and Mark Guy Pearse's *Rob Rat* (1879), another religious book for children about the horrors of canal life.

The links between *Canal Adventures* and *Two Girls* go beyond its appearance as a book-within-a-book: the *Industrious* fictionalised in *Two Girls* usually carried chalk from Harefield on its return journeys having delivered salt to London; Smith describes this very journey. The boats being loaded up are home to 'a number of children', boats which 'belonged to a firm at Droitwich, from whom I had hoped better things' (p. 76). In the third part of *Canal Adventures*, Smith refers to John Corbett, owner of *Industrious* in reality and in *Two Girls*, and then MP for Droitwich 'who owns, or at any rate employs, more boatmen than any other gentleman in the country' and the fact that he fines captains for working on the Sabbath (p. 171). *Canal Adventures* and *Two Girls* thus inhabit the same canal space, but the form and tone of their writing is to very different ends.

Canal Adventures is generically hybrid, featuring long dream sequences characterised by stream-of-consciousness religious and philosophical ideas, a style which brings to mind once more the work of George Borrow. In one of these dreams, he looks for the events which will demonstrate the dawning of the millennium: all land capable of cultivation will bring forth food for all humans and animals (and he is preoccupied by the hunger of canal children and horses); the population of the globe will be evenly spread; humans will have blended to become one race with skin similar 'to that of gipsies' and the stature 'of an Englishman'; the English language will be spoken as the 'language of the world'; the English form of government under a monarch will be universal; and 'our moral and intellectual nature [will] become a reflex of and assimilated to that of Christ'. Paradise looks a lot like the ideal of Empire in Smith's dreams, albeit with the kind of 'miscegenation' about which imperial Britain was generally nervous. Smith has another reverie about a pitched battle between Conservatives on one hill and Liberals on another, in the middle of which 'scores of thousands of little boat children' are dying in a valley like 'one of the worst kinds of African swamps' (p. 97). This, then, is *Canal Adventures by Moonlight*, which its author recovers from under the blacking with twinkling eyes in *Two Girls on a Barge*.

The captains of clean-looking barges doff their caps at Gershom, with a 'wordless deference' and 'implicit, unquestioning confidence'. The narrator of *Two Girls* describes the glimpsing of 'an undercurrent – some motive power sleeping silently between the boaters and ourselves, or such as we – something that made all things possible'. She notes that a dozen years ago, non-bargees on the canal would not have been welcome. Smith's philanthropy is proposed, in this rare, earnest passage, as a kind of mystical force that has made bargee and non-bargee relations possible, resembling in that power the intrepid explorer-missionary who makes first contact with strange peoples in a distant land (an 'alien people' as the narrator calls the bargees), to be followed by capital, institutions, or settler colonialism. This latent power relation that makes 'all things' possible – or, here, their sojourn and its textual retelling – is made legible in the bargees' wordless deference (pp. 97–101). Duncan, then, is reflective about the place of 'such as we' on the waterways in a way that previous canal leisure narratives do not manage. Reading this text in relation to her life and oeuvre suggests that her experiences as a women in Canada and India drive these nuanced considerations of philanthropy and responsibility, power and authority. Nevertheless, her conclusions are in many ways the same as those of Hughes and MacGregor: white, middle-class Christians at the end of the nineteenth century have a responsibility to civilize those who are 'beyond the pale', bringing them into a well-organised and hierarchical society where some will have time for leisure and others will provide the labour and resources that make 'all things possible'. In other words: everyone knows their place.

The narrator described a bargee girl with a gipsy face, and Smith's twin campaigns also cause the two groups – one defined by occupation and mode of living; one defined by ethnicity and culture – to textually overlap. The party go with Gershom to see a gipsy camp, turning the people into a spectacle.[83] There, they find 'Moorish-eyed babies' amongst the 'tribe'. Gershom is greeted 'in that curious rhythmic Romany that the centuries have cadenced and the Moorish suns have kissed'. This repetition is the sort of feature that Karyn Huenemann points to as evidence that the work is not actually Duncan's.[84] However, I suggest that its excess draws a distinction between the tourists and Gershom's more serious engagement with the residents of the camp. When they are unimpressed by Edna's 'cajoleries', the narrator compares the gipsy children's 'irresponsive spirit' to that of 'small grubby heathen gods permitting votaries' and calls them 'swarthy vagrants'. The romantic image the party have is disappointed by the fact that nobody 'proposed to tell [their] fortune'. The irony of the narrator's exotic picture is emphasised when the Cadet sits on a willow chair made by the gipsies and looks 'barbarically aristocratic' (pp. 104–5). This is not an exotic interlude separate from the rest of the narrative: the 'gipsiness' of the camp bleeds into depictions of the bargees. For instance, the narrator exclaims 'happy are they who have no history!', meaning not only holidaymakers but all those whose daily existence involves floating along the canal (p. 139).The statement echoes the stereotype of the timelessness of unchanging gipsy culture that pervaded nineteenth- and early-twentieth-century writing about Romani people and is, of course, a strange thing to think about canal boat life, which had such recent beginnings in Britain and whose history was regularly repeated.[85] Bargees are rendered as exotic others in *Two Girls* and, while Duncan does not put these words into the mouths of the narrator, the text's treatment of Gershom as an exception to irony leaves his values in place within the text: bargee life requires regulation and civilisation in the manner of a colony within Britain.

With its bold New Women characters, ironic tone, packaged marketing, ostentatious *fin-de-siècle* opulent aestheticism and middlebrow appeal, *Two Girls on a Barge* might at first appear to be anything but subtle. It depicted simply a short, entertaining leisure trip along the canal to Coventry. Nevertheless, its intertextual connections with a plethora of nineteenth-century representations of canal boat and Romani people, themselves constructed within an imperialist and often racist cultural hegemony, mean that the text's politics do require subtle reading and careful situating. The characters' class privilege and entitlement may be self-consciously ironic, but they have still colonised canal-land, seeing it as a playground with all its labourers ready to serve them thanks to the motive power between them and the boaters.

Putting Hughes's and Duncan's narratives in context and in dialogue reveals the connections between Empire, gender, class and
canals. The British Empire had not yet reached the peak of its spread
by the 1890s, but Britain was engaged in the scramble for Africa,
Victoria was Empress of India, white settler colonies like Australia and
Canada were part of 'Greater Britain', and it had developed strategic
protectorates and treaties in the Middle East to retain its dominance of
routes to India. While Porter has pointed to the ambivalent relationship between Britain's external imperialism and its domestic society
and culture, there were those in Britain who clearly and explicitly saw
Empire on the side of right: it was Christian, it was civilised, and it
would improve people's lives. Imperialists thought they had a responsibility to bring light to the dark corners of the globe. For authors like
MacGregor, canoeing felt like a personal act of responsibility, seeing
the wider world for oneself or bearing witness to its realities via travel,
which must be presented to an imperial audience. Hughes's narrative
(and that of Schofield before him) is less imbued with the responsibility of these works but takes up their spirit of exploration. MacGregor
was seen as the epitome of masculinity and Schofield and Hughes
seem to conform to that model of masculine canoeist-adventurer.
Duncan's irony in *Two Girls on a Barge* punctures the heroically individual journey of responsibility that developed in this genre of writing.
She thus presents a 'new kind of heroine' – not just in terms of female
literary representation but also for the canal travelogue. This is not to
say that her gender, nor her experience as a colonial subject, mean that
her characters' colonising of canal-land is any less assertive or entitled.
George Smith of Coalville had seen dark corners *within* England in
the 1860s, 70s and 80s, especially on its waterways; the canals needed
civilising. The putative success of that process of civilisation meant
that middle-class tourists were able to choose the canal as a space for
leisure by the 1890s, but they were not so cleaned up as to negate the
possibilities for intrepid adventure. To quote MacGregor, these tourists brought a new mode of seeing old lands, whether as earnest Boy's
Own adventurers or laconic observers.

There are others populating Schofield's, Hughes's and Duncan's
narratives: the workers of the waterways who sometimes come into
focus as amiable if simple mediators of the canal but are often no more
individualised than the water on which the narrators float. Workers
on the waterways and in the mines, mills and factories the waterways connected were imperial subjects: they were ruled by the class

of people who could afford to colonise the canal for their leisure. This subjugation is made legible by the genre of the canal travelogue, which inherits the depiction of the racial other from narratives of foreign exploration. The waterways thus made literal global connections, via the transport of materials and goods, and between imperial subjects in the metropolitan centre and the colony (or former and potential colonies); the texts this chapter has so far examined also make discursive connections between the representation of colonised others and workers in Britain. As I have already outlined, to read the waterways is always to make connections across time as well as space, and so the final section of this chapter cruises into the twentieth century to read where leisure use of the canal went next.

'Their use is an anachronism': Rolt's canal cruising

It is 1939 and I ply the Trent and Mersey, pulled by proud horse. This century, I soared again impossibly through the air: hauled by towering boat lift from river to canal. Valiant Victorian engineers had an answer to every watery challenge. The Liberty curtains and Japanese umbrellas of a previous journey have made way for bright paint and sturdy utility; the angles of my small cabin are reflected in polished brasses. I carry salt rather than gentlemen once more. The leisure journey was an eccentric false start. I slip past matronly bottle kilns at Middleport potbank. These waters have carried Burleigh ware from the Potteries to the world. Fellow boats carry coal and beer. I pass *Cressy*, and a man aboard – in a bathtub, in fact – is alive with the pleasure of living on the canal. He sloshes in water that has cooled *Cressy*'s engine, and perhaps there is some energy of past vivacity vibrating between its molecules, for he imagines parts of the waterways network alive in new ways. Not a false start after all.

Half a century separates Hughes's canal adventures and L. T. C. Rolt's 'tranquil voyaging' aboard the renovated *Cressy* with his wife.[86] Where Hughes and Duncan were by turns frustrated and delighted by the fact of co-existing with workers in an active industrial space, Rolt saw the ghosts of that activity everywhere. Holidaymakers on the canal in pedalos were like 'water-fleas' to Rolt and those in cruisers were littering, lolling nuisances (p. 93). Wanting to avoid the appearance of *playing* at boating (in which Duncan revelled), Rolt deliberately eschewed a colour scheme for *Cressy* which might seem 'precious'

(p. 29). Nevertheless, he paid a great deal of attention to, and took pride in, soft furnishings to an extent that would make the 'two girls' proud. He venerated the canal communities George Smith of Coalville deplored, mourned the loss of traditional crafts and values, hoped to protect canal heritage, yet shuddered at the world ushered in by industrialisation. Rolt believed that: 'if man had never discovered the mechanical arts by which he annihilates space and time he might never have acquired that tragic contempt for local environment, custom and tradition which has led him to break faith with the land' (p. 55). This assertion does not see the canal, the place of his reflection, as time-and-space-annihilating technology, in spite of the ways in which the industrial canal reorganised the time and space of commodities transport and made new connections between the coast and inland. Rolt does, though, explicitly note the contribution of the canals to the Industrial Revolution, comparing them to the spell which initiates chaos in Goethe's 1797 poem 'The Sorcerer's Apprentice' (p. 119).

Even with this denial of temporal annihilation, Rolt feels, on board *Cressy*, that he 'might have floated out of time', and the textual temporality of *Narrow Boat* is persistently paradoxical. Though the canals were built to connect cities, Rolt starts to feel their very existence improbable, it beginning to seem more likely that 'the canal would lead us to some enchanted Avilon "fair with orchard lawns", than to prosaic Leicester' (p. 69). Gehrke characterises Rolt as seeing the canals as 'an amalgam of industry and nature that had become central to Britain's identity, and yet was being overpowered as mechanised production was making inroads into the countryside as never before'.[87] *Narrow Boat* is therefore locked in an ambivalent relationship with the past that was Hughes's and Duncan's present, a key reason for reading this seminal canal text in dialogue with those older travelogues. Hughes and Duncan could never be described as direct influences on Rolt: in *Narrow Boat*, he acknowledges E. Temple Thurston as the *only* author writing about travel around England to have journeyed by water.[88] Similar to Hughes's thirst for adventure, though, Rolt wants to 'fulfil in the fullest sense the meaning of travel' – repetition of fulness here testifying to his desire to experience something *real* and be fully present in that experience (p. 12).

This emphasis on full presence catches at the temporal paradox of *Narrow Boat*: the authenticity for which the text yearns is rooted in an unreachable past. For instance, amongst the global epicurean pleasures of the twenty-first century, it is hard to understand Rolt's enthusiasm for the lost art of 'genuine English cooking', banished in the 1930s 'by the evil genius of the can-opener' (p. 77). He bristles at pastiche of the canal past in such symbols as 'Ye Olde Wharfe Inne' (p. 175). More seriously, though, it is enthusiasm for the life, community and crafts of 'canal folk' which sees *Narrow Boat* echo unconsciously and uncomfortably a 'specific branch of the dual ideologies of imperialism and racism' described by postcolonial scholar Patrick Brantlinger: extinction discourse.[89] In the colonial context of the long nineteenth century this discourse accounted for the apparently inevitable and tragic decline, and final extinction, of non-developed, uncivilised peoples as they were seemingly overtaken by white European modernity. On the English waterway, Rolt values the simplicity, directness and authenticity of working canal boat dwellers: they are his noble savages, that enduring European mythology designed to counter (amongst other concerns) materialism and cynicism.[90] By virtue of having come into being at the beginning of the industrial age, Rolt believes that traditional canal culture, remaining largely unchanged, has somehow retained the characteristics of pre-industrial England – acknowledging the strangeness of this suggestion (p. 119). While George Smith felt that this canal way of life had no place in a modern nation, Rolt pre-emptively laments modernity's destruction of folk continuity. His tone is different to some of the coldly racist nineteenth-century writings Brantlinger describes (including Trollope's *Castle Richmond*), but Rolt unwittingly harks back to Smith's (and Duncan's and Hughes's) depictions of primitive boatmen and industrial workers existing as savage others within Britain, and replicates the sentimentality of much extinction discourse.

En route to Middlewich on the Trent and Mersey Canal, Rolt encounters 'some fine types of the old race of canal folk' (p. 130). This racialisation is a recurrent theme, with Rolt referring to them as 'old proud stock' who will soon become an 'extinct race'. The extinction of canal communities acts as a synecdoche in *Narrow Boat* for a national loss of tradition, exceptionalism and refinement. Like Duncan, Rolt emphasises a perceived similarity between canal people and Romani people, mapping what he sees as 'true Romany' characteristics on to individual boaters, and by extrapolation on to the whole community: aquiline features, dark eyes, dark ringleted hair, graceful movements and gold jewellery appear several times in the travelogue, as if the gipsiness of the boatmen and women could be proven via these symbolic traits. Rolt suggests, too, that the famously colourful canal boat decoration was originally inspired by 'some old wandering Romany who exchanged his caravan for a narrow boat' (p. 24). As in the work of Smith and Duncan, the overlap of perceptions of canal folk (defined by occupation and mode of living) and Romani people (defined by ethnicity and culture) are made to seem common sense. I do not think that Rolt believed that canal boat people were literally Romani, but used widely understood connections between these groups to describe a folk aesthetic, the soulful freedom of mobility, a romanticised outsider status, and an anachronistic existence.[91] Modern life and the culture of the motor car will destroy both Romani cultural practices and the canal community Rolt frames as its kin.

One boatwoman, Mrs Horne, whom the Rolts meet while frozen in at Banbury, has married late on to the canal rather than being born and brought up to the waterway. However, according to Rolt, it is a milieu that suits her 'simple mind' far more than the 'synthetic attractions' to be had on land (p. 186). Rolt idealises a simplicity of life that is really only endurable, as he portrays it, to the simple of mind. Rolt even seems keen in this text to preserve illiteracy amongst canal boat people, preferring their 'forthright mother wit' to book learning, for education has not aided his bête noir: the uncultured townsman (p. 154). Rolt's persistent attacks against this figure are congruent with the twentieth-century manifestation of extinction discourse described by Brantlinger, the idea that progress would be its own undoing, with 'the masses' swamping society and 'subverting traditional values'.[92] To the twenty-first-century reader, social attitudes in *Narrow Boat* are jarringly of their time. For instance, Rolt uses racist language to comment on the appearance of coal-stained pitmen trudging home around Amington and Alvecote. His reference point is not directly imperialist; he thinks instead of seaside blackface minstrelsy of the kind popular in Britain since the 1830s (p. 173). It is a reference that nonetheless reproduces the image of the miner as a 'race apart' seen in Hughes's work and elsewhere in Victorian writing; the British worker is contained, decades later, in the ideological framework of race: class is still racialised.

Rolt as detailer of the state of the waterways sets himself up as the arbiter of taste, his views on everything from architecture to agriculture, pubs to propriety, class to cars invading his descriptions of the canal space. But it is *Narrow Boat*'s extinction discourse that discursively binds him to the other travelogues examined here. Regenia Gagnier has used Brantlinger's work to point out that, in the nineteenth century, 'advocates of Progress' were affronted by itinerant freedom at home and abroad, but for other writers at that time (and, I would add, for Rolt in the twentieth century), it was progress that destroyed instinctive, genuine, and independent cultures.[93] Brantlinger's focus on extinction promotes a nuanced understanding of the Victorian conception of race: 'in this model, the superficially white . . . could be structurally primitive, and therefore as inevitably disappeared as aboriginals of colour in the colonies'.[94] Rolt certainly did not celebrate such disappearing, but his authorial attitude towards canal boat people saw them as primitive others within Britain, destined to be lost under the wheels of progress. It was a culture at a dead end, without the capacity to adapt and develop as the world moved on and the lorry carried everything Britain and its industry required. There are twin ironies to *Narrow Boat*'s deployment of extinction discourse. First, the author has chosen to 'opt out' of progress by joining the ranks of boat dwellers, but his ideological framing in the text aligns him with it, the very social force he seeks to repel. Second, the canal communities he joins were a *product of* the technological and economic development that seem likely to cause their demise. We return again to the sorcerer's apprentice. Canal boat people were not, of course, literally a disappearing 'race' in the way that nineteenth-century imperialists understood this idea; they were a culture formed from technological and – more emphatically – economic contingencies. Yet Rolt imbues them with the characteristics of a doomed race in his literary effort to communicate the culture's authentic distinctiveness, most noticeably via historically recognisable tropes of the representation of Romani people in Britain which themselves drew, in the nineteenth century, on the rhetoric, imagery and mythology of Empire.

Thus, as with my readings of poetry in Chapter Two, my analysis of leisure or sporting journeys along the canals has been self-consciously situated in relation to the postcolonial, the transhistorical, and the lasting ideological and environmental effects of a system of industrial capital that demanded expansion and exploitation: the Anthroposcene.

Schofield's narrative, though peripheral to this chapter, manages to draw the transhistorical reader back into the eighteenth century with references that flag early industrial development (at Coalbrookdale, for instance) and slavery; *Two Girls* is tied up with the canals of the 1870s thanks to its moral anchor, George Smith of Coalville; Hughes's narrative cannot escape MacGregor's influence from the 1860s, and other earlier authors such as Livingstone. Rolt unconsciously inherits nineteenth-century extinction discourse in a canal travelogue that venerates the pre-industrial. Reading all of these works in the twenty-first century, they call out to (amongst other things) the politics of labour and identity today, to the Suez Crisis of 1956 and the end of Empire, to contemporary leisure use of the British waterways, to DuBois's hopeful future of a civilisation without coal. *I am* Industrious, *and the water flows on.*

The canal perennially has the waters of other times flowing through it; reading the waterways is always reading across time. The next chapter is, like this one, interested in the difference gender makes to writing about the work of the waterways, focusing on *new* new women of the waterways, and returns to Britain's relationship with its Empire and dominions – including Canada – in the run up to and during the Second World War. The globally-connected environmental impact of the materials carried by boats like *Industrious* shapes the Anthroposcene understanding of waterways and war in the twentieth century.

4

WOMEN, WAR, AND THE WATERWAYS

I am *Industrious* and now, in 1944, I boast the dark red, white and blue livery of the Grand Union Canal Carrying Company. I lie low in the stinking water; bits of Dunlop tyre and the bloated corpse of a dog, its legs in the air, float by.[1] Heavy with aluminium ingots baptised in colonial water and towing a similarly loaded butty, my rope tipcat bashes in to the wall of the canal. My propeller grinds into black mud; stemmed up. The tiller has been smoothed by the hands of women for decades, but this steerer seems jittery and unsure. We pass, for the umpteenth time, a coalmine. Coal is ubiquitous, dirtying the surface of the water; pollution leaks across liquid and land, covering the towpath flora like an apocalyptic ashy snow. The miners emerging from the hellish underground look like rocky monsters.[2] The aluminium is unloaded at a wharf, taken to a factory, and made into great flying machines: machines that will blast apart human limbs, human hearts, human minds.

New Naiads: Strength, Escape and Transformation

In 1941, the MP and author of *The Water Gipsies* (1930), A. P. Herbert, was quoted in the *Hull Daily Mail* as seeing no reason why women should not crew canal boats: 'In my opinion, women would be quite strong enough to undertake this work. Why, they are already doing it'. Those already doing the work are the daughters of women like 'Mrs Bargee' from *Two Girls on a Barge*, born to the cut and producing new heirs to the live-aboard life. An official of the Grand Union Canal Carrying Company (GUCCC) explained in the same article that the firm was having to turn down large numbers of applications received by women to contribute to the war effort on board their boats because, unlike Herbert, they doubted the women's strength.[3] In more recent reflections on the Home Front in the 1940s, the idea that ordinary women without a history of work on canals could fill the roles vacated by men (who had left to fight or for better-paid work in other war industries) is often attributed to one of the ministries, assumed to be another excellent piece of planning from the machine of wartime government. However, this change in waterways labour actually came about through pressure from women themselves. The number of women who eventually completed their training and were able to transport essential commodities along the waterways was relatively small, but the group looms large in the cultural imagination because, as literate women with the time and connections after the war to write and publish books, a surprisingly large proportion of them authored autobiographies, spoke to historians or recorded their thoughts in diaries.

Thanks to one of these texts in particular – *Idle Women* by Susan Woolfitt – the workers are now often referred to by this title, a joke on their 'I. W.' (Inland Waterways) badges, though others insist that this was not a moniker of the time.[4] The vast majority of the women worked on the Grand Union Canal, though a smaller number of workers were on the Leeds and Liverpool (where they were known as 'Judies'), Oxford, and Shropshire Union Canals. Kit Gayford noted in her autobiographical account of work on the Grand Union that at one time there were eleven pairs of boats working, 'all manned by girls' and that by the War's end there were six women still working, 'all of whom had joined in 1942'.[5] The published works have remained popular and in print, but have taken on new significance in the twenty-first century as women's history has been put back into the popular wartime picture. These experiences have also been taken up by romance novelists, keen to capitalise on what one dust jacket calls 'the romance and danger of World War II' and lighting on these workers as part of a series along with Land Girls, female munitions workers, WAAFs and Wrens.[6] The characters, forming a tight-knit three- or four-person crew living in very close quarters, are especially conducive to plots of sisterhood, gently uncovering secrets, and revelations about heterosexual relationships. They highlight the risks and opportunities of wartime labour, such as not knowing who people are, unlike their limited pre-war experiences of communities in which they had grown up.[7] Class, community and gender boundaries are muddied in these canal waters, and prove to be dangerous underwater obstacles as the women make their way along the cut.

The rest of this introductory section explains the historical circumstances of the canal trainee scheme, then the chapter moves on to think about the genre and form of the texts on which I focus: autobiography and romance fiction. The autobiographies are: Emma Smith's *Maidens' Trip* (1948) and *As Green as Grass* (2013), Nancy Ridgway's *Memories of a Wartime Canal Boatwoman* (2014), Eily Gayford's *The Amateur Boatwomen* (1973), Susan Woolfitt's *Idle Women* (1947), and Margaret Cornish's *Troubled Waters* (1987). Ridgway and Cornish are the prickly antitheses to Smith's narrative ingenue, while Gayford's narrative is a model of practicality. Ridgway's work is also something of an outlier because her role was on the Leeds and Liverpool Canal, while the others are predominantly based on the Grand Union. The romances are: Margaret Graham's trilogy (writing as Milly Adams) *The Waterway Girls* (2017), *Love on the Waterways* (2018) and *Hope on the Waterways* (2018), Margaret Mayhew's *The Boat Girls* (2007), Rosie Archer's *The Narrowboat Girls* (2018), and Molly Green's *A Sister's War* (2021). Picking up Chapter Two's assertions about different forms of knowledge, this discussion uses Lauren Berlant's affective meditation on genre to understand the way the texts in this corpus represent femininity, recognition and desire. I thoroughly enjoyed reading most of these romances and am sympathetic to Kim Wilkins's, Beth Driscoll's and Lisa Fletcher's explicitly generous approach to genre fiction, remembering that 'pleasure has been a generative principle in the writing and publishing of the text and is intended to be a significant reward in the reading of it'. This does not mean, however, that 'there is no room in genre worlds for critique' or, in this case, a thematic exploration.[8]

The chapter then digs into themes that recur across the corpus: preserving clean water, and the polluted waters of the canal. The question of access to potable water remains, even in the twenty-first century, one of gender. The UN points out that women and girls 'usually bear the responsibility for collecting water', and the lack of safe drinking water and sanitation facilities affects women's and girls' lives disproportionately.[9] It is, perhaps, hearing Abou Amani from the Intergovernmental Hydrological Programme speak about this that made me alert as a reader to the specific value of water even when surrounded by thousands of tons of it in these women-centred texts. The fact that the autobiographers, diarists and characters were unaccustomed to the canal environment means that they present shock and often disgust about its pollution; their urge to comment on this makes the cleanliness and dirtiness of water newly legible, and each of these texts is careful to detail the incredibly hard work of full-time canal boatwomen to keep boats, cabins and families clean. The final part of this chapter focuses on one of the commodities transported by the women. Their loads included coal, cement, wheat, timber, copper, steel, and scrap metal. Here, I pick up the threads of Empire discussed in the previous two chapters to consider the journey made by aluminium, in particular, on its way to the Limehouse Docks, where the crews would dodge rockets as they loaded up; the cargo's onward journey was to factories, and ultimately to be made into weapons to maim and kill human bodies.

The use of the waterways for wartime transport was not as straightforward as simply nationalising the canals. Many canals were, by this time, owned by railway companies, and in the late 1930s these looked likely to be automatically mobilised for the war effort as they had in the First World War. Indeed, the Emergency Powers (Defence) Act of 1939 brought control of the railways under the Railway Executive Committee, chaired by Sir Ralph Wedgwood, the great, great grandson of the potter Josiah Wedgwood discussed in Chapter Two – the intricacies of transport history have a habit of following the same lines, like those miles on the map where canal, railway and road run parallel. Independent canal carrying companies needed reassurance that they would be able to retain staff and compete for traffic against businesses whose rates were fixed by the state. This led to the Canal (Defence) Advisory Committee, focused on securing the best use of canals in the national interest in time of war, and then the Central Canal Commission in May 1941 when transport needs became more acute.[10] Labour on the wartime waterways was not, though, a nationally even picture; some regions felt a shortage of workers from 1939, while canal carriers in other areas complained of a lack of work. By December 1940, around 100 boats were 'lying idle for lack of labour in the North Western, Grand Union and South Western areas' (p. 204). Men, it seemed, were easily put off the difficult work of the canals: a 1941 newspaper advert garnered nearly a thousand enquiries, but only 13 men took and remained in employment. According to a Ministry of War Transport memorandum from June 1941, female applicants for canal work had been misled as to the 'hard manual labour involved' and their contribution was thought inappropriate (p. 205). Indeed, in August 1941 a newspaper article calling for greater use of the canals in the war effort lay directly beneath an advert advising women to have a perm while the 'materials are still available'; their place was the home or salon, not the cut.[11] As the labour shortage worsened, importing Irish labour was discussed and discounted due to anti-Irish sentiment and fears of IRA infiltration. Female labour was considered only as an absolute last resort, despite women's willingness to do the job. This can be understood as part of the tensions that Phil Goodman notes between gendered domestic ideology, an expanding war economy, patriotism and national male morale.[12] Nearly fifty years on from Sara Jeannette Duncan's New Women, women not born to the waterways were still considered literally and ideologically out of place when they boarded a canal boat to work.

While men in ministries and boardrooms procrastinated about women working on the waterways, Daphne March took the tiller. She and her brother owned a canal boat, the *Heather Bell*, that had been used for pleasure boating; she had it converted, and with another young woman began carrying cargo on the Worcester and Birmingham Canal and River Severn. The *Heather Bell* is an important boat in the story of female wartime trainees: first, its crew was pioneering; second, Kit Gayford, the well-known trainer of many of the recruits, joined the boat in 1941; and third, March became a poster girl for female labour on the waterways once the Ministry of War Transport decided to adopt the trainee scheme, and the Ministry of Information publicised it. A photograph now held by the Imperial War Museum shows Daphne shafting the *Heather Bell* away from the canalside as it carries flour from Worcester to Tipton. She is the picture of strength, forearm muscles bulging and using her entire body to manoeuvre the boat. Leaning heavily against the shaft, which is at least four times as big as her, she looks, in retrospect, like a combination of the marines raising the United States flag at Iwo Jima in Joe Rosenthal's famous image from 1945, and Rosie the Riveter with her iconic headscarf – now an important if nostalgic signifier for female labour and independence. The combination of this physical and semiotic strength and her name, Daphne, is a powerful condensation of images, especially in the context of the classical imagery read in Chapter Two because, prior to her metamorphosis, the mythological Daphne was a freshwater nymph. In reading the waterways through literary history, Daphne March becomes, after the New Woman, a New Naiad.

As well as privileging the *Heather Bell* as an object of Idle Women history, I would also highlight the advertisement that eventually called women to the water, a text that becomes retrospectively meaningful. For Nancy Ridgway, who would work on the Leeds and Liverpool Canal, that advert appeared in the *Manchester Evening News*; Emma Smith's friend spotted the article while they lunched in their War Office canteen in the grounds of Blenheim Palace.[13] For Woolfitt, the picture in the evening paper seems at first 'unexciting', but it nevertheless set her on the course of becoming a canal boatwoman.[14] Cornish saw the 'insignificant advertisement in a women's magazine' and knew immediately that that was what she wanted to do, partly, as she described in an oral history interview, because it lacked the authoritarian, institutional control of work in the forces.[15] In Archer's romance, *The Narrowboat Girls*, the advert becomes a clipping, dug out of a handbag to share dreams of escape with a friend. In Adams's fictional *The Waterway Girls* it is shown to concerned parents to explain the comparative safety of this war work. For Francis Carlyon in Mayhew's novel, the advertisement comes just at the right time: like the real-life Kit Gayford she has been frustrated in her desire to find war work as recruitment for other forces has been temporarily suspended. In the same novel, Prudence Dobbs's aunt produces the cutting like a winning card in one of their family Boxing Day games, as a way for Prudence to avoid a stifling future working in a bank with lecherous male colleagues. For Ronnie in *A Sister's War*, a Pathé News item invites her to join the waterways labour force just after she has been turned down by the Women's Land Army because of her youth.[16] For women both real and fictional, the advert proves textually talismanic, winking through the decades as a harbinger of change.

Femininity is a Genre

I am *Industrious*, puzzlingly referred to as 'she' by many, as if a boat should have a gender. But with that 'she' comes expectation; my journey through the waters of time surely defies all and any. The hand on my tiller is steadier now. I keep on keeping on, the minerals and metal lifted from me and burnt and bent into war. The hand lifts from the tiller to wave up at a plane dipping its wings. Its mission is death.

It is easy to see why these women's experiences make such popular texts; as Nancy Ridgway puts it: 'life on the barge was really a series of incidents; we'd go so long smoothly, then something would happen to shake us out of our reverie; sometimes nice, sometimes nasty, sometimes sad'.[17] This is almost a complete definition of story. Emma Smith, too, as she set out to write *Maidens' Trip*, found that a three-week round trip on the Grand Union naturally presented a structured textual shape and narrative drive.[18] The world on which the writing focuses, that of the canal, seems self-contained, helping to draw the boundaries of the text. In both autobiography and romance, the women arrive from different walks of life and previous experiences (often involving war-related tragedy) to form a crew, allowing for romantic character development in the novels as these pasts are revealed. In the life writing that inspired the fictional work, for instance, Margaret Cornish was annoyed by an offhand abbreviation of her name to 'Meg' because this had been a name reserved for someone important who had been killed, and to use it now 'was an intrusion into a private grief which had barely healed'.[19] In Adams's fictional *The Waterways Girls*, the twin brother of one of the trainees has been killed in action, as her mother's own twin brother had been killed at Ypres. Each trainee has a distinctive backstory that narrative draws out via the entering of a new world and being thrown into a team: in these texts, the narrative develops from the characters all being in the same boat.

The romance novels read in this chapter may draw heavily on the life writing of Smith, Gayford, Cornish and Woolfitt, but Smith presciently points out a key difference between non-fiction and romance novels: 'of lovers or of marriage we thought but dimly, and felt as yet no craving for a companionship other than that we gave ourselves or found along the way'.[20] Cornish, too, compares a palling romantic relationship with the 'basic survival existence' on the boats and finds it 'superficial' (p. 125). By examining these romance novels, I am not asserting that their version of wartime traineeship simply adapts personal stories to represent wider female themes. As Lauren Berlant points out, life writing already does this: 'the autobiographical isn't the personal', because the 'works of "women's culture" enact a fantasy that my life is not just mine, but an experience understood by other women'.[21] The very act of writing what seems to be a personal and particular female life is, by virtue of the ways in which culture operates, also to gesture to something gendered, cultural and shared. Here, each autobiography of a single person is also the biography of a group, of a moment in British social, industrial and national history, and a chronicle of women's work. What I do want to suggest is that, while the routine of a carrying trip drives the life writing in this corpus, the narratives of romance novels have other imperatives: personal discovery, love and desire, the security of marriage and/or a comfortable home. While the two genres are thus distinct in many ways, I also argue that they can be approached thematically together to read this period on the waterways.

The strict conventions of the mainstream female romance genre which, in the case of wartime trainee fiction, capitalises on the themes and knowledge of life writing, motivate a distinctive representation of gendered canal labour. The books are marketed, as Berlant predicts, on the premise that female identification with the expectation of a good life transcends the particular: the covers make promises of emotional recognition, such as 'new hope', 'courage', and 'strength in each other'. Berlant explains that a genre is 'an aesthetic structure of affective expectation' with the promise that anyone 'transacting with it will experience the pleasure of encountering what they expected'. Further, femininity itself can be understood like a genre because 'it is a structure of conventional expectation that people rely on to provide certain kinds of affective intensities and assurances' (p. 4). Narrative, gender and the canal share linearity. For Smith, the experience she writes about was happy because 'our living matched and even exceeded our youthful expectation of what life might be'.[22] In these structures of conventional expectation, then, we might look beyond 'romance' and 'life writing' to consider femininity as a genre. Indeed, Smith's and Cornish's work need not dwell on husbands and lovers because, Berlant predicts, 'normative femininity and aesthetic conventionality constitute the real central couple' both here and in the romances I read in this chapter. Romance novels do not, of course, allow for the explicit subordination by its central characters of sexual desire to labour and companionship, but both the novels and life writing repeat the conceit of wartime labour as a kind of moving pause, a time out, a brief moment to be something else, which is exciting but also inhibits the radical possibilities for permanent change in the women's understanding of what it is to be a woman in culture. Berlant makes clear that her analysis was 'depressing' to write because it shows 'what happens when a capitalist culture effectively markets conventionality' as the answer to a social existence that is stacked against most people (pp. 4; 19; 31). Sara Jeannette Duncan's publishers marketed *Two Girls on a Barge* as a continuity of feminine unconventionality; the wartime waterways romances ('gendering machines', Berlant would call them, p. 35) navigate the theme of 'women in the wrong place' with the compass of aesthetic conventionality and the effect of reasserting normative femininity despite (or, rather, because of) the 'unconventional women' on whose life experiences the novels are based.[23]

In what might seem a counterintuitive move, this section proceeds by centring a character who does not quite fit the script of normative femininity assigned to most of the other middle-class characters. I do this in order to make legible the genre of femininity. A version of the real-life Kit Gayford appears in almost all the Grand Union Canal texts in this corpus (save Green's *A Sister's War*). In Mayhew's *The Boat Girls* she is Pip Rowan. In Milly Adams's trilogy she is Bet Burrows. In Archer's *The Narrowboat Girls* she is just about recognisable as Dorothy Trent. In Smith's partly fictionalised *Maidens' Trip*, written in about three months at the end of the war, she is altered slightly to become Tilly. In Smith's later *As Green as Grass*, Kit is 'unmistakeably familiar': recognisable in her difference so that even the exception is structured by conventional expectation.[24] What follows, then, is not a fruitless comparison between fact and fiction, but an exploration of what Kit represents in the two different aesthetic genres as a route in to thinking about how these texts produce, reproduce and respond to normative femininity.

Gayford's *The Amateur Boatwomen* presents a supremely practical and hard-working woman who is deeply appreciative of canal culture and fully aware of her position as an outsider trying to master, within days, the intricacies of a job that have been passed down for generations. Cornish also recognised in the wartime recruits other women who worked to exhaustion to meet their own 'exacting standards of efficiency and perfection', a result, she reflects of 'a deep-seated feminine need to assert ourselves, to be "as good as the man" and even better'.[25] Kit is largely unshockable, even when, in November 1944, the boats are damaged by a bomb blast. In Adams's version of this in *Hope on the Waterways*, Bet characteristically tells everybody to stop fussing after the V2 hits, and instructs them to sort out the boats with her trademark 'chop chop'. This is typical of Adams's choice of language for this character, who also wants things to be 'tickety-boo'.[26]

Gayford details her chaotic initiation into canal carrying aboard the *Heather Bell*, quickly learning to manage the 70ft craft. Reading her account of the labour – and those that she inspired – I meet an overwhelming feeling of inadequacy: I have never worked as physically hard as those women and certainly lack the practical skill to steer a boat or mend an engine. Nevertheless, it is possible for the non-boater to identify with what we would today call the 'mindfulness' of those laborious days: 'the present was what counted and the daily acceptance of everything about this new and unfamiliar life'.[27] Woolfitt, one of Gayford's trainees, similarly remembers 'bodily work accomplished naturally', almost animalistically, with emotions subordinated to consuming physicality.[28] As she learns, Gayford is regularly self-conscious about being unhelpful and getting in the way, especially as she considers this period in retrospect. The rest of her career seems to have been dedicated to making up with efficiency any time she wasted in inexperience as a new recruit. She is even self-deprecating about her ability to accurately throw a rope – having spent her entire leave being instructed in this art by a sailing friend. Her first experience of training gives her the same performance anxiety, and the trip 'turned out to be a slightly embarrassing cavalcade', worrying about professional boatmen 'delayed by amateurs'. All of the texts in this corpus feature mortification as the women find themselves out of place and, often literally, in the way, marked out by their class, literacy, accents, inexperience and, as all-female crews, gender. None of the women were ever given a uniform (unlike their colleagues in the Women's Land Army and other services), so their cobbled-together attire forms part of all of the accounts. Gayford realised that delicate women's underwear was pointless, especially as the items turned grey from the conditions in which they were washed, so she invested in boys' pants and vests and dyed one pair bright blue and the other red. She borrowed her brother's bell bottoms from his First World War service, and being in the glove-making centre of Worcester offered the opportunity to acquire leather skins which were made into a shift.[29] This is a very literal way in which the women re-make their image for this new context. Almost every text I look at here sees trainees casting off the clothes made specifically for women and turning to men's working boots and brothers' discarded sporting or service items. They are not offered a new outward appearance to slip into, but must sew it together themselves.

One day, at the top of the Tardebigge flight of locks, Daphne March and Kit Gayford encountered a converted Shropshire Union boat – this was *Cressy*, owned by L. T. C. Rolt (discussed in the previous chapter) who would be so instrumental in the regeneration of the canals later in the century. It is possible that this incident and its connections inspired some of the cross-cultural love affairs between the recruits and professional boatmen found in the romance novels; Sonia Rolt (née South) was one of the women working for the GUCCC on the boats *Moon* and *Phobos* with two close friends, one of whom had spotted the talismanic newspaper advertisement. In her obituary in 2014, Veronica Horwell noted that Sonia became 'the grand dame of Britain's waterways'.[30] She met the golden-curled 'Adonis of the canals', George Smith (not the campaigner from Chapter Three), while she was a trainee and they married in 1945, she joining him on his boats *Cairo* and *Warwick*. Cornish notes that the other women 'half envied her the superior status of mate to a real boatman!'[31] Sonia separated from Smith, but not the waterways, when she left him for Tom Rolt in 1951.[32] In the romances, Archer's, Adams's and Mayhew's characters are all warned off falling for the good-looking, exotic boatmen who will only be truly happy with wives from their own community, reinforcing social boundaries and the sense that this waterways life is a moment of pause in real life rather than a moment of lasting change.

Transferring to the Grand Union in 1942, Gayford found few in the way of books to help accelerate her boating education, apart from Herbert's *The Water Gypsies*. This was, presumably, about as useful as Toad's adventures on the canal in Kenneth Williams's *Wind in the Willows* (1908), or those of Edith Nesbit's railway children (1906). Kit was, instead, to be practically trained up by a working couple, the Sibleys. The other versions of Kit all emphasise her profound respect for boatmen and women, their culture and community. In *The Amateur Boatwomen* she details their 'kindness and generosity', often masked to outsiders by taciturnity and inscrutability.[33] In *Maidens' Trip*, Emma Smith asserts that Tilly (her version of Kit) 'lived in mortal terror of offending the boaters for whom she would, at any moment, have spent her blood in battle'. She notes, too, Tilly's 'voice that came somehow manfully out of her stomach', and that the trainees eagerly competed for her praise. In *As Green as Grass*, Smith describes Gayford as 'bird-like', partly due to her mannerisms and size, but also because of the idiosyncratic peaked skiing cap she wore.[34] Adams gives the fictional Bet a booming laugh and brusque mannerisms.[35] Bird-like, with a manful voice and boys' underwear, Gayford clearly sits outside the constraints of normative 1940s femininity.

Adams's version of Kit in her waterways trilogy is a lesbian (usually couched in the period-appropriate terms of 'friendship'), but her location in the heterosexual romance genre means that this fictional relationship does not escape the power of heteronormativity. Christine

Wood's analysis of American romance novels from the 1950s and 60s found that a recurrent feature of these narratives saw the female protagonist embarking on a journey, 'often as the "new girl in town"', and encountering love and turmoil. She noted that the plots of hetero-sexual women protagonists followed a particular narrative formula, which is also clearly evident in wartime waterways romances, though they were written in the twenty-first century and feature sets of three heterosexual woman. The first part of the formula is the new scene, here: the canal. The second part is 'encounters', here with boatmen, servicemen or other men encountered in the course of their work. The third part of the romance formula is 'heat and smoulder', clearly in evidence in these novels. For instance: 'heat ran through her like molten metal' from Archer's *The Narrowboat Girls*. The fourth part is the 'cold shoulder', such as in Adams's *Hope on the Waterways*, when a trainee makes a silent deal with God to become a nun if a young boy's life is spared, thus renouncing her sexy fireman. The fifth part is reaction, and the sixth 'violence and turmoil', provided here either by the fighting front or criminally violent male characters.

Structurally, the final part of the narrative will usually be 'new ground', typified in *The Boat Girls*, for instance, by the fiancé of one of the trainees asking her, as she takes a last look at the canal, "Ready to go on?"[36] In the waterways romances, though, the endings are always anticlimactically doubled as the heroines tread the new ground of marriage (a triple wedding in *Hope on the Waterways*) or a satisfying new career (Izzy in *The Narrowboat Girls*) but are suddenly forced out of the context that brought them love and adventure by the abrupt termination of their contracts as the war ends (historically, the scheme continued until 1946). In *Hope on the Waterways* the women moor up at Alperton, well before their normal stoppage time: 'they could have pat-pattered on, but what was the point – now?' At the end of the novel (and the trilogy), with all three of the crew married, Sylvia notes that they are 'moored up at last . . . Home and dry'.[37] In one sense, this feels like a neatly conservative hetero ending, as the women have been labouring towards victory in war and romance, and the end of their life on water allows them to settle into a future of fruitful marriage. However, the sudden curtailment of a routine that brought them a novel sense of national usefulness at a time of crisis, exploration of the self, and fulfilling sisterhood hints at the compromise each of the engaged women makes by leaving the workforce: their national useful-ness now is to reproduce Britishness through motherhood, they are assumed to have found completion of the self with a male partner, and they must now prioritise their husbands over female friends.

The women's bodies can be seen as a site of contestation in this moment of transition: in both the life writing and romances, the trainees comment on what the heavy lifting and pushing of the job has done to their internal organs: will they be able to have children? And they have also become hard, fit and practical, the soft curves and curls of femininity lost to the labour (and trousers) of the waterways. Emma's weighty muscles in *Maidens' Trip* are denigrated as 'unwomanly' by a temporary male crew member and, despite Smith's assertion that they need not dwell on husbands or lovers, by the end of their tenure another crew-mate feels it is 'unnatural' for them to have been away from men for so long: 'we need them'.[38] They were out of place as trainees, but now their bodies are the wrong shape for feminine postwar 'new ground'. Though the cold winter work they undertake makes me ache to even think about it, the loss of this mindful physicality feels like one of the tragedies of the texts. Will the women, as Susan Woolfitt recounts, have shamefully to let out the arms of their (wedding) dresses to fit their bulging biceps? Emma Smith, towards the end of her time on the canal, '*yearn*[s]' to be 'a *real girl*'; they have spent so much time being dirty and smelly – in *The Waterways Girls* even sailors refuse the girls a kiss as they travel, unwashed, home on leave.[39] Nanette in *Maidens' Trip* sows seeds of doubt about peacetime marriage while dramatising the conflation of wartime romance and danger expressed on one of the romance covers when she daydreams about marrying a pilot: 'it must be much easier to go on loving a man who's always in danger' (p. 100). She points to the *un*naturalness of lifelong monogamy, rather than setting out marriage as the obvious female path. The overwhelming message from the romances is that physical strength is a side effect of the women's temporary independence, and both must be relinquished when peace is won. The life writing does not, however, communicate quite the same message, indicating that the genre of romance has added a layer of gender conformity to the experience of women's wartime work.

The one exception to these straight women's bodies apparently defeminised by labour is Tolly in Archer's *The Narrowboat Girls*, the most conservative of the novels in this corpus; once 'fat', Tolly's restricted diet and daily exercise has made her 'slim' enough to be acceptable as a beautiful bride – and her 'skinny young man' (formerly sufficiently deficient in strapping masculinity to court the 'rounded woman') has become broad-shouldered by 1945.[40] Her new, conforming, figure is celebrated in this twenty-first-century text – in other words, we cannot put this attitude down to outdated notions of gender. The *Daily Mail* of 1944 (a publication that is notorious for its sexist policing of women's bodies today) showed a similar interest in the size and shape of female GUCCC recruits in the article '1 Girl in 3 Fits a Barge: The Hatchway Decides'. A Ministry of War Transport Official is quoted as saying that applicants are mostly too old, too young, too short, too tall, or too fat. 'The fat girl is liable to be unwieldy in the tiny cabin', the article goes on.[41] Where Tolly might have been unsuitable to even enter the cabin in the 1940s (or so the *Daily Mail* would imply), in fiction she has the rather dubious privilege of accidentally losing lots of weight. When compared with the thin bodies of people freezing and 'having a very lean time' during the war, this retrospective glamorisation of thinness seems in particularly poor taste.[42]

That triple wedding as the culmination of Adams's trilogy matches the 'sister-brides' and 'best-friend-brides' conceit identified by Kate McNicholas Smith and Imogen Tyler in work on lesbian brides in popular culture. They explore the 'proliferation of "positive" and "ordinary," as opposed to deviant or pathological, mainstream representations of lesbian romance', and Bet and Fran's opaque relationship in the trilogy fits in to this category. In *The Waterway Girls*, they constitute a surrogate family grouping as stand-in parents one Christmas, welcoming two trainees, a boy they are looking after and his dog for roast goose. In the warmth of a cottage kitchen away from the cut, Bet calls Fran 'love' as they discuss a possible future in holiday boats once industrial loads are no longer carried by water. The night before the triple wedding, Fran and Bet do have their own room, but the narrative never enters it.[43] These novels follow, as I have just demonstrated, the script of the classic romance, and thus it is no surprise that Bet and Fran's manifestation of the 'lesbian normal' affirms, by the compromised terms of its visibility, the 'ideals of hetero-patriarchal, white, middle-class femininity'. In fact, 'the lesbian normal marks a convergence of the homonormative' and 'occludes queer commitments to anti-normativity'.[44] These heteronormative waterways romances thus allow for a lesbian character, but her sexuality is an open secret, never explicitly discussed in the terms of desire as voiced and enjoyed by the straight protagonists. While on the canal, with her partner living on land, Bet's sexuality is invisible. She lives alone in the butty cabin, apart from when a dangerous chest infection forces her away from work (thus pushing the other women into closer cooperation and independence). Three-quarters of the way through the novel (before their Christmas visit), one trainee is left wondering what 'home' means for Bet. Bet even refers to herself light-heartedly as 'an old maid'.[45] This produces, to borrow from Eve Kosofsky Sedgwick, an epistemology of the cabin in a text which writes around the edges of queer visibility. Bet and Fran explicitly share their love of the cut, but their desire for each other goes unspoken. What I'm sure a modern chest X-ray would reveal to be a shadow on Bet's lung clouds the long-lasting happiness and possibilities for voicing lesbian desire in the heterosexual romances of the waterways. Where the three straight woman are written into a comfortably conforming future, Bet's story ends with the other women's weddings.

In Cornish's autobiographical *Troubled Waters* (which finds an unexpected echo in the title of Judith Butler's classic *Gender Trouble*), queerness is represented as both deviant and pathological in the character of Jo. Margaret (whom I refer to by her first name here as the protagonist in a scene, a different voice to the reflective author) first encounters Jo's non-normative behaviour when she finds her with her head in the lap of Daphne, their trainer: 'was Jo a lesbian? Were they both lesbians?' The questions are left open for a chapter and a half until Jo embraces Margaret 'fiercely'. Jo tells Margaret that 'in fact, she was a man and that she loved [her]' and had done so since an incident when she had performed the male romantic role by picking up the injured Margaret and carrying her on to the boat. Margaret's diary recorded Jo as being 'almost a man yet not enough developed either physically or emotionally to feel certain of himself in any way'. In retrospect, Cornish sees the terms of her understanding as basically Victorian, though she was 'horrified and not a little frightened' at the time to be the object of Jo's urgent and almost violent desire. Jo's way of being is described as paranoid and schizophrenic – she is apparently an unpredictable fantasist in many regards – and this, according to Cornish's narrative, is centred on her predatory lesbianism and/or trans identity. This gets labelled, euphemistically, as 'Jo's problems'. The Jo of Cornish's narrative is, to match the book's title, very troubled (in that she seems mentally unwell), troubles normative femininity and heterosexuality, and troubles her initial identification (by Margaret) as a lesbian by describing herself as a man who desires women. Cornish writes a Jo who is plurally both/either lesbian and/or trans by referring to Jo as a lesbian and (just once) using a male pronoun. Jo's desire, combined with her dramatic mood changes and erratic behaviour, is considered beyond the bounds of what is acceptable on the boats ('a menace') meaning she 'disappeared into her own unknown future'. As with Bet in Adams's fictional work, the reader is not offered a glimpse of queer futures. However, Cornish does go on to describe the way in which female companionship replaces heterosexual relationships: 'Daphne's smile of welcome was more heart-warming' than male partners' 'torrid embraces' or 'poetic declarations' (pp. 87; 101–5; 133). Marriage promises only 'restraints and limitations' on the freedom Cornish found in a life on the boats (p. 181). That freedom, too, had its limits, in that same-sex desire was both strictly circumscribed and misunderstood.

Cornish notes (perhaps regretfully) that the content of her diaries 'has become the subject of nostalgic reminiscence to be revived in story and dramatic re-enactment' (p. 26). This presumably includes Alarum Theatre's very successful tour from 2016 of *Idle Women of the Wartime Waterways*, comprising Kate Saffin's play 'Isobel's War' and Heather Wastie's poem and song piece 'Idle Women and Judies', and Mikron Theatre's *Imogen's War*, performed in the 1990s. In other words, these wartime experiences continue to speak to new audiences as romance and drama, finding new meanings in these other contexts. The next section examines the ways in which the life writing and romances communicate not just what it is to live and travel on the water, but also the qualities *of* water in this context.

Clean and dirty waters

It is 1944 and I am *Industrious*, powered not by my usual motor but pulled. Pulled not by a horse but a woman, along the Bottom Road from Birmingham to collect coal in Coventry, a far cry from the kingfishers and otters of the bucolic journey towards the Second City. The air here is permeated by noisome vapours from the factories at the cut side.[46] The woman bow hauler creeps onwards through black mud, hands, shoulder and waist scarred by the rope; hair, lashes, nostrils and tongue dirtied by filthy air and water.

All of the romance and autobiographical texts in this chapter are, of course, set on the water and, as well as focusing on the extreme dirtiness of canal water, there are two ways in which this corpus explores the value of water, and that is via the preservation of water in locks, and the sourcing and reuse of potable water. The trainees' boating inexperience often leads them, at first, to muddle the sequence of closing and opening locks, meaning that tons of water are wasted; locks, despite being engineering marvels, are extremely inefficient in their use of water. Trainer Kit Gayford recounted an incident from when she started out on the *Heather Bell* – she left the paddle up on the top gate, so that water ran both out of the lock and into it. She managed to quickly bring it down, with 'an agonised look' to see if Daphne had 'spotted this unforgivable sin of "wasting water"'. In another similar incident she realises what is happening 'with a sickening jerk' (pp. 27–8). The anguish and guilt related to wasting the element on which their work relies demonstrates how emotionally invested the women were in not just contributing to the war effort, but in engineered water itself. The loss of water could mean limits on the number of boats going through a flight of locks (such as Tring in the summer of 1944) or a change in route such as on to the Bottom Road from Coventry, a horror described in all the romance novels, but especially vivid in Adams's trilogy.

The route involved bow-hauling the boats, turning the women into work horses. Adams leaves the marks of this labour on her characters' bodies, in welts, blisters, bruises, callouses and scars. These scars are even used in *Love on the Waterways* as a bodily mark of recognition and canal sisterhood by a woman deeply traumatised by brutal domestic violence: she pushes aside the collar of one of the trainees to see that the women before her can be trusted.[47] Kit Gayford reveals that the use of the Bottom Road in real life was indeed because of a water shortage, one that is here written on the body (pp. 87; 125). Smith also writes with disgust about the Bottom Road. She is sure that the flight of locks must be the dirtiest in England, and the tow-path is both sooty and covered with the dung of canal horses. Even the sliminess of the lock walls is of a different quality to elsewhere on the cut, here peculiarly black and oily. Everything they touch becomes covered in dirt.[48] The Bottom Road is not the only filthy portion of their journey, though. At Stanton the mud smells awful and a smothering green weed sticks to the boats.[49] This eutrophication – possibly from the nearby ironworks but also attributable to other industries, agriculture and human waste, will have upset aquatic ecosystems and enabled the uncontrollable growth of choking green weed. The pollution is invisible, but its effects are not.

The women had quickly to try to memorise the location of fresh water taps on the journey as drinking water supplies were often hard to come by. It was 'no joke to find the cans empty, the next tap miles ahead, and a dreary wait before we could even have a mug of cocoa'. Gayford notes the water economies they made, like using the hot water from cooking vegetables for a hot water bottle to warm the bed, and then using this water a third time in the morning to boil eggs for breakfast. On the occasions she boiled an egg in fresh water, she would then use that water to make a cup of cocoa, 'with apparently no ill effects', though the crew in *Maidens' Trip* are warned that this practice will give them warts. Gayford reflects that water conservancy was something that 'became absorbed into the general pattern of life', just as water wastage is the pattern for most in the West today.[50] They even learn the location-specific qualities of fresh water, saving their laundry for the soft water of Warwickshire.[51] Though its authors ply what Jamie Linton would call the 'modern' water of the engineered canal in support of a thoroughly modern war, this life writing's attention to the heterogeneity and human value of water mingles society and nature in an older form.[52] We might be less laudatory about their lavatory: they must use a bucket on board, with the canal as their sewer. They have to repress knowledge of this relationship between their waste and the cut when they wash parts of their body with water scooped from it.[53]

The dirty water is never confined outside the boat – for one thing the engines are water-cooled, so there is constant intake. When objects get tangled in the propeller, someone has to get in to the water and cut it away. Because of its dirtiness, trainer Bet advises trainee Polly in *The Waterways Girls*: 'if you ever fall into the cut, keep your mouth shut', and the action of the Waterways trilogy results in many characters ending up submerged.[54] The real Kit Gayford fell into the canal early in her career, and recalled filthy mud and water and a lingering odour (p. 41). In Adams's rendering of the girls' first trip to the public baths – an experience in which both romance and life writing wallow – Polly looks at the dregs of her dirty bathwater and was 'disgusted with herself'.[55] The dirt of the cut has been translated into disgust with the self; the girls may rail against the children who lean over bridges and call them dirty, even spitting on them, but this statement demonstrates an internalisation of judgments about cleanliness, dirt and social attitudes to dirty work. This moment of disgust is textually complex because of the genre in which it sits. There are no two ways about it: Polly is covered in her own shit, and in the waste of other animals and industry. Such moments do not belong in romance fiction – Berlant would say that we do not expect it. The disgusting pollution of water is a moment when conventionality fails, the conventional (clean) woman in the conventional romance is made toxic. The internalisation of the toxicity of the canalscape is literal in *Maidens' Trip* in a moment of bodily contamination: Nanette gashes her hand on a rusty nail while they navigate the Bottom Road and realises her blood may be poisoned.[56] The scarcity of clean water and the absolute filth of the canal water are persistent themes in this corpus; not only does that draw attention to the actual facts of pollution, it highlights that contamination is culturally thorough: it turns the body bad, disrupting both the character's sense of self and expectations of the gendered body and self that exist as and in textual genre.

The Waterways Girls treats another particular type of dirty and dangerous work as quietly heroic: coalmining. When the women load up with coal, as in 'Through Canal-Land in a Canadian Canoe', those on the water witness the miners, but this time in a state of exhaustion from work rather than frustration from underemployment. The labour tells on their bodies not just in weariness, but, again, enters the body itself, the coal grit in teeth, throat and lungs. The text does, then, cause readers to think about where the commodities the women transport come from, and the human and environmental cost of their extraction. The next section, however, considers how the cost of aluminium specifically exists largely beyond the pages of this corpus.

From the black mud of the Bottom Road to the red mud of Guiana

I am *Industrious*, carrying aluminium from London up a flight to Marsworth. I carry ingots which whisper their own stories, hints of elemental Guiana, water and earth, mud and fruit, race and Empire.[57] Like the coal whose dust still lingers on my boards, this cargo has been cleaved from the ground, but on another continent and with feverish new purpose. Aluminium is the metal of a modern war.

The very first load in the hold of Adams's waterways trilogy refers the reader to the risky wartime transatlantic journey of essential metal supplies, this rusty shipment having escaped the U-boats, with others in the convoy not being as lucky.[58] The first load of the second book in the trilogy is aluminium, unloaded again from merchant ships at Limehouse Basin in London and trans-shipped on to the women's boats for the onward journey by canal. Polly reflects on the type of aeroplane it will be made into once they deliver it to Tyseley Wharf in Birmingham and is reassured that the cargo contributes to the war effort.[59] Even when the girls are trapped in a cellar after a V2 explosion, Bet shouts down to them (in an exchange that could come straight from a 1940s filmic depiction of the stiff upper lip) that they must get themselves out because the country needs them, and they have aluminium to be collected.[60]

Aluminium was, indeed, one of the cargoes transported by the female crews, as their life writing testifies. Cornish mentions bars to be delivered to 'Maffas' (Marsworth), and Woolfitt describes 'aluminium bars which look so like chocolate bars wrapped in silver paper, with neat little nicks in them to make them easier to break!' for the same destination. A load of 42½ tons is considered very light for this particular cargo.[61] An online discussion forum has suggested that the final destination for the ingots may have been the Bifurcated and Tubular Rivet Company, working day and night for the aircraft industry during the war.[62] Besides historical accuracy, aluminium is also a useful thematic choice of cargo for Adams because it is so clearly connected to the war effort.

A post-war history of *The Control of Raw Materials* records that the peak year for wartime aluminium was 1943, with munitions taking 99% of this: 'no commodity, with the exception of magnesium, bore comparison with it in its complete or virtually complete diversion to service needs'.[63] In the final novel of the *Waterways* trilogy, Sylvia's pair of boats have, once more, holds full of aluminium. She notices her 'fingers scraped raw by the rope, and blistered, calloused and frozen'.[64] Again, women's bodies are figured as smooth and unblemished in their 'natural' state but here hardened and roughened by unfamiliar labour. The focus of this section, however, is on the politics of the labour that produced the aluminium on the boat, the hands it blistered before reaching Limehouse but whose location is kept out of the frame of the narratives described thus far. This commodity on the cut brings with it the exploitation of land and labour elsewhere.[65]

The aluminium in the holds of those boats crewed by women was likely shipped from Canada: the country supplied 90% of British and Commonwealth wartime imports of the metal; this was by no means, however, the start of its journey.[66] This is a commodity history worth detailing, from Guiana to Canada to London, in order to trace the geopolitics and environmental damage lurking in the background of texts featuring wartime canal transport.

Aluminium is smelted from bauxite which, at this time, came mostly from British Guiana (now Guyana). Bauxite, formed from the weathering of rocks over millions of years, was first discovered by the French geologist Pierre Berthier in 1821 and is mainly aluminium oxide bound in different forms with various impurities (e.g. iron oxide and silica). Robin Gendron, Mats Ingulstad and Espen Storli assert that the 'history of the bauxite industry is also essentially a history of economic globalization'.[67] Its wartime production is also a story of Britain's twentieth-century imperial politics. The British had captured the two Dutch colonies of Berbice and Demerara-Essequibo in 1803 – seven years after the opening of the Grand Junction Canal, the precursor to the Grand Union Canal, to locate us in waterways time. They amalgamated the colonies as British Guiana (which would be the country's name until independence in 1966) and maintained a system of plantation slavery followed by the introduction of indentured Indian labour. Like Guiana's slaves, the Indian labourers on sugar plantations were 'treated as less than human'. As in many of its imperial territories, the British used strategies of divide and rule between black and Indian Guyanans, meaning that enduring post-war political divisions are now viewed by commentators as a pervasive 'legacy of slavery'.[68]

Guyana has a particularly textual relationship to Europe, with David Dabydeen suggesting that it 'came into modern being, in a sense, through literature', specifically via Walter Raleigh's 1596 *Discoverie of Guiana*.[69] While canal literature may seem a surprising continuation of Guyana's textual relationship to Europe, a focus on aluminium as a wartime commodity connects the waterways of Britain, Canada and Guyana and serves as yet another reminder that the functioning of the English canals can never be read simply as happening in a contained 'inland'. The waterways had long connected the interior of the country to the rest of the world; here we see the fruits of Empire brought right to the heart of England in the service of war industry.

Andrew Perchard has called the British and Canadian aluminium industries 'an important, and overlooked, part of Britain's military-industrial complex', with the links in the commodity chain formed as much by politics as global bauxite deposits.[70] Before the First World War, the British government had little interest in bauxite because there was such a small demand for aluminium. Guyana, for Britain, represented, for the most part, sugar – and Britain still imports millions of pounds worth of sugar from Guyana today. Sugar – or rather its wartime absence – is a preoccupation for the women working on canal boats in the texts so far examined, but the novels express little if any personal feeling about aluminium as a commodity beyond its indispensability to the war effort. In describing the difficulties of obtaining spare parts, Susan Woolfitt noted that they 'were almost impossible to replace in those days when all metal was being commandeered for more lethal purposes', but this is not directly connected to the aluminium ingots her boats carry.[71] Woolfitt's reference to the ingots as bars of chocolate elides (with a sugary product) rather than acknowledges their ultimate purpose. In contrast, Gayford notes the germination of grains of wheat they have spilled from a cargo, and reflects on the feeling of 'personal insult' when they see any bread floating in the canal, 'made from some of the flour from those sacks over which we had sweated our guts'.[72] The commodity chains of grain and flour are much more visible, and that of coal is obvious as the women collect it from mines where they see miners, and burn coal in their own cabins. Aluminium is much harder for them to think and feel about because of its far-flung mining and smelting, and because its transformation into deadly machines of war does not bear thinking about.

The implications of this are not just emotional and political, they are also ecological. Matthew Evenden points out that the aluminium commodity chain reveals some of the environmental history of war 'because it unfolded over vast distances and imposed different environmental burdens on several locations'.[73] In explicitly situating the aluminium cargo managed by women who worked on English canals in the Second World War to its long journey from bauxite in the ground to bomb-dropping aircraft, I hope to make it heavier than its literal 42½ tons: it is ideologically heavy with the weight of colonialism, exploited labour, environmental carnage, and its potential as a death machine. We are a long way, now, from the 'romance' of the Second World War touted on the cover of a novel.

After the First World War, Britain began putting measures in place to assure supply of commodities in the event of a new war, and in 1920 David Lloyd George pressed British colonies to secure mineral resources. The British and Colonial Bauxite Company was registered in 1927, with an agreement for the Demerara Bauxite Company to mine Guianese reserves reached in 1936.[74] Domestic production met Britain's aluminium needs prior to the Second World War, but could not hope to keep pace with requirements for the metal in the 1940s. The quality of Guianese bauxite was questionable: problems were reported at the British Aluminium Company (BACo's) Larne works, for instance, because of high iron content in the supplies; BACo preferred supplies from France and the Gold Coast (Ghana). France, of course, was occupied by the Nazis when Britain needed its bauxite most to defeat those occupiers, and Gold Coast bauxite had the disadvantages of high mining costs and a long rail journey to port. The story of bauxite/aluminium is reminiscent of the driving forces of canal development: proximity of and access to fuel/energy, raw materials and manufacture. Bauxite is bulky and therefore costly to transport, but deposits are rarely located near sources of the massive amounts of power required for the smelting process. In the 1980s, Raymond Dumett pointed out the tendency of Anglophone scholars to ignore, in the mobilisation of Africa's mineral resources (such as Gold Coast bauxite) for Allied victory over totalitarianism, 'the colossal waste and destructive purpose in virtually all wartime metals fabrication and petro-chemical production by the belligerent powers'. In fact, the war could be viewed 'as an economic struggle for the control and exploitation of the world's strategic minerals'. It certainly 'called forth the extraction of raw materials [. . .] on an unprecedented scale'.[75] Martin Gutmann agrees: 'the modern warfare of the Second World War was global in its environmental footprint'.[76] For Britain, then, its historic colonial acquisitions and centuries-old transport technology were brought together to access a relatively new material that had become crucial to fighting an all-consuming modern war.

The texts in this chapter featuring aluminium see it transported by water inland in Britain. Water is also key to the production of aluminium. Commercially viable hydro-electric schemes for the production of aluminium had peaked within the United Kingdom by the late 1930s. The British government began to work with Alcan (originally the Northern Aluminum Company, a subsidiary of the American Alcoa), who dammed rivers in Canada's Saguenay region to produce hydro-electricity, altering the seasonal flow regime, the sediment load and aquatic ecology, such as fish habitats, in the process. All of this was seen as 'unavoidable collateral damage in the mobilization of rivers for war'. The effects of the smelting process on water systems are long lasting, including the accumulation of polynuclear aromatic hydrocarbons (PAHs) which continue to affect species such as the beluga whale.[77] These environmental effects were seeded in agreements made in 1930 that, should another global conflict occur, Canada would be the main supplier of aluminium to Britain, and that the supply of metal for the Empire should come *from* the Empire.[78] That conflict did occur, and the supply was needed. For instance, 12,000 aircraft were primed for D-Day. Each aircraft required up to fifteen tons of aluminium.[79] That makes 180,000 tons of aluminium for that decisive moment in the war in Europe, aluminium that came from a colonised tropical landscape via the hydro-electric power of a former colony (now dominion), Canada. Water, then, was vital to the 1940s production and transport of aluminium, whether in the form of steam-powered vessels, hydro-electricity, or canal carrying. To return to ideas floated in the Introduction about the way we think about water, I suggest that the water used to produce aluminium should be considered 'colonial water', because Empire produced the geographies of mining and smelting for wartime production.

The environmental cost of production was and is enormous. Bauxite mines involved the felling of tropical forests, the removal of sand and clay 'overburden', then surface mining. In Guiana in the 1940s, this was in the context of 'permissive colonial conditions' and 'low-waged workers', the people who (borrowing from Gayford) 'sweated their guts' to mine bauxite.[80] These workers mainly lived in the company town of McKenzie, named for the Scottish American engineer who prospected for bauxite there. McKenzie is 65 miles up the Demerara river from the coastal capital, Georgetown. The Demerara Bauxite Company financed and controlled almost all of the amenities in McKenzie and wielded a huge amount of power which, Maurice St Pierre notes, it 'exercised in typical colonial fashion'; the town was segregated along racial lines, with white people living in South McKenzie (apart from live-in domestic staff) and non-white people in North McKenzie.[81] The work of bauxite mining is dangerous, with prolonged exposure to bauxite dust potentially leading to respiratory ailments and pulmonary diseases.[82] As the aluminium cargo on the canal becomes ideologically heavy, Bet's chest complaint back on the English waterways can be heard as a rattly echo of those suffered by bauxite miners. To think about the journey of the metal on the boats is to connect characters in Britain to their counterparts off the page, allowing the reading to flow beyond its inland setting. 'Red mud', a waste product of the refining process is also toxic to humans and the environment, being caustic and metal-rich.[83] It makes the black mud of the Bottom Road seem positively benign. Gendron and co-authors note that the environmental impact of mining and refining bauxite is evident in 'the scars left on the landscape by strip-mining, deforestation, or the holding ponds for red mud'.[84] Evenden looks even more expansively at aluminium's waste stream, encompassing not just the razed tropical forests of British Guiana, the red mud and air pollutant by-products of the Bayer process and smelting in Canada, but also the 'discarded and destroyed shells of airplanes'. It was the wartime expansion of aluminium production that accelerated its environmental effects.[85] In its journey from Guyanese ground to British factory (and on to plane and exploded flesh), aluminium has devastating ecological and human consequences.

The tropical forests of Guyana may seem as far from English countryside and industrial cities as it is possible to imagine, but the jungle finds its way into the wartime canal life writing, as if the ingots brought part of their bauxite-laden ground with them onto the boats. Gayford, for instance, notes that 'great woody tendrils were hanging down from a great height on some of the trees. We wondered what it could be as it looked strong enough to swing on'.[86] It is, in fact, the hedgerow clematis Old Man's Beard, but a sudden image of other places, with different light and soil, is conjured. This is not, of course, a deliberate authorial reference to Guyana, but its presence is a product of tracing aluminium's journey. Smith produces the tropical forest more metaphorically in *Maidens' Trip*. The English canal space feels, in these autobiographical narratives, like a largely closed off world. For instance, Smith notes the paradox that without the war they should never have experienced the canal in this way, yet the war 'was little more than a distant noise in our ears' – often quite literally: 'aeroplanes were droning out of sight in the grey sky'. The pattern of the changing seasons she observes on the cut are, for Susan Woolfitt, 'as far removed from war or thoughts of violence as one could conceive'.[87] But Smith describes the letters the women are able to pick up at particular points on their journeys as missives from beyond its boundaries: 'we, every now and then, broke from the jungly bounds of our canal to snatch up these precious waiting packages'.[88] One way or another, the landscape of Guyana, the starting point of their cargo's long voyage, makes its way onto the canals, with the aeroplanes overhead marking the cargo's destination.[89]

Journeying to the Midlands, Smith notes that 'the idea of a Saturday afternoon in Coventry was the real root of our discontent'.[90] The characters of David Dabydeen's *Our Lady of Demerara* (2004) might know just what she means. The form of Dabydeen's novel could not be more different from the life writing and romance novels so far assessed in this chapter, but it makes unexpected connections between the industrial canals of Coventry and the social and environmental legacies of colonialism in Guyana, connections that are almost hidden in the journey of wartime aluminium cargoes. I introduce the novel to this chapter in order to demonstrate the cross-textual insights made possible by reading canal texts together, and how this thematic reading makes the politics of canal literature newly visible: what do canals carry, where did it come from, and what forms of exploitation do generic conventions hide in their representation of the canals? *Our Lady of Demerara*'s epigraphs come from a nineteenth-century social reformer and a missionary, both critiquing native belief in reincarnation and its challenge to Western Christian 'expectations of the linear, the stable, the steady and reasonable development of plot and character'.[91] This is a clear warning to the reader: unlike the romance novel, all expectations of stable and linear plot and character should be left behind. Instead, there is Derridean wordplay and character disappearance and reappearance. There are fakes and explicitly unreliable narratorial strategies. There is dissembling and deceit. Where conventional life writing and romance novels are usually predicated on straightforward readerly identification with protagonists, every 'I' in Dabydeen's novel is discomforting, a point of view the reader shrinks from inhabiting.

The first part of the novel follows the murderous misogynist Lance in Coventry and his short marriage to Elizabeth, whose great-grandfather, a sugar planter in Demerara, had a child with a young widow who had arrived on a coolie boat from India. The patriarch owned a thousand acres with 'as many natives beholden to him for their livelihood' (pp. 13; 68). Elizabeth compares her ethnicity, an apparent whiteness that is demographically dominant in Coventry, to 'raw sugar, pungent in its brownness, becoming an aromatic white through the process of refinement' (p. 14). Guiana is an inconvenient and dark secret for this character, and it is also the hidden origin of canal cargoes in the romances and life writing so far explored. Its very prospect is appalling to Elizabeth, 'not just the savagery of the place but the journey into [her] own past' (p. 98). While seeming to distance her refined whiteness from the raw savagery of Guiana, Elizabeth acknowledges that this darkness is within her own past and her own body. She embodies the fallacy of an 'English' story divorced from British power and influence abroad. She is a hybrid export, smelted into something no longer Guianese and living an unsatisfactory life in post-industrial Coventry – the kind of 'mobilization of fragments' and dispersal in which Shivani Sivagurunathan says the novel revels.[92] To put it crudely: Elizabeth's family have not been the winners by their colonial inheritance. By contrast, two of the women in Mayhew's *The Boat Girls* find happiness by marrying into families of vast fortunes, one made via privateering and the other in cotton: in romance fiction, inheriting the spoils of state-sponsored piracy and slavery is no obstacle to a happy ending. There are no happy-ever-afters in Dabydeen's novel, but reading his work alongside that of Mayhew (and others) draws attention to the inconvenient truths of British history repressed by romance plots.

The second part of Dabydeen's novel is Lance's imagined autobiography of a priest, with figures from his life in Coventry reincarnated in Ireland, England and Guyana. Lance's voyage is prompted by an Indian migrant named Samaroo, who, like his father, had joined the British army and moved to racist England in 1959, a place which reminisces about war but ignores the wartime roles of these men (p. 54). Following his ritualistic murder of Samaroo's adopted niece, Corinne, Lance escapes 'the scene of the grime', hoping to find some 'form of cleansing' of the 'accretions of Coventry dirt' in Guiana on the trail of the trainee Catholic priest whose 'autobiography' is apparently bequeathed him by Samaroo (pp. 73; 110). In direct contrast to narratives which centre female experience and desire (however circumscribed) in the life writing and romances of this chapter, the women of *Our Lady of Demerara* represent, for Elizabeth Jackson, a 'relentless catalogue of men's historical and contemporary brutality to women in Guyana, Britain and India'. Jackson notes, however, that the text is self-conscious about this, and can also be seen as a male perspective on the radical feminist idea of heterosexuality being the 'basis of women's oppression'.[93] Though some of the passages in Dabydeen's novel are difficult to read, it nonetheless offers a more profound comment on patriarchal social and religious structures, sexuality and violence towards women than texts limited by the romance genre can hope to, even when they seem to be ostensibly *all about* women escaping violent partners, female desire and women finding freedom.

For Dabydeen, Coventry, 'all puddles and gutters and canals' is Guiana's strange twin, and this is nowhere more evident than in the novel's representation of ecological damage (p. 227). In Guiana, as well as the mistreatment of African slaves and Indian indentured labourers, Lance recognises that the priest whose trail he follows 'would have realised the real origin of evil, which lay in the clearing of spaces in the jungle, the draining and ploughing of the land' (p. 82). Alvin Thompson has pointed to the 'indelible marks' of slavery in Guyana, including a heavy emphasis on export crops (i.e. sugar) rather than food crops, the location of the population in areas opened up to produce and export sugar, and a typical infrastructure of dikes, dams and canals used by the Dutch and British during slavery (p. 194). Spaces in the jungle were also cleared on a large scale to mine bauxite. Dabydeen finds centuries of rot in the cuts around Coventry too, its white underclass and immigrant workers caught in a vicious intergenerational trap of poverty, ignorance and superstition. The priest's grandfather moved to the city; months of digging in Coventry made him sick, but the narrative does not attribute this to overwork alone: 'the wounds he inflicted on the earth', Lance's false narrative claims, are just as damaging (p. 147). The trainee priest's mentor, Father Harris, believes that Nature limits the damage done to it, so it is not wounded beyond recovery, allowing humans to survive in and through it. Human sickness is thus a cosmic punishment for 'all that digging and slashing and laying down of bricks', disrupting a natural equilibrium.

Father Harris connects the canal extension scheme to the original building of the Coventry canals, which 'so many hundreds died shovelling' on meagre wages. Meanwhile, 'the rich looked on, waiting for them to drop and rot so they could suck their bones, having already sucked their flesh'. The new scheme shows 'the same disdain for nature' in its construction and purpose, because the canals were built to transport coal (p. 205). The trainee priest notices trees bleakly stripped of life because, he thinks (via Lance's imagining) his grandfather had 'maimed the earth, making unnatural canals', his shovel awakening spores to 'vindictive life' as he carelessly tossed the earth aside. This carelessness brings disease which 'would spread all over Coventry and beyond'. Even the coming war has the same cause; indeed, the sickness and war become completely conflated. 'Father Harris knew it', thinks the priest, which is why he is being sent to Guiana, 'beyond the reach of plague' (p. 259). The spore sickness is likely to be a literal reference to aspergillosis or a similar fungal illness, but Coventry's canals, dug by one exploited labour force and then replaced by another, are, in Dabydeen's novel, an analogue for the clearance of land for sugar plantations in Guyana by African slaves and then Indian coolies. The sickness in both locations is not simply fungal, but moral and ecological. I have used the details of a wartime commodity chain in the background of literature about women's work on the waterways to highlight the enduring colonial politics of war industries. *Our Lady of Demerara* relocates the pervasive pollutions of a plantation economy to the industrial Midlands. Dabydeen does this via a priest who escapes the plague of war in Guiana only to end in his own bones being sucked dry in and by the forest. He writes the relocation via the English fortunes (and offspring) made on the plantations. Dabydeen's construction of multiple crossings and relocations in this exploration of the lasting moral and ecological sickness of colonialism can be conceptualised as a 'trans-plantation'.

Guiana appears as the figure of a dark other in England a number of times in the second part of the novel, Lance's invented autobiography of the priest consolidating the image of the trans-plantation. For instance, before being sent to Coventry, Father Harris spent a tenure in Falmouth, where the grocer led a relief society for the natives of Guyana. One day, a widow swore she was attacked by a 'black thing from head to toe, black as a... as a... toad', a 'dark stranger who had leapt straight out of the pages of the Old Testament in the shape of the devil. Or out of the map of Guiana in the shape of a savage' (pp. 188–90). When the grocer is implicated in a cuckolding plot, he is described as having 'taken on the qualities of the very savages whose souls were in his custody' (p. 197). After the second Corinne's death, Enoch is pictured as 'settled on his haunches like a feeble savage put out to die' (p. 258). Lance has followed 'his' priest, a man who left Coventry hoping to escape war and plague – the First World War in this case – and landed 'amidst people afflicted by history'. But it is in Europe that Lance's priest sees 'the doomed fate of that earth because of war among men', the 'ending of the world' in 'aeroplanes, tanks, huge batteries of guns, screaming metal' (p. 105). Aluminium is the metal that screams throughout the Second World War. It screams of the afflictions of history in its colonial production, it screams of a maimed earth, and the screams echo along the waterways of the English Midlands.

Identifying the colonial water of a trans-plantation economy

In *Maidens' Trip*, Nanette throws her bicycle down at a lock which has the date '1863' on it, causing Smith to reflect that 'the rain that splashed her legs as she ran lay in hollows worn into the stone by generations of boaters' boots' (p. 55). Smith connects the layered history of the waterways, via rainwater, with her friend's body. If we read off the page of wartime trainee life writing and its reinterpretation as romance, it is possible to read the afflicting histories of other waters and other bodies. Enjoying the boating experience during summer, Smith felt guilty that she might take enjoyment in her liberty, while 'almost everybody else in the world is entangled one way or another in a horrible war'.[94] She neither sees nor hears this 'everybody else', but she cannot forget the men, women and children in danger. They face death, in many cases, from the metallic machines of war that her labour has helped bring into being as part of a long chain of exploitation and destruction. The line of thinking that connects British colonialism in Guyana, deforestation, toxic bauxite dust and red mud, dammed Canadian rivers and the chemical residues of smelting, women working on the English waterways and bomb-dropping planes made of aluminium is available to those reading beyond the bounds of a national war effort and the constraints of what particular genres allow us to know. It is not a line of thinking available within Smith's text, whose moment of sunny relaxation is punctured by the thoughts of 'horrible war', and this is enough to contend with. We might compare this to the experience of living through a global pandemic (as when I wrote this chapter), just about managing to get through each day and then suddenly remembering the thousands who have died. Thinking beyond that to climate crisis and the labour conditions under which one's food, clothing and electronic devices have been produced (in, say, Senegal, Bangladesh and China) is a very hard emotional and cognitive task. Smith decides that she has 'simply to keep going, keep going, in imitation of the boating fraternity'.[95] The 'keeping going' is, narratively and historically, towards the next drop off point for their cargo, and towards the end of the war. However, to keep something going is also to reproduce it: the power imbalances that feed Britain's aluminium consumption; the capitalist culture that markets conventionality; the expectations of heterosexual femininity.

The war, points out Cornish, provided the liberty that Smith enjoys, 'this chink of opportunity, this narrow slice of experience'. Cornish, a pacifist, says that the female boat teams were 'in no way involved' in the destruction of war, and yet their labour is unavoidably complicit not just in the dropping of bombs, but also part of a trail of destruction beginning in Guyana (p. 135). In taking this deliberately broad view of the ways the waterways are connected to global politics and environments, and drawing on Dabydeen's postcolonial fiction, this reading ultimately locates the life writing of Cornish, Smith and Gayford, and the romances of Adams, Archer and Mayhew in a 'trans-plantation' economy. I mean by this an explicit recognition of the ways in which the British imperial possession of Guiana, motivated by control of sugar-producing slave plantations and later indentured labour, has brought about particular incidents, images, and relationships in Britain itself: transplanted, transported, transshipped. During the Second World War, hands were required to take aluminium from Limehouse along the Grand Union Canal so that it could be turned into planes; the shortage of labour and a national war effort brought together women who formed new relationships and had new experiences, which they captured in memoir. These, in turn, inspired romance novels which reinscribed expectations about femininity, heterosexuality, and conformity. The textual manifestation of these women's work has given them a lasting place in literature of the waterways, enabling a reflection on particular aspects of the war effort, such as where the aluminium came from: it came from Guyana because the British government was intent on using minerals from its imperial possessions as a security strategy. This trans-plantation economy includes a reckoning with 'colonial water', by which Empire has also produced the geographies of mining, smelting and transporting aluminium, and thus affects all the waters that flow into and out of those processes. Colonial water is a polluted water, dyed red with bauxite dust and blood and still pumping out PAHs downstream. It functions as an analogue to the toxic waters of the British industrial canal on which the autobiographies and romances float. If you fall in, keep your mouth shut.

It is 1945 and I am *Industrious*. The woman steering my course along the Grand Union considers her time aboard like the tick of a clock across the history of a dream.[96] This new way of thinking about life on the canal will not be the last reinvention of this space and these waters.

5

WATERS OF LIFE AND DEATH

Another bell tolls at midnight; 1962 frostily becomes 1963 and I am *Industrious*, carrying coal. I do not float; I am encased in ice like a glacier-entombed craft from millennia ago, waiting to be discovered by future archaeologists as the global temperature rises and frozen wastes reveal their secrets. The icebreaker has not yet passed this section of Cut, and the depth of frozen water has increased inch by inch, day by day. When finally the air turns warmer, it will also blow in winds of change. The couple aboard cannot continue this life, this work. Already marginal, it has become too, too hard. They discuss moving on to the land. Centuries of change and industry, what itinerary will I follow next? Who will keep boat time?

The 'Big Freeze' of 1962/3 is often used as a marker for the end point of industrial traffic on the canals.[1] The nationalised waterways, already struggling to be at all competitive with rail and, more significantly, road transport, found their very lifeblood frozen in the veins for weeks that winter. However, L. T. C. Rolt's *Narrow Boat* had inspired the creation of the Inland Waterways Association, a body which, along with local organisations and the seemingly bottomless enthusiasm of volunteers, would resuscitate life on the waterways as industry withdrew. Their work enabled the continuing existence of the network one can walk, jog, cycle, paddle board and boat along today. The canals' visibility, desirability as waterscape, and popularity has brought a fresh flush of waterways writers, some of them personally invested in the space as home. Many of the books published this century are part history, part travelogue, such as Jasper Winn's *Water Ways* (2018). There are also a good number of romances, such as Cressida McLaughlin's *The Canal Boat Café* (2016). Sarah Jasmon's *You Never Told Me* (2020), meanwhile, is a family drama with a boat, *Skíðblaðnir*, at its centre. The focus of this chapter is two genres that may seem to represent the canals in very different ways but, I argue, are in fact generic responses to the same twenty-first-century, postindustrial condition. These are New Nature Writing (NNW) of the canals, and canal noir. Both of these genres *revisit* the waterways, understanding them as both anachronistic and novel modes of transport, spaces of habitation, and landscapes for explorations of the human psyche, politics, and social ills. NNW figures the industrial waterway as both revelatory and contradictory, while the noir novels highlight a related idea, ambivalence, as they work through individual and social guilt and complicity.

Joe Moran has advanced a cultural history of NNW, from its influences such as Collins's New Naturalist series of the 1940s, to the 2008 edition of *Granta* which popularised the term, through to its offshoots and controversies: critics have argued that the works are neither 'new' in their form, nor properly 'nature writing' in their content (preferring, for instance, 'place' to 'nature').[2] Despite the wide-ranging themes and styles of books placed on this shelf, they do, Moran suggests, have 'shared concerns that all speak to anxieties about human disconnection from natural processes'.[3] Moran also points to the unifying themes of exploring 'the potential for human meaning-making . . . in our everyday connections with the non-human natural world' (p. 50). Similarly, Phil Hubbard and Eleanor Wilkinson see these works regularly eschewing nature as a 'pristine idyll' in favour of the deindustrialised edgelands. They see the autobiographical writing in this vein exploring the 'relation between landscape, self-hood and ethics'. As a sub-genre it has been 'dominated by stories of male self-discovery and exploration' – the 'lone enraptured male' as Kathleen Jamie has it – but the NNW of the canals on which this chapter focuses is written by women.[4] These texts are: Alys Fowler's 2018 *Hidden Nature*, Helen Babbs's *Adrift* (2016) and Danie Couchman's *Afloat* (2019). Indeed, Fowler comments on the appropriateness of the canal (rather than the towpath) as a safe space for the female urban explorer: out on the water no one can get you.[5] These works are not generally marketed as NNW, rather as memoir or hybrid forms including nature writing. I have also seen them shelved as 'travel', and as specialist interest amongst other boats and trains. Nevertheless, the relationship between writing the self and writing the canal environment is clear in these three works.

Of the five strands that Kate Oakley, Jonathan Ward and Ian Christie identify in NNW, these three works, or rather the aspects of the works I highlight, fit the bracket of 'close natural history observation as psychotherapy'. Critique of the sub-genre has claimed that this writing commodifies or instrumentalises the natural environment, 'particularly as a balm to troubled psyches', and that it focuses on the individual at the cost of the social.[6] '*Close attention*', critics argue, 'conveyed by "fine writing", is both a marker of personal sensitivity and attunement, and also a means to ecological consciousness-raising'.[7] This aesthetic is accused of problematically appealing to only a limited readership with the knowledge, time and means to emulate such immersion in nature. If the natural environment becomes a set of commodities for the 'individualised, positional consumer', NNW implicates it 'in the circuits of late capitalism which have done, and are doing, so much to bring about ecological crisis' (p. 14). NNW of the canals is in danger of making this implication twice over, drawing the nature and wildness of the twenty-first-century waterway into the consumerism of late capitalism, but also in valorising the canal *as* a natural space and thus belatedly miswilding the waterways of industrial capitalism. The industrial origins of the canal and its coal-carrying purpose are erased in order to emphasise the ecologies it now sustains. Fossil-fuelled British industrialisation fails to look insidious in a rosebay-tinted cloak of willowherb. However, Oakley, Ward and Christie note that post-industrial sites have the potential to 'force us to see the imprint of power and corruption' (p. 14). The crumbling industrial ruins with which we are often confronted beside the canal rebuke, says Tim Edensor, 'scenarios of endless progress'.[8]

The unregenerated canalside factories I have passed, with buddleia sprouting from chimneys and shattered ornate windows, speak at the same time of Victorian industrial confidence (to fashion such permanent structures) and economic hubris (this workshop of the world stands idle). These sites lay bare not just what *was*, but what was *hoped*, just as the Aikins' eighteenth-century poetry used depictions of Roman might and ingenuity at the birth of the industrial revolution to suggest both hope and hubris. Push the Himalayan balsam aside and find a marker of the Anthropocene. This canal wildness is a contradictory space for individual nature therapy: an author recounts the process of finding herself, or maybe losing herself (in nature), but in this context one also always finds signs of decline; imprints of loss.

Loss is the starting point for the key figures in the canal noir texts on which the second section of this chapter focuses: Kerry Hadley-Pryce's *Gamble* (2018), Andy Griffee's *Canal Pushers* (2020), and Faith Martin's *Murder on the Oxford Canal* (2017). These texts, in their focus on crime, secrets, and the undesirable aspects of human nature, also draw attention to the 'imprint of power and corruption' in the canal space. For Lee Horsley, defining features of literary noir include: the protagonist's subjectivity and her/his function as victim, transgressor or investigator; the protagonist's difficult relationship with society; and the text as socio-political critique.[9]

Intriguingly, Timothy Morton has pointed out that the loss and mourning inherent in this century's ecological awareness functions like noir fiction, as one realises one's human complicity in climate crisis like the detective who is also a criminal.[10] This awareness is perhaps the motivation for recent scholarship at the intersection of crime fiction studies and ecocriticism.[11] In asking 'what might it mean for noir to be green?', Lucas Hollister posits the ecological awareness Morton compares to noir fiction as a 'pervasive traumatic or pretraumatic imaginary, one that forces us to rethink the scales of our stories and their causal logics'. This means thinking about 'how crime fiction or violent popular fiction might narrativise (or fail to narrativise) our traumatic ecological awareness'.[12] Hollister also notes noir's 'capacity to foreground what is usually considered background', drawing attention to setting and place' (p. 1021). It is therefore no surprise that noir might revel in canal locations. Harry Pitt Scott has noted that noir 'depends on energy forms and infrastructure in constructing plot, character, and narrative impetus'.[13] He is specifically focused on postmodernity's hotels, highways and hinterlands, but the observation holds true for the legacies of a coal-powered industrial past and waterways infrastructure in canal noir. Interpretation of the text's 'energopolitical unconscious' is a means, then, of discerning the imprints of power and corruption in the postindustrial, Anthropocene canal landscape, and that is precisely what the 'canal noir' section of this chapter does (p. 3). As a whole, then, the chapter finds two genres of twenty-first-century narrative waterways writing framing the industrial canal as a contradictory and ambivalent space.

A Fluid Place: New Nature Writing of the Canal

Two and a half centuries have passed since a poet witnessed my wondrous flight above the Irwell; thousands of miles and tonnage across and up and down the country since then. Many decades have passed since I last hauled coal through this industrial urban giant. Now I rest in a warm and quiet fold in the flesh of the city as my steel collects rainwater as useless cargo, and I grow my own strange ecology: flag irises, water dock, a disposable coffee cup.[14] Weeds nearby are burnt by the effort of growing through heavy-metal pollution, and the flash of cobalt as a kingfisher darts over the water is as sad as it is electric – high in the food-chain the bird is at serious risk from eating poisoned fish, and its small body may be dead in the grass by the end of summer.[15] Coots weaving nests from twigs and twine take a break on my metal sides and I will be the first to see the punky juveniles make their way into a watery world.[16] A narrowboat – all cabin; the cargo only humans and their belongings – cuts a path through dark green weed, but the weed zips itself back up as if the boat had never passed at all.[17] I am . . . post-*Industrious*, all my history undone.

It is impossible to read about the 'new' British nature writing without encountering Richard Mabey, whose *The Unofficial Countryside* from 1973 was (and still is) inspiration to many authors, readers and walkers. That work has canals running through its pages, with a then-revolutionary vision of the postindustrial waterway as an opportunity to access nature that has now become official policy. On one pedestrian foray, Mabey describes feeling encouraged to find 'native riverside flowers of the old herbalists', including gipsywort. He quotes the seventeenth-century botanist Caleb Threlkeld's views on the plant and its namesake; it seems that Romani people once used this plant to dye their own or others' skin darker (though the motivation for this is unclear – perhaps for performance, perhaps the practice is myth). The fact that gipsywort should end up by a canal seems strangely appropriate considering the cultural links non-Romanies have made between people of that ethnicity and canal communities. For instance, from the previous chapter, *The Narrowboat Girls* erroneously refers to live-aboard boaters as 'gypsies' throughout, and Mayhew's *The Boat Girls* features a primal sexual memory for Frances who, aged nine, was hypnotised by a glossy-haired 'dark and smiling gypsy'.[18] This memory motivates Frances's exoticising interest in canal boat people in her adult sojourn on the waterways. 'Water gypsies' was a fairly common appellation for canal boat people in the nineteenth century, and was the title of A. P. Herbert's famous book which floats to the surface of several of the novels discussed throughout the present work. The term has found new life in Julian Dutton's 2021 book, *The Water Gypsies* which, the author notes, refers to people choosing to live and work on rivers and canals, not to any ethnicity.[19]

It was with this entangled botanical etymology in mind (the sort of plant species storytelling that seduces perhaps any writer if you read enough nature writing) that I set out to find gypsywort on the banks of the Huddersfield Narrow Canal one wet May Monday during the pandemic. Reading Mabey's book, I had been keenly aware of just how many species listed had declined in the intervening decades. I am no naturalist, relying on an app to be sure of what I'm seeing, but I exclaimed with joy on identifying the distinctive spiky leaves on either side of stems sticking out of the water. I was also placated to learn that Alys Fowler, a plant expert, had needed to use *Collins Flower Guide* to identify gypsywort from the canal once she had narrowed it down to a member of the Lamiaceae family.[20] I saw, too, dense patches of water horsetail, which Mabey describes as having 'scarcely changed at all from those huge feathery trees' of the Carboniferous Period 300 million years ago, 'whose rotting remains helped build up our coal deposits' – deposits which would be mined and transported along the very canal where I excitedly noted down descendant fauna.[21] Breathing deeply along this stretch of the canal I inhaled the sweet and savoury combination of bluebells and wild garlic, and then a not-unpleasant chemical pear-drop scent. This part of the canal hides sections of sylvan enchantment, featuring herons and woodpeckers then, around the corner, a worker from a nearby factory leant against the bridge smoking half a cigarette on his break: humans always share this space with nature.

In an updated introduction to *The Unofficial Countryside*, Iain Sinclair calls these collections of flora and fauna logged by Mabey – yellow water lilies on the canal's surface, newly hatched fish in the shallows, hemp agrimony on the towpath, angelica on the bank – 'the tough fecundity of the margin'.[22] Mabey clings, though, to a sense that canals and other marginal spaces lack the authenticity of proper nature: they are not the 'real' countryside, no substitute for an actual meadow, stream or woodland. In thinking about water, Mabey (much like the eighteenth-century poet Henry James Pye, mentioned in Chapter Two) counterposes the 'rancid canal' with the 'chalk stream between two villages', calling on a liquid purity running between units of pre-industrial Englishness that becomes horribly polluted in the later waterway. As Graham Huggan notes of the New Nature Writers that followed Mabey, 'wildness is as much a temporal as a spatial category'.[23] The *post*industrial and *re*wilding are overlapping temporalities of wildness. In the twentieth-century, Mabey noted that for those responsible for the upkeep of the canals, wildness was an enemy, choking water and towpath alike and crumbling the banks (p. 65). These days, the Canal & River Trust often use coconut fibre to construct soft banks to support wildlife such as water voles.[24] Wildness is the enemy no longer – though badger excavations require careful negotiation. In *Edgelands* (for which Mabey is a 'presiding spirit'), Paul Farley and Michael Symmons Roberts consider the 'double life' of the twenty-first-century canal, at once natural, 'barely distinguishable from rivers', and the urban version: 'wet skips'.[25] Such is the complex inauthenticity of the canal: unnatural, like rivers but not really, an already-compromised space of reflection, that the following paragraphs explore in relation to examples of New Nature Writing.

Babbs's London-centred book is as much about people as non-human nature: other boaters, towpath users, people in the communities near the canal – though as a live-aboard boater she sometimes feels that those on land cast her as less-than-human, granting little respect or privacy. Babbs sees human beings as a fundamental part of the canalscape – something one rarely hears said about rivers; they existed, after all, long before humans made any appearance on the planet. She makes the distinction clear between the 'true' River Lea and the canalised Lee Navigation. For instance, the latter is 'wide and straight', the former meanders 'prettily' (p. 15). Of the same waterways, Couchman likes 'the gentle flow of the river rather than the stillness of the canal' (p. 81). Compared to the Thames, thinks Babbs, Regent's Canal is fake and tame (p. 78). There are, of course, real physical differences between canals and rivers, but in this genre of writing these differences are frequently ushered into direct oppositions in order to produce literary paradox. Canals are unnatural *and* wild, inauthentic *but also* the source of profound truths, beautifully ugly, disappointing *yet* full of hope. If one is supposed to 'find oneself' in this environment, the reflection in the water is broken into 'a thousand copper and silver shards'.[26]

Babbs's feelings about living on a boat on a canal are complicated and contradictory – as they should be: Bowles, Kaaristo and Caf make clear that dwelling on water challenges the 'terra-centric logics' with which we are familiar.[27] Drawing on Mabey, Babbs asserts that such a life demands one be both 'settled native and adventurous pioneer'.[28]

She reflects on her many house moves – twelve in thirty years, and all emotional. Couchman draws up a similar list: eight homes in four countries by the age of seven; seventeenth (unsatisfactory) home by 2013. Now, Babbs's home, *Pike*, and Couchman's home, *Genesis*, go with them but those moves are fortnightly (by virtue of continuous cruiser licences). Reaching the age of thirty, Babbs found that relationships and views of the world shifted, an instability she answered by unfixing her home and defying terra-centric logic in a way that can only be expressed via seeming contradiction. In her life on board, Babbs reflects that she has become very *at* home, but also very afraid. Now profoundly interested in the plants of the towpath, she is conscious that she has subjected herself to a constant domestic 'uprooting', an astute semantic choice in the context of the close observation of plants unexpectedly rooted in the city, and also one that imagines a literal withdrawal from terra firma (p. 111). Couchman describes her own adaptation to nomadism as being 'like a hardy plant that can grow in the crevices of rocks' (p. 10). Her reflections are full of liquid and natural simile like this, but her work differs from most nature writing (and the work of Babbs and Fowler) in the tone with which she notes her observations of the natural world: there are few authoritative species identifications, which in other nature writing come with implications of taxonomic expertise, bringing non-human organisms into a managed world of knowledge. Babbs's uprooting, meanwhile, is mitigated by the fact that moving is also a persistent homecoming; in fact, when a permanent mooring becomes available, the cons of this plan seem to come under the heading of 'giv[ing] up by rooting down'.[29] The tension between settled native and adventurous pioneer is tight in this moment, and the call to water is strong.

The dirt and pollution of coal that has dusted every chapter of this book is finally relinquished here, replaced in *Pike*'s stove with a smokeless fuel. In many ways, this narrative, like Couchman's, tells an ancient human story of finding enough fuel and water, getting tasks done in daylight, and disposing safely of human waste – but these are individual stories, based around one household's consumption rather than planetary possibilities for sustainable energy and potable water. We can't all live on a canal boat, after all. The hybrid memoir/nature writing form demands this individualist reflection as Oakley, Ward and Christie identify. However, Babbs connects this experience to the global, explaining that life on land elides the fact that hot showers and electric lights always involve 'someone, somewhere' burning something (p. 12). Live-aboard boating, asserts Babbs, is an exercise in understanding the finitude of resources and our relationship with the natural world (p. 125).

Bowles, a social anthropologist, has found that live-aboard boaters do spend a 'great deal of time and energy trying to prove that they are ecologically responsible agents, and tend to react badly to suggestions to the contrary'.[30] In other words, positing canal life as ecologically responsible is a narrative in which people – and texts – are deeply invested. The contradictory London waterways of *Adrift* are, I suggest, a product of the post-industrial nature writing genre, when clear boundaries between wild/tame, rural/urban, self/environment, native/ non-native are explicitly investigated (though sometimes reinforced in the process), and these contradictions are made more acute when the focus is mobility via water. As Bowles, Kaaristo and Caf note, the 'laminar quality of water' may make various mobilities possible, 'but it also creates frictions, immobilities and moorings', which in turn complicate 'the boundaries between moving and staying, scarcity and abundance, "nature" and "culture"'.[31] A 'true artifice' exists on the Regent's Canal, in Babbs's description, for instance, with the landscape slipping from 'hostile to benign' and 'romantic to weird' (pp. 72; 76). The Lower Lea is both 'unexpected pleasure and a bit of a mess'; beloved and abused (p. 25). In interpreting landscape and surroundings in different conditions, seasons and lights, Babbs draws on Woolf's *A Room of One's Own* (Babbs, too, reads the waterways) and echoes Woolf's question: 'which was the truth, which was the illusion?' Babbs answers that each passing canal moment is neither and both (pp. 187–8). She finds she cannot 'quite grasp hold of the Cut', a quasi-rural existence in Zone 2, in all its representational fluidity (p. 17).

And what of that nature that locates *Adrift* in the genre of NNW? For Babbs it is simultaneously attraction, distraction and source of reassurance. The Lea Valley is presented as a healing force, keeping Londoners sane. Like many of the places Babbs enjoys, however, there is an urgent reminder that this area is at constant threat from land grabs and development. There is a long lament for what has been lost under the bulldozers clearing ground for the 2012 Olympics. The mature trees of Kensal Green Cemetery overlooking the Grand Union Canal are at risk from plans for Old Oak Common. In the wake of corporate development, Babbs notes, 'water often becomes a passive thing, decorative detail'; the watery genius loci, discussed in detail in Chapter Two, is 'laid waste' in this veneered new city (p. 60). The precarity of urban blue and green spaces thus lends the healing force a jittery quality.

Babbs notes the lichen *Xanthoria parietina* on a concrete bridge: yellow-orange, common, and useful as an indicator of air quality as well as being an attractive hint of wall-favouring wildness.[32] The British Lichen Society notes that *Xanthoria parietina*'s visibility is thanks to its need for nitrogen – prior to the UK's current levels of nitrogen pollution from vehicle exhausts, it was mainly found on bird perches.[33] A compromised identification within nature writing, this, that relies on pollution. The content and quality of air, land and water is constantly changing, offering scientists and casual observers alike new data. The 'newness' of NNW is, I suggest, an acknowledgment that nature writing must encompass this constant change – including the mourning that comes with climate crisis, pollution, and species loss. The change is moment to moment – the Cut shifting from 'smoked glass' to 'sharply crumpled' or 'ribbed and ruffed'.[34] The change is season to season, year to year. It is also century to century: monstrous boat-sized buddleia are charmingly relabelled 'singing bushes' from the sparrows emitting a noisy chirruping chatter, and the sparrow population takes the reader of *Adrift* to the Victorian history of the canals, and Victorian natural history, when the little birds were plentiful, collecting in 'chapels' (p. 97).

On a flora-spotting trip with a botanist-boater, Babbs lists over fifty species on the towpath between Victoria Park and the Islington tunnel, including black lovage or Alexanders – introduced by the Romans for culinary purposes. The list certainly contains enough variety for a salad, but diners beware! Hemlock and hemlock water dropwort are amongst this collection. Hemlock, *Conium maculatum*, will always be appealing to the nature writer because of its cultural resonance, becoming a botanical shorthand for continuities of human experience across the passage of time. Socrates used hemlock to end his life, the speaker of Keats's 'Ode to a Nightingale' describes his drowsy state using the effects of hemlock as a simile, and it was an ingredient in the medieval anaesthetic, 'dwale'.[35] In Shakespeare, the 'hebona' that kills Hamlet's father is often considered to be hemlock, the landscape wasted by war in *Henry V* is typified by the plant (along with darnel and rank fumitory), a similar collection comprises Lear's crown of weeds, and, of course, it is an ingredient in *Macbeth*'s witches' brew.[36] That it appears alongside the canal is indicative of one of the key contradictions inherent in twenty-first-century writing of the waterways:

Babbs goes in search of wild*life*, and in it finds a classic course to oblivion. For the nature writer considering any space 'managed' by humans, Rachel Carson's *Silent Spring* (1962) is an obvious reference point, the shadow of the Anthropocene haunting descriptions of insects, wrens and wagtails, just as death haunts the white blooms of hemlock. In the Anthropocene, the constant change that NNW catches is not just moment to moment, season to season, century to century, but epoch to epoch.

I am completely biased towards Alys Fowler's *Hidden Nature*: it has one of the most apt titles I have ever encountered, it returns me to the Midlands, she explores the canals as an outsider to that world (men keen to tell her all the facts crop up regularly), and it speaks an emotional truth about major life changes. It is also the work in this triad most identifiable as 'nature writing'. Fowler's canoe is rather different from John MacGregor's (bright red, inflatable), but she admits that in her early life she longed to be an explorer like Gertrude Bell, who mapped Jordan and Iraq. The book nestles quite neatly into Oakley, Ward and Christie's category of 'close natural history observation as psychotherapy': Fowler speaks of a powerful need to be in a landscape that 'wasn't part of [her] heart', to throw herself into the detail of a new environment that will fascinate and 'soak up some of the unsettledness' that she, like Babbs, feels – though for different reasons (pp. 84; 29). Many of Babbs's and Fowler's botanical reference points are plants of disturbed ground, a scene of uprooting that mirrors the emotional context they are writing through. At this moment in her life, Fowler paddles away from gardening (her professional specialism), unable to tend and cultivate. Fowler also posits the built canal landscape as being as unsettled as she is, 'barely holding itself together' thanks to the growth of nature over time, a landscape that cannot decide what it is, 'wild but not natural'; 'old but not old enough' (p. 29).

These contradictions of the canal are thoroughly explored. In a drained portion of the canal, Fowler finds live mussels – the inside of their shells are gleaming and pearlescent, while the outside is coated in stinking industrial slime. Like *Xanthoria parietina*, these duck mussels are both hopeful and depressing: an unexpected organism, but one that really only survives here because they are adapted to sieve out waste material, cleaning up the waters in which they live (pp. 11–13). Nymphs and larvae swim in black waters that reflect the bright lights of Birmingham's Mailbox (p. 214). In the canal a stone's throw from Smethwick, Fowler finds watercress growing. This is no 'Hampshire chalk stream', a vision of water purity that returns to Mabey's image of rural perfection, but still a 'heartening sign' deep in post-industrial Birmingham – a tasty vegetable that you really don't want to try eating (p. 101). In Dudley, there are eels; from the Sargasso Sea to the Black Country swims this biological enigma (pp. 170–6). In Tipton, an industrial unit expels a scent like washing powder, offering an incongruent smell of 'cleanliness and order in an environment that was quite the opposite' (p. 186). On the water, Fowler attempts to find her sense of self as a lesbian, while losing herself in the landscape. Her sense of loss, for a marriage and husband, for a home and certainty, mirrors the broken remnants of industry, but also the imprints of environmental loss in the Anthropocene.

Couchman's experience of living on water causes her to imagine 'what might lie beneath [her] in the silty murk'. As well as images of 'shopping trolleys, broken bottles, pike, eels', she is visited by 'fragments of buried memory' that rise through the 'sludge of [her] subconscious' (p. 65). Gradually, the peace and community she finds on water buoys her enough to share her trauma: childhood abuse and rape by a seventeen-year-old and his friends. Couchman slowly reaches the right emotional place to return to these terrible events, while Fowler urgently uses the waterways and their nature to distract her from the unravelling she experiences on land. In both cases, the waterways become spaces of deep emotional engagement. Fowler howls under bridges, spinning in her inflatable boat, barely able to keep afloat. At the end of her book, she realises that her journeys on water were about 'finding an external correlation' to what was happening within, a 'fluid space' in a life full of change.[37] All three women emphasise the fluidity of that period of their lives when they were drawn to life on water. Water is, for them, a new way of thinking and living that also brings new connections to nature and a sense of one's place in the natural world when the human world is full of rush and confusion. The water may not be clear, but it can make *life* clearer.

Implicit in these three works is the beginning assumption that the Cut is knowable: its maps were drawn long before the first ton of water poured in. The fiction in the next section of this chapter is also well suited to this milieu, as Hollister points out: 'crime fiction has always delighted in drawing maps, and it is often thought to have a privileged relation to cartographic, geographic, and spatial representational practices'.[38] In this nature writing, however, cartographic representation is a kind of lost-and-retrieved knowledge; the space of the canal had been literally built over and filled in with other things. Each author has her moment of 'finding' the waterway: a friend suggests to Fowler that the canal might be a place of escape within her city-bound life; for Babbs, a boat home is a daydream that becomes research that becomes a reality; Couchman takes a spring walk home from work rather than the sweaty Tube and is charmed by the Regent's Canal. Each text also makes clear that, in its complexity and contradiction, this ever-changeable space is mapped anew by each human and non-human journey: the live-aboard boater, the eel, the gypsywort. The industrial canal is positioned in these three books (and others like them, from Mabey onwards) as unexpectedly full of life.

However, there is always the sense that this is a compromised experience of nature, each narrative yearning for the Hebrides, a chalk-stream, Waltham Abbey rather than central London. Couchman's first encounter with the canals sees her visually filtering out litter, oil on the water and the chaotic towpath in order to appreciate 'the lush-ness of the trees, the colourful floating homes and the wildlife enjoy-ing the water' (p. 15). Fowler even asks 'why exalt concrete?' when one could be in *real* nature (p. 202). The New Nature Writing of the canals leaves me feeling that this is all we can wearily expect in the twenty-first century, a dead tench floating through the reflection of an amphitheatre of trees.[39] The authors' lives are full of hope by the end of each narrative, but the landscape where they found it is not. Analysis of this genre takes us, then, from waters teeming with life to a realisation that this life is always at risk, always on the edge of being ruined (by development, toxins, litter or other people), that death is everywhere. The waterways space itself is liminal, Couchman points out, meaning that life there is often 'dangerously unpredictable'. It is, she notes, 'a place where people with intentions you'd rather not think about could wander in the city's darkness'; it is also 'a place where people who didn't want to be found could hide'. It is even 'a place you could disappear, or lose yourself' (p. 64). In other words, the perfect setting for noir fiction.

Canal Noir

Stourbridge. Grey winter. The surface of the water unravels swirls of violet and blue-black and yellow. A warmish sourness on the wind smells like death.[40] This watery system that once seemed miraculous and airy, carried aloft by the sheer power of audacious new ideas,

then became permanent and quotidian, now seems to be strain-
ing with the weight of it all – it might give way at any moment.[41]
Is this an end? For now, dark shadows lie beneath. A giant pike? A
drowned rat? A human corpse? Or perhaps just the murky secrets
of the industrial canal.

There has long been an association between canals and dark intentions, accidents and death. Allan Scott-Davies's *Death on the
Waterways* (2011) is a gruesome catalogue of murders and accidents,
and R. H. Davies's *Canal Crimes* (2010) delights in pickpocketing,
drunkenness, robbery, rape and murder. Whenever I want to engage
an audience of schoolchildren in their local canal history, misdemean-
ours and injuries reported in the local newspaper are always a good
place to start. The Gothic canal was exploited by figures in the early
canal restoration movement, with ghost stories clearly inspired by trips
through abandoned tunnels. Elizabeth Jane Howard's compelling and
atmospheric story 'Three Miles Up' (1951), for instance, draws on the
experience of 'canal busting' – which demonstrated that waterways
were still viable routes.[42]

There were a number of popular-novel contenders for fuller discussion in this section on the British industrial canal and twenty-
first-century noir, which has its own intricate relationship with the
waterways. Chris McGeorge's *Now You See Me* (2019), for instance,
uses Standedge Tunnel on the Huddersfield Narrow Canal as the basis
for a locked-room mystery. Felicity Radcliffe's *Union Clues* (2020)
finds death on the waterway. Stephen Booth's 1990s-set *Drowned
Lives* (2019) loosely connects canal mania with the dotcom boom,
two new networks which changed the fabric of work and where serious money was won and lost. *Drowned Lives* features a limp hero
who has sunk a fortune into an ill-advised online auction site. The
novel brings readerly focus back to Lichfield, home to Anna Seward
and Erasmus Darwin in the eighteenth century, as the intrigues of the
narrative take place between the abandoned canal and the shadow
of the cathedral. Excavations to rebuild the canal literally dig up the
past. A family feud dating to the building and operating of the canal
causes death and violence in the novel's present. In one of the novel's
final scenes, the combination of 'tumbled brickwork' and 'overgrown
scrub' produces a 'complex of dark corners'; a fitting location for a
noirish denouement.[43] My focus in this section, however, is three
novels whose 'energopolitical unconscious' is discernible, revealing a

complex cultural relationship between the twenty-first-century canal and the Anthropocene.

Kerry Hadley-Pryce situates her own writing as 'Black Country fiction', inhabiting that hard-to-define place of South Staffordshire and North Worcestershire.[44] Between 1750 and 1850, Barrie Trinder has noted, industry turned the heaths of what would become known as the Black Country into a 'tortured landscape of blast furnaces, pit headstocks, canals and waste tips'. The Earls of Dudley oversaw large-scale mining, ironworking and other industry on their estates, and they enthusiastically promoted canals to enable access. North of Stourbridge, glassworks with conical kilns grew up on the banks of the canal, memorialised now (as in so many of the industrial geographies described in this book) by pub and suburban street names as well as the White House Cone Museum of Glass.[45]

Hadley-Pryce's 2018 novel, *Gamble*, could not be said to be *about* the Anthropocene, nor ostensibly about energy or climate crisis. The defining use of energy for mobility is nothing to do with the canal here, either: it is the personal motor vehicle as an extension of the self, a place to retreat and *be*. Gamble is one with his car, proudly able to make a turn without changing gear, for instance. Nonetheless, the novel's postindustrial canal setting prompts a reflection that connects an individual sense of how one gets to crisis point in one's life with broader understandings of energy, industry, and our current condition. The enfolding complicity of noir fiction produces just the guilty realisation about climate crisis that Morton describes, and Gamble's murky guilt is an analogue for our hard-to-pin-down, disseminated and ongoing complicity in that crisis. The canal, the free indirect discourse tell us, 'contains lots of things'. These are literal items from the past 'sunk right to the bottom' and 'embedded in the silt and soil and mud', or ideas, feelings, and experiences 'that linger in the dark water, suspended'. The water is also 'greasy with things from the present' including oil from Black Country factories.[46] The industrial past and its effects are suspended in canal water, surfacing now and again like toxic bubbles in a rubbish-strewn watery present. Hollister's Anthropocene reading of noir points to a disruption in the 'causal logics' of stories. Is Greg Gamble a product of a Black Country trying to survive its industrial past? Is his misogyny caused not simply by a violent patriarchal culture or personal trauma but by a locale in which there is no defined sense of future beyond the fossil-fuelled heyday? Where 'something about the shut-down factories and the over-optimism of the shops' is 'intensely sad' (p. 169)? The air and water of the Black Country stagnates in Gamble, producing a dislikeable central character whose actions are not only unpredictable but impossible to trace to a reliable cause.

Unfaithful, possibly murderous, Gamble casts himself initially as a hero, the rescuer of Mara after she is slapped by her boyfriend, but this is immediately unconvincing, undermined by the recurrent formulation 'he'll say'. This idiosyncratic syntactical device of uncertainty casts the reader as a detective, slowly finding out what events have transpired but obscured by what Gamble will (or would) say in a formal and excusatory statement. The text lies between the grimy truth of his interior thoughts and their positioning as external voicing. Gamble makes the words themselves seem grubby, as he rolls them around in his mind. The repetition of particular phrases further undermines their authenticity, as if Gamble hasn't really thought these thoughts but considers them an appropriate or poetic addition to the statement he formulates. Gamble is an older version of *Our Lady of Demerara*'s Lance, representing all that is corrupt in masculinity. He feels he *deserves* the female bodies he encounters, undresses, hurts. He is also, like humanity in the Anthropocene, constantly aware of the slow death that awaits him, worrying away at a lump in his testicle but refusing to read the diagnosis letter.

One of the most troubling moments in the novel is when the narrative directly addresses the reader, and it is on the subject of the canal: 'something about the water, though, might make you, *you* want to plunge your face and hands into it', letting 'it touch you' and 'feel movement underneath', the 'pulsing' (p. 34). It is discomfiting to feel interpellated in this way, embroiled in the revelations of Gamble's erotic and ethical inner life. Just how dirty are the reader's hands, now? The Stourbridge Canal, built in the late 1770s to connect mines to the Staffordshire and Worcestershire Canal, is overburdened with meaning in Gamble's thoughts; he projects his desires and anxieties on to it. The water itself is 'alive, watchful' and 'the colour of the blood of strangers' pp. 41; 97). The canal is a 'border' between his old and new selves. It looks back at him – 'through him' (p. 78). It is flat enough to write on – the novel is written on the water of the canal (p. 97). In the Anthropocene, the canal running through the novel is also the route to the text's energopolitical unconscious; whatever guilt we find of Gamble's reflected in its waters, we also see our own, for a culture built on coal. 'You might say', the novel addresses the reader, that the scene by the canal was a peaceful one: 'You might. But you'd be wrong' (p. 10). The placidity of the water hides horrors; the industrial past stores up future problems.

The action of Griffee's *Canal Pushers* takes place on and near the Stratford and Worcester and Birmingham Canals, 'a perfect place to get lost from the world'.[47] There are two ostensibly unconnected crimes that motivate the plot: a man who pushes victims into the canal and drowns them, and drug growing and manufacture. Jack Johnson is a typically disaffected would-be detective: 'forty-five years old, divorced, jobless, childless and with nothing more to show for twenty years of marriage than a rented canal boat' (p. 11). He is unheroic, not least because of his open lusting after a recently bereaved and traumatised young woman. He adopts the boat, *Jumping Jack Flash*, about eighteen miles from Alys Fowler's inflatable adventure in central Birmingham, and it sustains massive damage in a deliberate 'cilling' at the book's dénouement. Both Jack and his competent but mysterious companion, Nina, come from backgrounds of greater privilege than most noir protagonists, but the simplicity of their residence on the boat brings them into alignment with the genre. An initially minor character, Sam, whose death via both canal pushers propels Jack and Nina into their detective work, is a reminder of the tenuousness of a life with a stable income and home. Sam reminds Jack that people walk past the homeless because 'they're all shit scared that it could happen to them' (p. 54). We are a culture in denial, Sam affirms, of where our comfort comes from. Live-aboard boating is one clear reminder of the processes by which we access power and potable water, as is Sam, squatting in an abandoned cottage without mains water or electricity.

When Jack and Nina discover his murder via the local newspaper, Jack wonders if the boat has inadvertently cruised over his remains, 'lurking somewhere in the silt and weeds under our hull, being stirred and disturbed in the water's murky depths by the blades of our propeller' (p. 97). Silt is a troubling substance in the noir novels, indeterminate in make up and depth, the bottom of things but not quite, muddying the waters, swallowing and hiding. Jack and Nina work to uncover the conditions of Sam's life and the reason for his death, disturbing society's murky depths as they make their journey: 'dysfunctional junkies', drug dealers, murderous psychopaths, media intrusion, and naked gardeners (p. 137). In a classic moment of noir complicity, Jack also wonders if the cash he gave had 'inadvertently helped Sam to his doom' (p. 104). This image of disturbing murky depths, and

Morton's assertion about noirish complicity and our own role in climate crisis, enables a fuller consideration of the thriller's 'energopolitical unconscious'. The novel's setting of the Stratford Canal, built, as with most of the industrial canals in this book, to transport coal, suggests an unexpected twenty-first-century analogue: the oil and gas pipeline. Form, setting, character and Anthropocene reading come together to narrativise, as Hollister predicts, a traumatic ecological awareness.

Like *Gamble, Canal Pushers* demonstrates our ongoing reliance on the petrol engine as a means of transport: while moored in Stratford, Nina and Jack are reliant on Sergeant Milk's car and taxis; movement along the canal is not, for the most part, what drives the narrative, though it is the means of a 4mph flight out of Stratford to escape armed drug lords. Jack even notes the combustion engine as the 'undisputed champion' of Birmingham's post-canal development and remarks on the 'car-choked arterial roads' of the city (pp. 298; 334). The energopolitical unconscious of the novel can be pursued from the petrol-guzzling four-wheel-drive vehicles of the drug dealers to Nina's reason for escaping on *Jumping Jack Flash*: six weeks after their marriage, her husband was killed in Afghanistan, in 'a war that's just a joke' (p. 182). Nina is deeply critical of the war in Afghanistan and, whether it is the novel's intention or not, this points the reader to arguments that America and Britain's invasion of the country had more to do with oil than terrorism or the Axis of Evil.

Dick Cheney's National Energy Policy Report of April 2001 had 'projected a dramatic increase in U.S. dependency on imported oil over the coming two decades', with growing global shortages.[48] A stable government in Afghanistan would have allowed for a faster route to the Gulf from the Caspian Sea oil reserves in states such as Turkmenistan and Uzbekistan. The American oil firm Unocal even wooed the Taliban until the US relationship with the Taliban soured (in part because the Taliban suggested that pipelines might serve Afghan energy needs) and reached crisis point with the 9/11 terrorist attack. President Bush appointed a former aide to Unocal as special envoy to Afghanistan in 2002, and another, Hamid Karzai, as provisional Afghan president.[49] The rapidly-disgraced firm Enron was also negotiating pipeline routes through Afghanistan.[50] Journalist Frank Viviano called oil the 'hidden stakes in the war against terrorism', and Bülent Gökay notes that 'within a week of the commencement of war in Afghanistan, the Bush administration discussed the shape of a post-Afghan government to do deals over oil and gas pipelines' (p. 10). Gökay is not sure that all of these details add up to a conspiracy theory, but that there is certainly a 'significant money subtext to "Operation Enduring Freedom"', a military campaign that would cost Nina her husband (p. 11). The global imprint of power and corruption inspired by energy demands is brought to the apparently sleepy Stratford Canal via Nina's widowhood. It is an appropriate space for angry reflection on the violence of fuel supply, because the canal was itself built to satisfy nineteenth-century industrial demands for coal. In noir fiction, the industrial waterway can act as an historic analogue for the oil and gas pipeline, an innocuous setting managing to draw attention to the pervasiveness of fossil fuels in our lives, literature and politics.

Like Jack Johnson, DI Hillary Greene's residence on board *Mollern* in Martin's *Murder on the Oxford Canal* is inspired not by enthusiasm but reluctant financial necessity. Tarnished by her ex-/late/missing husband's bent copper reputation, Greene dismisses the idea of cycling from her boat to the canal crime scene because she does not want to look like some 'new-age greenie', and it is throwaway comments like this that act as breadcrumbs to follow the text's energopolitical unconscious.[51] Anthropocene reading of the text as part of 'canal noir' (rather than reading the text in isolation) allows for new inter-pretations of popular crime fiction that speak of wider twenty-first-century interests and anxieties. The novel, after all, draws attention to its own place in culture, with regular reference to television detective series and the coincidences and clues of detective novels. As in *Canal Pushers*, the crimes ostensibly centre on the drug trade (though the narrative gradually reveals other motivations), and Greene's concern (ironically) about seeming green can be connected to other addic-tions in an Anthropocene reading: from where do the things to which we are addicted come, and what are the effects of their supply? This might mean murder suspect Jake Gascoigne with his 'druggie mother' and then being 'in and out of Juvie', or it might equally be a culture addicted to fossil fuels (p. 58). Another minor detail points us in this direction. The body in the lock to which Greene refuses to cycle is identified as being that of a rapist, and the brother of one of the women he attacked is noted as being 'in oil. An engineer in Saudi Arabia' (p. 78). An innocuous aside in a witness statement – but this is a criminal inquiry, and the detective (or Anthropocene literary critic) must chase down every detail on the hunt for the text's linkage of centuries-old coal routes and today's pursuit of oil.

Unlike *Canal Pushers*, which centred on the canal but tended not to consider its mobile potential, *Murder on the Oxford Canal* uses boats as a mode of transport that propels the narrative. Similarly to *Canal Pushers*, though, the canal is posited as a quiet backwater rather than edgy urban hinterland. On the canal, even Oxford 'might have been a million miles away' (p. 97). It is a place where middle-class holiday-makers talk 'pretentiously' about 'getting back to nature'. But this was 'all bollocks of course' (p. 58). As the previous section of this chapter demonstrates, there is no simple return to nature via the waterway. The police soon realise that the canal network is actually a clever route for drug-running: 'slow but sure. And just think how much stuff you could store in a narrowboat'; its pace and historical connections throw a veil of innocence and respectability over its craft because 'who'd think of raiding a narrowboat?' (p. 58). It is easy to think of the past as safe, of heritage as cosy. How could something like the waterways be contentious or political? All of my experience researching in this area has dispelled any such notion. *Murder on the Oxford Canal* demands that we think again about the meaning of the industrial canal; it is not, of course, a 'million miles away' from the city, from people, from crime and politics, and neither is it divorced from the climactic conditions that it helped to produce and in which we read.

When I take a break from writing about this canal, I read that the American West is now caught in a cycle of 'heat, drought and fire'.[52] Engineered water 'made the west', but now 'climate crisis threatens to break it'.[53] People are dying, and it is climatologists outlining the cause of death, not the police surgeon. I cannot be a reader divorced from this reality, lulled into the tranquillity of the Oxfordshire countryside and the satisfaction of a narrative resolution. Coal and the Anthropocene may not seem to be part of this story, but the themes of noir and the time in which I read disrupt the causal logic of narrative as Hollister predicts.

The Oxford Canal, admittedly picturesque, takes us back to Brindley, coal, and the beginning of this book's story. Brindley designed the canal (but died before it was completed), with the aim of moving coal from Coventry to Oxford and the Thames before the Grand Union Canal opened. Detectives look for footprints; this chapter has looked for imprints. As I noted in the introduction, quoting Andreas Malm, 'every impact of anthropogenic climate change carries the imprint of every human act with radiative forcing, . . . the aftermath and the source – intimately coupled yet strangely discon-nected'. Twenty-first-century drug supply in noir fiction couples our addiction to fossil fuels to its eighteenth-century source when we consider the 'historical totality of the fossil economy'. None of these books explicitly links the death and destruction of climate crisis to their dark contemporary canal setting, but the canal as the source of coal for an overwhelming range of industries, whose success would set Britain and its Empire on a planet-burning path, is the content of these works' energopolitical unconscious. Their abstract references to oil and control of its supply reveal continuities across the centuries this book covers. These are waters of doom. Every corpse in the lock, every odour of 'metal and bone and blood', should send a shiver down the reader's spine – not through noirish thrill, but the recognition of where all that coal has led.[54] Not only does ecological awareness function like noir fiction because one realises one's human complicity in climate crisis, ecologically aware readings of noir – for instance, interpretation of the text's 'energopolitical unconscious' – reinforce a sense of guilt, disillusionment and anxiety about our capacity to avert climate crisis while existing in a culture addicted to fossil fuels.

Coal, oil, water

As I noted at the beginning of this chapter, critics have said that close attention and fine writing in NNW mark the author out with personal sensitivity and ecological consciousness. I have argued that close atten-tion to *genre* writing is what brings the text's energopolitical uncon-scious into readerly ecological consciousness. Coal and industry are not in the past; we still fight over oil pipelines and catastrophically heat the planet by burning fossil fuels. Again, I noted that critics of NNW fear it commodifies nature, implicating it in the circuits of late capitalism and thus ecological crisis. This is indeed an individualistic contradiction in NNW; noir (via Morton and Hollister) complicates what we can mean by individual responsibility in the Anthropocene, inducing guilt on behalf of a species, economic systems, and our past. I am not suggesting that this guilt is a personally productive response to climate crisis, but that contemporary canal noir symptomatises the way in which writing and reading implicate diverse aspects of our cul-ture and landscape in this very real threat to our existence. To simplify: for all the soul-baring that happens in NNW, noir novels feel more honest in their darkness for the position we find ourselves in today.

For instance, I suggested that coal had finally been relinquished in *Adrift* – it was never relinquished, merely submerged. NNW's exploration of the relation between landscape, self-hood and ethics is just as acute in noir fiction, connecting the industrial histories of the canal landscape with the postindustrial economy, complex complicity in the Anthropocene, and cultural addiction to damaging ways of fuelling our warm, well-fed, safe lives.

It has got dark. It is the third decade of the twenty-first century and I am *Industrious*, survivor of centuries, borne aloft by a precious resource, carrying a fuel now overwhelmingly heavy with meaning. I am surrounded by diverse species: birds, fish, plants, fungi. Will I outlive the one that built me? A posthuman craft rotting slowly into oblivion as my maker species tears itself apart?

6

THE BASIN, OR CONCLUSION

Reading the industrial canal from the eighteenth century to the Anthropocene reveals that textual representations of the British waterways can be usefully understood via four networked ideas: 1) energy cultures; 2) Empire; 3) geology; 4) water. The identification of these ideas demonstrates the ways in which the waterways are built in and of culture, society, literature and text. This cultural embeddedness means that questions of gender occur throughout the texts I have examined: it is a fact of their textuality rather than a theme. Similarly, the affective and the personal are, as I explored in the Introduction, a mode of reading rather than a thematic approach to the literature of the waterways. The Anthropocene pervades it all, for it is *when* we read.

First, energy cultures. My reading of the waterways across the centuries leads me to call for a rethinking of the waterways not simply as a transport system, but as an energy system. This might be, I suggest, the starting point for other cultural approaches to the industrial canal. In an analysis of 'petroculture', Imre Szeman notes that 'the history of modernity has seldom been narrated in relation to the massive expansion of socially available energy (specifically fossil fuels)', nor has modernity been understood via 'the social practices, behaviours and beliefs that have accompanied accessible energy'. While this book opens with the epistemological shifts of the Enlightenment, as well as other features associated with a dawning European 'modernity' (Empire, industrialisation), I would not describe the current work necessarily as a history of modernity, nor even a history of one of modernity's components. Nevertheless, I agree that 'leaving energy out of our picture' means we misunderstand 'the forces and practices animating . . . politics and economics, as well as . . . social and cultural life'.[1] Energy has, indeed, been left out of the literary picture. In the US, for instance, 'oil is simply what makes the country "go", and in a way that doesn't necessitate comment or concern', meaning it is 'relegated to the background', acting like 'furniture, or the asphalt covering the streets' (p. 282). Literature can, though, says Graeme Macdonald, 'reveal energy's "hidden" ubiquity'.[2] The industrial canal has hitherto formed the background to countless literary and cultural texts, rather than being the focus of reading. Not only have I brought the canal to the foreground, by doing so I have drawn attention to the fuel that made industrial Britain 'go': coal.

Burned as fuel since around 4000 BCE in China, it was also burned in England during the Bronze Age, and the Romans used it to heat their baths. It was, however, a 'minor resource' until the Industrial Revolution.[3] Then, it was the industrial canal's original raison d'être, by far its largest cargo (by tonnage), and often the last thing to be transported before canals were closed. It is one reason that the boat appearing in every chapter is named *Industrious*, for the coal-fired industry that changed the economy and culture of Britain. Paying attention to this 'resource of literature' demonstrates the ways in which coal created, organised and enabled modes of 'living, thinking, moving, dwelling and working'.[4] Macdonald asks whether literature changes 'in accordance with the dominant energy forms of the era it registers', whether it reproduces or resists a predominant energy culture (p. 6). The Industrial Revolution opened the era of coal as our energy culture. The eighteenth-century poetry discussed in Chapter Two can certainly be seen to shape itself to the contours of the new cut, but does not uniformly respond to the era of coal-fired industry. Barbauld's 'The Invitation' has its eyes wide open to all the unknown possibilities of a new energy culture. Though the 'Coalbrook Dale' of Seward's poetry does not get its name from the fuel, it became central to the industry of the place and now seems extraordinarily fitting. Seward's response to the industrial changes in the Dale is to imagine not a return to nature but a post-coal collapse – even at the dawn of coal energy culture, its end is envisioned.

Two lines and the notes from Darwin's Second Canto of *The Botanic Garden* about the treasures found underground are particularly striking when thinking about the end of the coal epoch imagined from its beginning. Darwin describes 'sable Coal', whose 'massy couch extends/ And stars of gold the sparkling Pyrite blends'. His extended note takes us back to Coalbrook Dale, and a 'fountain of fossil tar, or petroleum' discovered in 1786, the details of which were sent to the poet by his son, Robert. Workmen were 'making a subterranean canal into the mountain, for the more easy acquisition and conveyance of the coals which lie under it'. In the process 'they found an oozing of liquid bitumen' or 'fossil tar'. The evidence yielded by the new canal leads Darwin to suggest that 'a *natural distillation* of this fossil in the bowels of the earth must have taken place at some early period of the world', some 'antient time'.[5] The potential exploitation of petroleum as a fuel (and the dawning of a new energy culture) is not considered in this note, but Darwin's enthusiasm for new and future imagined modes of conveyance in the poem, from submarines to rockets, is a reminder that the use of petroleum for fuelling cars, in heating, for electricity generation, and for making plastics and synthetic materials, was not yet a given. Our world of gas-guzzling vehicles and islands of plastic in the ocean was not, of course, Darwin's world. The journey from the industrial canals, scientific investigation, burgeoning geo-logical discovery, global trade, manufactories and invention to the Anthropocene was not, at the moment Darwin wrote, an inevitable one by any means. Darwin's poem calls out to our energy culture from the still exciting possibilities of his own. The industrial canal helped to define an energy culture of coal, and the texts of the waterways articu-late the culture and its edges and alternatives, from Darwin, Seward and Barbauld through to canal noir in our own century.

The nineteenth-century travelogues of Chapter Three work hard to repress the energy form that enables a life with leisure, resisting yet benefiting from the predominant energy culture. Coal is much more present in the life writing and romances of Chapter Four, and they unproblematically and retrospectively reproduce twentieth-century coal culture. In a foreword to Gayford's account of the trainee scheme, Smith calls Gayford's *The Amateur Boatwomen* 'a small brightly flutter-ing flag at the conjunction of our industrial past and future', perhaps showing that these texts demonstrate a latent realisation of the nearing end of an energy era.[6] The New Nature Writing of the waterways thus positions itself as post-coal and post-industry in Chapter Five, but canal noir lives up to its 'sable' name by bringing us back to the power and violence of energy supply, the geopolitical dark side of coal and oil. I have posited the events and processes in and surrounding the texts in these chapter as (after Malm) moments in the historical totality of the fossil economy, from the opening of the Bridgewater Canal to invasions in the Middle East and climate crisis. Not only this, the 'fossil economy' that transects the energy cultures of coal and oil plays, as Szeman notes, 'an important role in managing and maintaining (post) colonial control'.[7] The industry and economy made possible by the transportation of coal by the industrial canal is intimately connected to Britain's Empire.

The industrial canal was, from its early stages, not just a linking network within the country, but a connection to the world, and for Britain in the eighteenth and nineteenth centuries the wide world was a place to wield power, acquire land, spread 'civilisation' and acquire natural resources. My exploration of a Second World War commodity chain in Chapter Four suggested that the water used to produce aluminium should be considered 'colonial water', because Empire produced the geographies of mining and smelting for wartime production. The functioning of the British canal system can, therefore, no longer be understood as happening in some contained 'inland'. I suggest that, because of the power and influence to which the waterways contributed, the industrial canal should be considered colonial water throughout the centuries under discussion here, because Empire was projected, imagined and celebrated in Barbauld's, Seward's and Darwin's poetry, clearly shaped Hughes's and Duncan's Victorian travelogues (and influenced Rolt's), enables the supply chains motivating the life writing and romances of Chapter Four, and exists as a neo-colonial oil pipeline analogue in Chapter Five. It is impossible to ignore the way in which the long arms of the canal network reach around the globe and return to Britain, such as Seward's imagining of an invading force. In Chapter Three, the global journeys of the imperial canoeist flow back to the Grand Union Canal and the Leeds and Liverpool Canal when British-based travelogues are read in imperial context. Further work on the colonial water of the canal might trace commodities and their cultural and social significance (as I did with aluminium) from sites of Empire to the inland waterway, and the role of British products manufactured inland that played a part in the ocean-going imperial project.

Ralph O'Connor has described how early 'geological writers engaged readers' imaginations with vivid descriptions of the vanished past'.[8] As the climate scholars cited in the Introduction make clear, the Holocene may also belong to that vanished past. The very human – textual – history of the industrial canal is now entangled in the geologic time of the Anthropocene. To read across the development, peak, decline and reinvention of this important facet of industry is also to read geologically, if one allows for shifting scales of analysis in the Anthropocene. In the case of my analysis, reading geologically becomes noticeable because of the close ties between the industrial canal and geology. Cutting through the land to make new canals meant that the layers of what existed beneath Britons' feet were suddenly presented in cross-section. The canals, as has been noted, had coal (to quote the Duke of Bridgewater) 'at the heels' of them, and the search for coal was also, Donald Prothero says, 'the foundation for some of the earliest geological studies in Britain or anywhere in the world'. Proto-geological studies of major coalfields led to recognition of Britain's 'Coal Measures', the basis for the 1822 term 'Carboniferous' or 'coal bearing'.[9] This period is also suggested by the plants Richard Mabey identified in the canal, mentioned in Chapter Five: the water horsetail that calls back to its huge, coal-forming ancestors. Jasper Winn described the geologist Sir Roderick Murchison's 1849 speech in Dudley Canal Tunnel proposing the geological period called the 'Silurian' when Dudley's limestone was formed; miners had been digging up and selling fossilised *Calymene blumenbachii*, which came to be known as 'Dudley Bugs'.[10] Canals, coal and fossils are never textually far apart thanks to the their geology.

Scholars such as O'Connor, Noah Heringman and Adelene Buckland have convincingly demonstrated the intersections of literature and geology. I assert that writing about the canals is also geological writing, in part because of the cut through the earth in their construction, and in part because such writing is consciously or unconsciously orientated towards mineral resources in the service of industry. Writing about the waterways in the eighteenth and nineteenth centuries connects a vividly described vanished past (even when some of the science delineating that past was still opaque) with a vividly imagined future wrought from industry, engineering and technology (for good or ill). While the fossils, clay, bauxite and limestone of canal writing may have lain beneath the surface of previous readings, reading waterways texts collectively as a network allows us to see the way in which references to these substances newly configure disparate texts, geographies and timescales, from 'the stiff opposing clay' through which the Bridgewater Canal was built, to the strata of limestone Darwin and Wedgwood examined, to the bauxite first identified by Pierre Berthier in 1821 – an identification that calls back over millions of years.

When Gideon Mantell wrote of the *Wonders of Geology* in 1838, he recounted finding a specimen of fossilised wood on the banks of the Regent's Canal, complete with grain and shells. Wood of this kind, he said, is often ravaged by 'a species of teredo, resembling the recent *Teredo navalis*, or *borer*, which inhabits the seas of the West India islands'.[11] *As Mantell stands on the towpath, admiring the brilliant pyrites caught in the shells, I, Industrious, float past, laden with sugar from the West Indies, the bloodied means of its production an inconvenient fact boring through nineteenth-century culture.* The canal is here a passageway to the geological past, but simultaneously to the structuring ideas, things, relationships, and symbols by which we know our world. Wedgwood considered that his fossils were 'silent and innocent'.[12] '*On the contrary, Josiah,*' whispers Industrious. '*They speak of the past, present and future, of the stories we tell to make sense of the apparently inexplicable, like shellfish buried in the Midlands. And like other things found in the canal, they are anything but "innocent", caught in the power structures of language, economy, and culture. Even the water on which I float is modern, colonial, economic, emplaced*'.

Think of water. It rushes and swells, trickles and pounds, boils and freezes, sustains and takes life. Derek Gregory asserts that by the end of the nineteenth century, hydrology and hydraulic engineering were able to tame wild 'nature' into mathematical formulae. In these, he says, 'there would be no place for "local" knowledge, and the hydraulics of irrigation channels and the mechanics of dam construction could be made the same the world over'.[13] This may have been the way one was *supposed* to think about water, but the human relationship to water could not be confined to formulae, even in the highly engineered space of the canal. As Jane Costlow, Yrjö Haila and Arja Rosenholm put it, 'techno-scientific discourses frequently exclude or erase human affects, memories, and dreams'.[14] I would modify the deliberate sense of exclusion and erasure, and suggest instead that such discourses *in isolation* are unable to capture our diverse and nuanced responses to water, but that those discourses are always part of a cultural network (an 'artful maze', to return to Barbauld) that includes poetry, travelogue, fiction, life writing, drama, nature writing and more. These forms and genres 'engineer' rising, swelling feeling into something that connects us to each other, a passage of communication from one human's affects to another's.

Just because water is engineered into the reliable channels of the industrial canal does not mean, as we have seen, that it is all the same. For instance, the double meaning of 'genius' (a genius of engineering and genius loci) meant that, from its inception, the waters of the industrial canal were and are considered very much of a place: Wigan, Manchester, Birmingham, Stourbridge, Worcester, Huddersfield. The waters of the industrial canal emerge from caves, tunnel through limestone, soar overhead via aqueducts. It can freeze – terrifying if your livelihood depends on movement through it – and flood. It is black, brown, phosphorescent, bright green with weed, reflective of blue skies, 'pitted with silver stars'.[15] It meets and collects waters from high-up reservoirs, streams, rivers, and the sea. It turns Britain's 'mainland' into an archipelago (transecting from Leeds to Liverpool and Inverness to Corpach). It takes the oceans and their cargo inland. Water may be ingeniously managed by engineering, and it will always be H_2O, but it is still unique for every animal that encounters it, in every time and place.

The water of the industrial canal is historical and social; its flow, for instance, was routed to serve particular historical contingencies and for particular economic reasons. Its presence as both cleanser and carrier of effluent was remarked on by women who found themselves unexpectedly working on the canals thanks to the rise of fascism in Europe. It is looked to as a mental balm in an overheated twenty-first-century urban working world. The water is situated in the places I note above. It is relational, connecting person to person, city to city, Britain to the world. It is material: floating and sinking boats (and with them belongings, hopes, livelihoods); demanding inspired engineering solutions to its physical qualities; frozen, murky, wet, thick. Here, it is also scaled to encounter vast nonhuman entities: the world's oceans, carbon emissions, pollution, ecosystems. Particular human experiences of the waters of the canal are communicated in writing, enabling that particularity to flow across time and space. For instance, A. N. Wilson's depiction of the canal towpath, when first introduced in *The Potter's Hand*, is a romantic riparian space. He details the flowers of the hedgerow: meadow-sweet, bramble, rest-harrow and kidney vetch, campion and groundsel, vivid tufts of green grass, part of 'damp, fertile, mysterious England'. Kingfishers and voles are spotted more than once.[16] Such biodiversity is a reminder to the reader that the industrial canal at this moment wends through a landscape not yet affected by the floral-cleansing of industrial agriculture, a presentist self-awareness towards which the novel frequently nods as it depicts a version of England that did not yet know industrial cities, nor sulphurous pollutants, nor railways. As Wilson so accurately puts it, 'none of the consequences of Jos Wedgwood and friends' Industrial

Revolution could yet blight the calm, the grey, the green of that sublime England which they saw' (p. 141). *The Potter's Hand* therefore fits in with the post-industrial, ecologically aware impulses of the New Nature Writing of the canals, celebrating Wedgwood and co's genius and the England they inhabited at the same time as offering the dark foreboding of pollutants and industrial burning. While Wilson's novel bridges the canal's beginnings and its after effects in a sophisticated transhistorical appeal to the reader, the present work has charted the *flow* of the industrial canal's meanings across time and space. It offers – especially via *Industrious* – a sense of liquid history, of the flow of the past into the present. It begins to map the textual network, and read the waterways.

Almost every text analysed here makes explicit or implicit reference to at least three more – all of these authors, from Barbauld and Darwin to Fowler and Babbs, are reading the waterways. This also means that it is more appropriate to describe, as I have done above, a network of texts centred on the industrial canal rather than a corpus, though I suggest that thinking of this network in similar ways to a literary corpus is productive in tracing themes and continuities. My examples have often, by nature of the reason people write, focused on the exceptional rather than quotidian experiences of the canal: when they were new, by canoe, during war. I have also, though, drawn attention to *why* these experiences are exceptional, and the usual experiences from which they stand out: working in mines, factories and docks; generations of canal carrying expertise; the 9-to-5.

What, then, do the canals *mean* if they stop being background and if I reassert that the waterways network is a tool to help describe something, not simply what is being described?[17] In short, they powerfully signify the passage of time – geologic, seasonal, human, epistemological, of cultural eras and norms, of energy cultures. Margaret Cornish lamented that as she wrote her memoir she now felt like an anachronism on the canal.[18] At the same time as wanting to hear her feelings of placelessness and loss, I would also answer that the canal's unique indexing of time means that everything and nothing is anachronistic when reading the waterways; all exists in a passage from the past to the future, every boat and its cargo a marker in the transition from one period, era, culture to another. Reading the waterways enables us all to board *Industrious* and travel impossible routes through history.

NOTES

Notes to Chapter 1

1 Jo Bell, 'Working Pair', *Waterlines: Canal and River Poetry*, *https://waterlines.org.uk/poems/* (accessed 1 August 2022).

2 Helen Babbs, *Adrift: A Secret Life of London's Waterways* (London: Icon, 2016), p. 153.

3 Philip Bagwell, *The Transport Revolution 1770–1985* (London: Routledge, 1988), p. 4.

4 J. M. W. Turner, *Lancaster, from the Aqueduct Bridge* (*c.*1825).

5 J. M. W. Turner, *Kirkstall Lock, on the River Aire* (1824–5), *http://www.tate.org.uk/art/research-publications/jmw-turner/joseph-mallord-william-turner-kirkstall-lock-on-the-river-aire-r1146209#fn_1_2_1* (accessed 1 August 2022).

6 'On the Canal', *Household Words*, 11 September 1858, 442.

7 William Black, *The Strange Adventures of a House-Boat* (London: Sampson Low, 1893).

8 Emma Smith, *Maidens' Trip* (London: Bloomsbury, 2011).

9 Manuel DeLanda interviewed in Rick Dolphijn and Iris van der Tuin, *New Materialism: Interviews and Cartographies* (Ann Arbor, MI: Open Humanities Press, 2012), p. 41.

10 William John Charles Moens, *The Voyage of the Steam-yacht 'Ytene' through France and Belgium by River and Canal* (London: n. pub., 1876), p. 128.

11 For more on the ship of Theseus and logic and intuition, see Christopher M. Brown, *Aquinas and the Ship of Theseus: Solving Puzzles About Material Objects* (London and New York: Continuum, 2005).

12 Virginia Woolf, *Orlando* (London: Penguin, 2016).

13 Tristan Gooley, *How to Read Water: Clues and Patterns from Puddles to the Sea* (London: Sceptre, 2017).

14 Patricia Ticineto Clough, *The Affective Turn: Theorizing the Social* (Durham, NC and London: Duke University Press), p. 2.

15 Elisha Cohn, 'Affect', *Victorian Literature and Culture* 46/3–4 (2018), 563–7.

16 Ben Anderson, 'Affective Materialism', *Dialogues in Human Geography*
    8/2 (2018), 229–31 (p. 230); *Encountering Affect: Capacities, Apparatuses,
    Conditions* (London: Routledge, 2017), pp. 7; 14; 60. For Anderson,
    'mediation involves constant (dis)connections between affects and the
    complex mixtures that make up ways or forms of life' (p. 6). Mark Guy
    Pearse, *Rob Rat: A Story of Barge Life* (London: Wesleyan Conference
    Office, 1879).

17 Clough, *Affective Turn*, p. 2.

18 Anderson, *Encountering Affect*, pp. 87; 105; 167.

19 Elizabeth Carolyn Miller, *Extraction Ecologies and the Literature of the
    Long Exhaustion* (Princeton University Press, 2021), p. 23. I have pre-
    viously read transhistorical textual encounters in detail in *The Gypsy
    Woman: Representations in Literature and Visual Culture* (London: I. B.
    Tauris, 2018).

20 Alan Liu, English 238: Critical Infrastructure Studies (Fall 2018), *https://
    alanyliu.org/course/english-238-critical-infrastructure-studies-fall-2018/*
    (accessed 1 August 2022).

21 Bruno Latour, *Reassembling the Social: An Introduction to Actor-Network-
    Theory* (Oxford University Press, 2005), pp. 128–33.

22 Patrick Jagoda, *Network Aesthetics* (Chicago University Press, 2016),
    pp. 5–42; 221.

23 Caroline Levine, *Forms: Whole, Rhythm, Hierarchy, Network* (Princeton
    University Press, 2015), pp. 17; 9; 113; 122–5; 130.

24 For just how much coal, see B. R. Mitchell, *British Historical Statistics*
    (Cambridge University Press, 1988), especially chapter four.

25 Cited in Bagwell, *Transport Revolution*, p. 11.

26 Hugh Malet, *Bridgewater: The Canal Duke, 1736–1803* (Manchester Uni-
    versity Press, 1977), p. 92.

27 Donald R. Prothero, *The Story of the Earth in 25 Rocks: Tales of Important
    Geological Puzzles and the People Who Solved Them* (New York: Colum-
    bia University Press, 2018), p. 64.

28 Jesse Oak Taylor, 'Anthropocene', *Journal of Victorian Literature and Cul-
    ture* 46/3–4 (2018), 573–7.

29 Kenneth Pomeranz, *The Great Divergence: China, Europe, and the Mak-
    ing of the Modern World Economy* (Princeton University Press, 2000),
    p. 44; Marcia Rocha et al., *Historical Responsibility for Climate Change –
    from countries' emissions to contribution to temperature increase*, Climate
    Analytics (2015), *https://climateanalytics.org/media/historical_responsi-
    bility_report_nov_2015.pdf* (accessed 1 August 2022).

30 Philip T. Hoffman, 'The Great Divergence: Why Britain Industrialised
    First', *Australian Economic History Review* 60/2 (2020), 126–47 (pp. 127–
    8; 141).

31 Andreas Malm, *Fossil Capital: The Rise of Steam Power and the Roots of Global Warming* (London and New York: Verso, 2016), pp. 4; 13; 156; 222. I make a number of references to Malm's lucid and rigorous work here but, as my approach to the Anthropocene illustrates, not all of Malm's assertions align with my arguments about 'reading the waterways' and the industrial histories on which they draw.

32 Miller, *Extraction Ecologies*, p. 17. Further, the water in the canals could be used in steam engines' condensers.

33 A. Rogers, N. Castree and R. Kitchin, 'Anthropocene' in *A Dictionary of Human Geography* (Oxford University Press, 2013).

34 David Wallace-Wells, *The Uninhabitable Earth: A Story of the Future* (London: Allen Lane, 2019), p. 4.

35 Malm, *Fossil Capital*, p. 5.

36 Juha Schweighofer, 'The Impact of Extreme Weather and Climate Change on Inland Waterway Transport', *Natural Hazards* 72/1 (2014), 23–40.

37 See 'Flood Damage on Calder and Hebble Canal', *Examiner* Live, 4 January 2016, *https://www.examinerlive.co.uk/incoming/gallery/flood-damage-calder-hebble-canal-10685492* for photographic evidence (accessed 1 August 2022).

38 Schweighofer, 'Impact of Extreme Weather', p. 24.

39 Alice Harvey-Fishenden, Neil Macdonald and James P. Bowen, 'Dry weather fears of Britain's early "industrial" canal network', *Regional Environmental Change* 19 (2019), 2325–37.

40 Helen M. Hanlon, Dan Bernie, Giulia Carigi and Jason A. Lowe, 'Future Changes to High Impact Weather in the UK', *Climatic Change* 166/50 (2021).

41 Celia Deane-Drummond, 'Rivers at the End of Nature: Ethical Trajectories of the Anthropocene Grand Narrative', in Jason M. Kelly et al. (eds), *Rivers of the Anthropocene* (Oakland, CA: University of California Press, 2018), pp. 55–62 (p. 56).

42 Bronislaw Szerszynski, 'The Anthropocene Monument: On Relating Geological and Human Time', *European Journal of Social Theory* 20/1 (2017), 111–31 (p. 123).

43 Deane-Drummond, 'Rivers at the End of Nature', p. 57–9. Deane-Drummond explicitly parts company from Bruno Latour's reading of the Anthropocene narrative in this chapter, insisting that he has conflated the Anthropocene with Gaia theory.

44 Szerszynski, 'The Anthropocene Monument', p. 127.

45 Dipesh Chakrabarty, 'The Climate of History: Four Theses', *Critical Inquiry* 35/2 (2009), 197–222 (p. 198).

46 Chris Otter et al., 'Roundtable: The Anthropocene in British History', *Journal of British Studies* 57 (2018), 568–96 (p. 571).

47 Taylor, 'Anthropocene', p. 575.
48 Jacques Derrida, *Writing and Difference*, trans. Alan Bass (London and New York: Routledge, 2003), pp. 266–9.
49 Cody Marrs, 'Dickinson in the Anthropocene', *ESQ: A Journal of Nineteenth-Century American Literature and Culture* 63/2 (2017), 201–25 (p. 202).
50 Robert Marzec, 'Reflections on the Anthropocene Dossier', *MFS Modern Fiction Studies* 64/4 (2018), 585–616 (pp. 602–3).
51 Wallace-Wells, *The Uninhabitable Earth*, p. 18.
52 Marzec, 'Reflections on the Anthropocene Dossier', pp. 602–3.
53 Jamie Linton, *What is Water? The History of a Modern Abstraction* (Vancouver and Toronto: UBC Press, 2010), pp. 7–34.
54 Radhika Seshan, 'Representing Water: Travel Accounts, Water and the Constructions of Difference', *Water History* 7, 151–8 (p. 151).
55 Seshan, 'Representing Water', p. 151.
56 Astrida Neimanis, *Bodies of Water: Posthuman Feminist Phenomenology* (London and Oxford: Bloomsbury, 2017), pp. 2; 23.
57 Veronica Strang, 'Forum: What to do about "Flow"?', *Suomen Antropologi: Journal of the Finnish Anthropological Society* 2 (2014), 92–6.
58 Neimanis, *Bodies of Water*, p. 4.
59 Strang, 'Forum: What to do about "Flow"?', p. 93.
60 'Introduction: Toward a Hydrological Turn?', in Cecilia Chen, Janine MacLeod and Astrida Neimanis (eds), *Thinking With Water* (Montreal and Kingston: McGill-Queen's University Press, 2013), pp. 3–23 (p. 3).
61 S. E. Wolfe, 'Fear, Anger and Responsibility: The Emotional Content of Historical Speeches about Water and Water Policy', *Water History* 9/3 (2017), 317–36 (p. 318).
62 Eily Gayford, *The Amateur Boatwomen* (Harrow: Belmont, 2008), p. 135.
63 See, for instance, P. Mathias, *The First Industrial Nation: An Economic History of Britain 1700–1914* (London: Methuen, 1969).
64 Barrie Trinder, *The Making of the Industrial Landscape* (London: Dent, 1982), pp. 12; 53; 118.
65 Adam Rogers, 'Water and the Urban Fabric: A Study of Towns and Waterscapes in the Roman period in Britain', *International Journal of Nautical Archaeology* 41/2 (2012), 327–39.
66 See G. W. Crompton, 'Canals and the Industrial Revolution', *The Journal of Transport History* 14/2 (1993): 93–110 (p. 94) for a summary of these views.
67 Malet, *Bridgewater*, pp. 30; 51.
68 John Blair, *Waterways and Canal-Building in Medieval England* (Oxford University Press, 2008), pp. 4–5.

69 W. B. Stephens, 'The Exeter Lighter Canal, 1566–1698', *Journal of Transport History* 3/1 (1957), 1–11.

70 W. A. McCutcheon, 'The Newry Navigation: The Earliest Inland Canal in the British Isles', *The Geographical Journal*, 129/4 (1963), 466–80.

71 'History of the Sankey Canal', *Pennine Waterways*, http://www.pennine waterways.co.uk/sankey/sa2.htm (accessed 1 August 2022).

72 Trinder, *Making of the Industrial Landscape*, p. 131.

73 Simon Bradley, *The Railways: Nation, Network and People* (London: Profile, 2015), p. 9.

74 Bagwell, *Transport Revolution*, p. 13.

75 Liz McIvor, *Canals: The Making of a Nation* (London: BBC Books, 2015), p. 8.

76 Bagwell, *Transport Revolution*, p. 6.

77 Anthony Burton, *The Canal Builders* (Stroud: Tempus, 2005), p. 132.

78 John Cassidy, *The Ship Canal Digger* (1892). Cast bronze. Manchester Art Gallery.

79 See also Bagwell, *Transport Revolution*, p. 21.

80 Trevor Hill, 'From Packhorse to Railway: Changing Transport Systems from the Seventeenth to the Nineteenth Centuries and their Impact upon Trade and Industry in the Shropshire Area' (unpublished PhD thesis, University of Leicester, 1998), pp. 133–5.

81 Jules Gehrke, 'Countryside, Recreation, and the Transformation of Canals in Britain in the Mid-Twentieth Century', *Journal of Tourism History* 11/2 (2019), 167–86 (p. 174).

82 Joseph Boughey, 'From Transport's Golden Ages to an Age of Tourism: L. T. C. Rolt, Waterway Revival and Railway Preservation in Britain, 1944–54', *The Journal of Transport History* 34/1 (2013), 22–38 (p. 23).

83 'Holidays Afloat', *The Times*, 4 March 1948, cited in Gehrke, p. 183.

84 L. T. C. Rolt, *Narrow Boat* (Stroud: The History Press, 2014).

85 Charlotte Mathieson, *Mobility in the Victorian Novel: Placing the Nation* (Houndmills: Palgrave, 2015), p. 5.

86 Adrienne Gavin and Andrew Humphries, *Transport in British Fiction: Technologies of Movement, 1840–1940* (Houndmills: Palgrave, 2015), p. 1.

87 Steve Mentz, *Shipwreck Modernity: Ecologies of Globalization, 1550–1719* (Minneapolis and London: University of Minnesota Press, 2015), pp. xiii–xxvii. I see similarities between Mentz's understanding of history and my own (despite my emphasis on the Anthropocene), in particular the tension between the persistent claims of novelty that emerge from texts about the industrialisation of Britain and an acute awareness of historical continuity (p. xiii).

88 Nick Middleton, *Rivers: A Very Short Introduction* (Oxford University Press, 2012), p. xv.

89 Michael Ferber, *A Dictionary of Literary Symbols*, 2nd edn (Cambridge University Press, 2007), pp. 170–3.

90 T. S. McMillin, *The Meaning of Rivers: Flow and Reflection in American Literature* (Iowa City: University of Iowa Press, 2011), pp. xii–xiv.

91 Katharine Norbury, 'The Top 10 Books about Rivers', *The Guardian*, 18 February 2015. *https://www.theguardian.com/books/2015/feb/18/ top-10-books-about-rivers-katharine-norbury* (accessed 1 August 2022).

92 Robert Burroughs, 'Travel Writing and Rivers', in Nandini Das and Tim Youngs (eds), *The Cambridge History of Travel Writing* (Cambridge University Press, 2019), pp. 330–44.

93 See my 'Thousands of these floating hovels: Picturing Bargees in Image and Text', *Nineteenth-Century Contexts* 35/2 (2013), 121–42 for examples.

94 Lee Rourke, *The Canal* (New York and London: Melville House, 2010), p. 135.

95 Anthony Cartwright, *The Cut* (London: Peirene, 2017), pp. 40–3.

96 Paul Gilroy, *The Black Atlantic: Modernity and Double Consciousness* (Cambridge, MA: Harvard University Press, 1993), p. 11.

97 Lisa Fletcher, *Historical Romance Fiction: Heterosexuality and Performativity* (London: Routledge, 2016), p. 2.

98 Deborah Philips, *Women's Fiction: From 1945 to Today* (London: Bloomsbury, 2006), p. 1.

99 Joe Moran, 'A Cultural History of the New Nature Writing', *Literature & History* 23/1 (2014), 49–63, p. 50.

100 Moran, 'A Cultural History of the New Nature Writing', p. 50.

101 See Jos Smith, *The New Nature Writing: Rethinking the Literature of Place* (London: Bloomsbury, 2018).

Notes to Chapter 2

1 Anna Letitia Barbauld, 'The Invitation', *Poems* (London: Joseph Johnson, 1773), pp. 13–24 (p. 14). Hypertext version edited by Lisa Vargo and Allison Muri available at *Romantic Circles*, *https://www.rc.umd.edu/editions/ contemps/barbauld/poems1773/title_page.html* (accessed 1 August 2022).

2 Rachel Hurley, James Rothwell and Jamie Woodward, 'Metal contamination of bed sediments in the Irwell and upper Mersey catchments, northwest England: exploring the legacy of industry and urban growth', *Journal of Soils and Sediments* 17/11 (2017), 2648–65.

3 'Account of the Duke of Bridgewater's Navigation across the Irwell', *The Oxford Magazine*, June 1771, 234–6.

4 Peter Maw, Terry Wyke and Alan Kidd, 'Canals, Rivers, and the Industrial City: Manchester's Industrial Waterfront, 1790–1850', *Economic History Review* 65/4 (2012), 1495–1523.

5 Barbauld, 'Invitation', p. 13.

6 Sonia Hofkosh, 'Materiality, Affect, Event: Barbauld's Poetics of the Everyday', in William McCarthy and Olivia Murphy (eds), *Anna Letitia Barbauld: New Perspectives* (Lewisburg, PA: Bucknell University Press, 2013), pp. 80–102.

7 Barrie Trinder, *The Making of the Industrial Landscape* (London: Dent, 1982), p. 53.

8 Ron Broglio, *Technologies of the Picturesque: British Art, Poetry and Instruments, 1750–1830* (Lewisburg, PA: Bucknell University Press, 2008), p. 15.

9 Richard Holmes, *The Age of Wonder: How the Romantic Generation Discovered the Beauty and Terror of Science* (London: HarperCollins, 2008), p. xix.

10 Lisa Jardine, *Ingenious Pursuits: Building the Scientific Revolution* (London: Abacus, 2000), p. 6.

11 William McCarthy, *Anna Letitia Barbauld: Voice of the Enlightenment* (Baltimore, MA: Johns Hopkins University Press, 2008), p. 8. As it is the name by which she is remembered, I generally refer to her as Barbauld, unless referring to her collaboration with her brother.

12 McCarthy, *Barbauld*, p. 16.

13 The first Duke of Bridgewater had commissioned the civil engineer, Thomas Steers, to explore the possibility of linking up his mines' drainage soughs and Worsley Brook to the Irwell; this plan was curtailed by improvements to the River Douglas. See Cyril J. Wood, *The Duke's Cut: The Bridgewater Canal* (Stroud: Tempus, 2002), p. 11.

14 Hugh Malet, *Bridgewater: The Canal Duke, 1736–1803* (Manchester University Press, 1977), pp. xii; 55; 62. Malet attributes the mythologising to 'journalists', 'gongoozelers' and the Victorian author Samuel Smiles.

15 1754 circular letter soliciting subscriptions, quoted in McCarthy, *Barbauld*, p. 63. Warrington at this time provided places of worship for Catholics, Presbyterians, Anabaptists, Methodists and Quakers, as well as the parish church. See John Aikin, *A Description of the Country from Thirty to Forty Miles round Manchester* (London: John Stockdale, 1795), p. 306. Digitised at *https://archive.org* (accessed 1 August 2022).

16 See, for instance, Ellen Moers, *Literary Women* (London: W. H. Allen, 1977) and Moira Ferguson, *First Feminists: British Women Writers, 1578–1799* (Bloomington, IN: Indiana University Press, 1985).

17 McCarthy recounts Barbauld's journey to being 'made classical' by Wedgwood in some detail, including her sitting for a portrait during

the Christmas season of 1774, and eventually appearing in the Wedg-wood catalogue in 1777. 'Her own family used one [of the cameos] on a brooch'. McCarthy, *Barbauld*, p. 116.

18 'Five terminals, limitless solutions', Manchester Ship Canal (2022), *https://www.peelports.com/our-ports/manchester-ship-canal* (accessed 1 August 2022).

19 John Goodridge, 'Hell, Hull, and Halifax: John Dyer Visits the Work-house', *Literature & History* 21/2 (2012), 1–15.

20 John Freeth, 'Birmingham Navigation: An Ode', *The Political Songster* (Birmingham: Baskerville, 1771), p. 109. Available at *https://books.google. co.uk* (accessed 1 August 2022). This poem is titled 'Inland Navigation: An Ode' in other editions.

21 John Phillips, *A General History of Inland Navigation*, 4th edn (London: Baldwin, 1803), pp. 97; 100.

22 For more detail on Barbauld's relationship with Belsham see McCarthy, p. 79. Edmund Spenser, 'The Shepheardes Calendar', *Renascence Editions* (1996; based on facsimile of the first edition, 1579). *http://www.luminarium. org/renascence-editions/shepheard.html* (accessed 1 August 2022).

23 John Hassell, *Tour of the Grand Junction* (London: published privately, 1819), pp. vi–vii.

24 Thomas Whately, *Observations on Modern Gardening*, 4th edn (London: Payne, 1777), p. 62. Digitised at *https://archive.org* (accessed 1 August 2022).

25 Barbauld, 'Invitation', p. 17.

26 Henry James Pye, *Faringdon Hill: A Poem in Two Books*, 2nd edn (Oxford: Daniel Prince, 1778), book I, p. 15. Penny Fielding suggests that '*Faringdon Hill* marks a separation of the river as nature and the canal as the bearer of economic improvement, social rank, and national prosperity. The historical river that "naturally" connects points of social sameness now comes to be defined against its industrial other, an act that produces the river as purely natural'. Fielding, '"Usurpt by Cyclops": Riv-ers, Industry, and Environment in Eighteenth-Century Poetry', in Evan Gottlieb and Juliet Shields (eds), *Representing Place in British Literature and Culture, 1660–1830: From Local to Global* (Farnham and Burlington, VT: Ashgate, 2013), pp. 139–54 (p. 146).

27 Jane Austen, *Persuasion*, ed. Patricia Meyer Spacks (London and New York: Norton, 1995), p. 64, and quoted in Noah Heringman, *Romantic Rocks, Aesthetic Geology* (Ithaca, NY and London: Cornell University Press, 2004). ProQuest Ebook, p. 3.

28 John Aikin, *Essay on the Application of Natural History to Poetry* (War-rington: Eyres, 1777), p. 33.

29 Heringman, *Romantic Rocks*, p. 15.

30 Hillary Eklund (ed.), *Ground-Work: English Renaissance Literature and Soil Science* (Pittsburgh, PA: Duquesne University Press, 2017), pp. 4–5.

31 Frances E. Dolan, 'Compost/Composition' in Eklund, *Ground-Work*, pp. 21–39 (pp. 21–3).

32 See, for instance, Cyril T. G. Boucher, *James Brindley, Engineer* (Norwich: Goose, 1968) and Nick Corble, *James Brindley: The First Canal Builder* (Stroud: Tempus, 2005).

33 McCarthy, *Barbauld*, p. 65. The majority of the works in the collection were penned by Barbauld, but the motto on the title page reads '*Si Non Unius, Quaeso Miserere Duorum*'. For this detail, and a scrupulously precise elaboration of the Aikins' 'joineriana', see Daniel E. White, 'The "Joineriana": Anna Barbauld, the Aikin Family Circle, and the Dissenting Public Sphere', *Eighteenth-Century Studies* 32/4 (1999), 511–33.

34 John and Anna Letitia Aikin, 'The Canal and the Brook' in *Miscellaneous Pieces in Prose* (London: Johnson, 1773), p. 79.

35 Both the portrait and one of the copies are owned by the National Portrait Gallery. Francis Parsons, *James Brindley*, oil on canvas (1770), NPG 6170, see *npg.org.uk* and Robery Dunkarton, after Francis Parsons, *James Brindley*, mezzotint (1773), NPG D13400.

36 Aikin and Aikin, 'The Hill of Science' in *Miscellaneous Pieces*, pp. 33; 36.

37 Brindley is, of course, not the only figure to be represented in this conflated-genius mode. Beneath a large stone classical urn in the grounds of Croome Court, Worcestershire, the Earl of Coventry was memorialised in 1809 in some lines of formulaic verse. The memorial is 'sacred to him, the Genius of this place/ Who reared these shades,/ and form'd these sweet retreats'. Croome is known for being the first of Lancelot 'Capability' Brown's picturesque landscapes, so the 'genius' invoked is that of this particular corner of England, of the aristocrat whose money and vision enabled its fashionable transformation, and the designer.

38 Phillips, *General History*, p. 94; emphasis added.

39 Barbauld, 'Invitation', p. 17.

40 Julia Saunders, '"The Mouse's Petition": Anna Laetitia Barbauld and the Scientific Revolution', *The Review of English Studies* 53/212 (2002), 500–16, p. 503.

41 Jamie Linton, *What is Water? The History of a Modern Abstraction* (Vancouver and Toronto: UBC Press, 2010), pp. 77–81.

42 McCarthy, *Barbauld*, p. 87; Rachel Hetty Trethewey, 'The Progressive Ideas of Anna Letitia Barbauld' (unpublished PhD thesis, University of Exeter, 2013).

43 Samuel Smiles, *James Brindley and the Early Engineers* (London: Murray, 1864), pp. 196–7. Meetings at which Brindley spoke were also regularly reported on in newspapers.

44 Joseph Drury, 'Literature and Science in Enlightenment Britain: New Directions', *Literature Compass* 14 (2017), p. 9.

45 Saunders, 'The Mouse's Petition', p. 507.

46 Hofkosh, 'Materiality, Affect, Event', p. 82.

47 White, 'The "Joineriana"', p. 526.

48 Aikin and Aikin, 'Canal and the Brook', pp. 82–3.

49 For more on Dyer's optimism, see Goodridge, 'Hell, Hull, and Halifax'.

50 Phillips, *General History*, p. 99.

51 James Thomson, *The Castle of Indolence: An Allegorical Poem Written in Imitation of Spenser* (London: Millar, 1747), II.xx (p. 51). Digitised at *https://archive.org* (accessed 1 August 2022). I am indebted to Ivanka Kovacevich's reference to these lines in a very long poem, which may have otherwise gone unnoticed. See 'The Mechanical Muse: The Impact of Technical Inventions on Eighteenth-Century Neoclassical Poetry', *Huntingdon Library Quarterly* 28/3 (1965), 263–281.

52 Francesco Crocco, 'The Colonial Subtext of Anna Letitia Barbauld's "Eighteen Hundred and Eleven"', *The Wordsworth Circle* 42/2 (2010), 91–94.

53 The poem imagines England in ruins following the Napoleonic Wars

> England, the seat of arts, be only known
> By the gray ruin and the mouldering stone;
> That Time may tear the garland from the brow,
> And Europe sit in dust, as Asia now.

Anna Laetitia Barbauld, *Eighteen Hundred and Eleven, A Poem* (London: Johnson, 1812). Available at *http://www.gutenberg.org/cache/epub/14100/pg14100-images.html* (accessed 1 August 2022).

54 Human-induced climate change warms the world's oceans. Hurricanes draw their energy from warm seas, and Ocean Heat Content has soared since 1970. Hurricanes are therefore more likely and will become stronger, slower and wetter in future. See Daniel Levitt and Niko Kommenda, 'Is Climate Change Making Hurricanes Worse?', *The Guardian*, 10 October 2018, *https://www.theguardian.com/weather/ng-interactive/2018/sep/11/atlantic-hurricanes-are-storms-getting-worse* (accessed 1 August 2022).

55 O. Hoegh-Guldberg et al., 'Impacts of 1.5°C global warming on natural and human systems', in *Global warming of 1.5°C. An IPCC Special Report on the impacts of global warming of 1.5°C above pre-industrial levels and related global greenhouse gas emission pathways, in the context of strengthening the global response to the threat of climate change, sustainable development, and efforts to eradicate poverty.* 2018. *https://www.ipcc.ch/sr15/* (accessed 1 August 2022).

56 Andreas Malm, *Fossil Capital: The Rise of Steam Power and the Roots of Global Warming* (London and New York: Verso, 2016), p. 5.

57 Letter from Anna Seward to William Hayley, 6 October 1787. Cited by Donna Coffey in 'Protecting the Botanic Garden: Seward, Darwin, and Coalbrookdale', *Women's Studies* 31/2 (2002), 141–64 (p. 141) and by Sharon Setzer in '"Pond'rous Engines" in "Outraged Groves": The Environmental Argument of Anna Seward's "Colebrook Dale"', *European Romantic Review* 18/1 (2007), 69–82 (p. 69). The close association between letters and poetry is particularly pertinent in the case of Seward's legacy, as she deliberately rewrote letters to form an epistolary autobiography.

58 Trinder, *Making of the Industrial Landscape*, p. 71

59 Trinder, *Making of the Industrial Landscape*, p. 68; Richard Hayman, 'The Shropshire Wrought-Iron Industry *c.*1600–1900: A Study of Technological Change' (unpublished PhD thesis, University of Birmingham, 2003), p. 44. For the date of 1787, see the letter to Hayley cited in Coffey, 'Protecting the Botanic Garden'.

60 'lay', n.4 and n.1, OED; Lichfield District Council, 'About Minster Pool and Walk', *Lichfield Historic Parks*, [n. d.], *http://lichfieldhistoricparks. co.uk/minster-pool-walk/about-minster-pool-and-walk/* (accessed 1 August 2022).

61 Teresa Barnard, *Anna Seward: A Constructed Life, A Critical Biography* (Farnham: Ashgate, 2009), p. 21.

62 Sylvia Bowerbank, 'Seward, Anna [*called* the Swan of Lichfield] (1742–1809)', *Oxford Dictionary of National Biography* (2004).

63 Barnard, *Anna Seward*, p. 5. Speculation about Seward's sexuality has long been fuelled by her admiration of and visits to the 'Ladies of Llangollen' – Eleanor Butler and Sarah Ponsonby.

64 Anna Seward, *Elegy on Captain Cook*, available at *Digital Archives and Pacific Cultures*, *http://pacific.obdurodon.org/CookElegy1780.html*, ll. 17; 36–7 (accessed 1 August 2022).

65 Bridget Orr, '"Maui and Orphic Blood": Cook's Death in Contemporary Maori Poetry, *The Eighteenth Century* 49/2 (2008), 165–79.

66 Barnard, *Anna Seward*, pp. 133; 177–8.

67 John Sargent, *The Mine: A Dramatic Poem*, 2nd edn (London: Cadell, 1788), preface pp. xxii; xvii; xxvii.

68 Anna Seward, *Original Sonnets on Various Subjects; and Odes Paraphrased from Horace* (London: Sael, 1799), p. 49. Digitised at *https:// archive.org* (accessed 1 August 2022).

69 Both Barbauld's and Seward's geniuses find a preceding intertext in Michael Drayton's *Poly-Albion* (1612), whose antediluvian Genius aids the Muse.

70 Seward, 'To Colebrook Dale', *Original Sonnets*, p. 65.

71 Trinder, *Making of the Industrial Landscape*, p. 69.

72 Hayman, The Shropshire Wrought-Iron Industry, p. 27.

73 Melanie Giles, 'Making Metal and Forging Relations: Ironworking in the British Iron Age', *Oxford Journal of Archaeology* 26/4 (2007), 395–413.

74 Todd Borlik, 'Iron Age as Renaissance Anthropocene: Periodization and the Ecology of War in Shakespearean History', *Early Modern Culture* 13 (2018), 115–26.

75 Malcolm McKinnon Dick, 'Discourses for the new industrial world: industrialisation and the education of the public in late eighteenth-century Britain', *History of Education* 37/4 (2008), 567–84, p. 580.

76 Borlik, 'Iron Age as Renaissance Anthropocene', p. 116.

77 Trinder, *Making of the Industrial Landscape*, pp. 72; 88.

78 'Coalbrookdale Museum of Iron', Ironbridge Gorge Museum Trust (2022), *https://www.ironbridge.org.uk/visit/coalbrookdale-museum-of-iron/* (accessed 1 August 2022).

79 Fielding, 'Usurpt by Cyclops', pp. 145; 154.

80 Anna Seward, 'Colebrook Dale', *The Poetical Works of Anna Seward*, ed. Walter Scott, 3 vols (Edinburgh: Ballantyne: 1810), vol. II, pp. 314–19 (pp. 314–15).

81 Dick suggests that Seward may have been 'the first writer to use the word "pollute" to refer to environmental contamination' (pp. 580–1).

82 Emily Eden, *Up the Country: Letters Written to her Sister from the Upper Provinces of India*, new edn. (London: Bentley, 1867), p. 67.

83 See, for instance, the effects on water courses of nineteenth-century gold mining in Australia in Susan Lawrence, Peter Davies and Jodi Turnbull, 'The Archaeology of Anthropocene Rivers: Water Management and Landscape Change in "Gold Rush" Australia', *Antiquity* 90/353 (2016), 1348–1362, and in New Zealand in Alastair Clement et al., 'The Environmental and Geomorphological Impacts of Historical Gold Mining in the Ohinemuri and Waihou River Catchments, Coromandel, New Zealand', *Geomorphology*, 295 (2017), 159–75.

84 Seward, 'Colebrook Dale', pp. 315–16.

85 Coffey, 'Protecting the Botanic Garden', p. 157.

86 Seward, 'Colebrook Dale', p. 318.

87 Dick, 'Discourses for the new industrial world', p. 584.

88 For twenty-first-century examples see, for instance, Alan Weisman, 'Earth Without People', *Discover Magazine*, 6 February 2005, *http://discovermagazine.com/2005/feb/earth-without-people* (accessed 1 August 2022).

89 Seward, 'Colebrook Dale', pp. 318–19.

90 Seward, 'Colebrook Dale', p. 316.

91 Peter Jones, *Industrial Enlightenment: Science, Technology and Culture in Birmingham and the West Midlands, 1760–1820* (Manchester and New York: Manchester University Press, 2008), pp. 26–8.

92 Seward, 'Colebrook Dale', p. 316.

93 Jenny Uglow, *The Lunar Men: The Friends who Made the Future* (London: Faber, 2002), p. 157.

94 Jones, *Industrial Enlightenment*, p. 82.

95 Uglow, *The Lunar Men*, p. 162.

96 Jennifer Tann, 'James Watt (1736–1819)', *Oxford Dictionary of Literary Biography* (2014).

97 Jennifer Tann, 'Matthew Boulton (1728–1809)', *Oxford Dictionary of Literary Biography* (2013).

98 Uglow, *The Lunar Men*, p. xix.

99 Seward, 'Colebrook Dale', p. 316.

100 Seward, 'Colebrook Dale', pp. 316–17.

101 Jones, *Industrial Enlightenment*, p. 14.

102 Seward, 'Colebrook Dale', p. 318.

103 Erasmus Darwin, *The Botanic Garden* (Menston: Scholar Press, 1973), Part I, Third Canto, IX, ll. 330 (p. 141).

104 For details of the Frog Service and Wedgwood's promotion of the canal see Robert Copeland, *Wedgwood Ware* (Botley: Shire, 1995); and Susanna Cole, 'Space into time: English canals and English landscape painting 1760–1835' (unpublished PhD thesis, University of Columbia, 2013).

105 In particular see Uglow, *The Lunar Men*, but it is rare to find Darwin written about without thorough discussion of his social/intellectual network.

106 Uglow, *The Lunar Men*, p. 95 and Desmond King-Hele, *Erasmus Darwin and Evolution* (Sheffield: Stuart Harris, 2014). Erasmus's grandson, Charles, makes no reference to his grandfather's work on evolution in his own more widely-read and referenced work on a theory of evolution.

107 Cited in King-Hele, *Erasmus Darwin and Evolution*, p. 55.

108 On the opposition from Revd Thomas Seward to the implications of this motto, see King-Hele, *Erasmus Darwin and Evolution*, pp. 20–5.

109 Philip K. Wilson, Elizabeth A. Dolan and Malcolm M. Dick (eds), *Anna Seward's Life of Erasmus Darwin* (Studley: Brewin, 2010), p. 95.

110 King-Hele, *Erasmus Darwin and Evolution*, pp. 55–64.

111 Erasmus Darwin, *The Temple of Nature*, ed. Martin Priestman, Canto IV: Of Good and Evil, ll. 430–50. *Romantic Circles* electronic edition, *https://www.rc.umd.edu/editions/darwin_temple/* (accessed 1 August 2022).

112 King-Hele, *Erasmus Darwin and Evolution*, p. 20.

113 Canal & River Trust Instagram feed, 29 November 2018. *https://www.instagram.com/canalrivertrust/?hl=en* (accessed 29 July 2021).

114 William White, *History, Gazetteer, and Directory of Leicestershire* (Sheffield: Robert Leader, 1846), p. 522.

115 Darwin, *Botanic Garden*, Part I, 'Apology', p. vii.

116 Letter from Josiah Wedgwood to John Wedgwood, 11 March 1765. *Letters of Josiah Wedgwood* (transcribed), vol. I, p. 42. Wedgwood Museum and Archive.

117 Uglow, *The Lunar Men*, pp. 109–10.

118 Brian Dolan, *Josiah Wedgwood: Entrepreneur to the Enlightenment* (London: HarperCollins, 2004), pp. 104–5.

119 Dolan, *Josiah Wedgwood*, p. 155.

120 Letter from Josiah Wedgwood to John Wedgwood, 3 April 1765. *Letters of Josiah Wedgwood* (transcribed), vol. I, p. 42.

121 Bentley's Pamphlet on Inland Navigation', *Letters of Josiah Wedgwood* (transcribed), vol. I, pp. 172–202.

122 'Bentley's Pamphlet on Inland Navigation', *Letters of Josiah Wedgwood* (transcribed), vol. I, pp. 172–202.

123 For the origins of Wedgwood investigation into clays and glazes see Dolan, pp. 3–32. Intriguingly, 'the red clays so striking within the Staffordshire landscape came from a geological formation (now called the "Etruria Formation") lying immediately above the coal measures – a formation and clay unique to the English Midlands' (p. 29).

124 Letter from Josiah Wedgwood to Thomas Bentley, 5 January 1766, *Letters of Josiah Wedgwood* (transcribed), vol. I, p. 207; 27 September 1767, vol. II, p. 75.

125 King-Hele, *Erasmus Darwin and Evolution*, pp. 15–16.

126 Letter from Josiah Wedgwood to Thomas Bentley, 8 September 1767, *Letters of Josiah Wedgwood* (transcribed), vol. II, p. 67.

127 Letter from Josiah Wedgwood to Thomas Bentley, 16 January 1768, *Letters of Josiah Wedgwood* (transcribed), vol. II, p. 110; 'fossil', *n.* 2.a., *OED*.

128 Letter from Josiah Wedgwood to Thomas Bentley, February 1768, *Letters of Josiah Wedgwood* (transcribed), vol. II, p. 117. Liz McIvor attributes the coinage of 'strata' to William Smith, sometimes called the 'Father of English Geology'. He, too, made geological discoveries while engaged in canal engineering. In 1791, visiting Coalbrookdale, he noted which other conditions made it possible to predict where a coal seam would be. He also found different types of fossils at different levels of rock. As McIvor points out, canal histories often neglect him, despite his later geological fame. He produced a national geological map of stratification in 1815. See Liz McIvor, *Canals: The Making of a Nation* (London: BBC Books, 2015), pp. 133–40. He followed John Strachey who, Donald Prothero notes, published one of the first ever geological cross sections in order to establish his rights to a coal lease. See Donald R. Prothero, *The Story of*

the Earth in 25 Rocks: Tales of Important Geological Puzzles and the People Who Solved Them (New York: Columbia University Press, 2018), p. 62.

129 Tristram Hunt, *The Radical Potter: Josiah Wedgwood and the Transformation of Britain* (London: Allen Lane, 2021), p. 107.

130 Letter from Josiah Wedgwood to Thomas Bentley, 1 November 1779, *Letters of Josiah Wedgwood* (transcribed), vol. XIII, p. 146.

131 Wedgwood certainly knew Da Costa's work, citing his *History of Fossils* in a piece he wrote for the Royal Society in 1783. See Wedgwood, 'Some experiments upon the ochra friabilis nigro susca of Da Costa, Hist. Foss. p. 102;. and called by the miners of Derbyshire, Black Wadd', *Philosophical Transactions of the Royal Society of London* 73, January 1783, pp. 284–7.

132 Darwin, *The Botanic Garden*, Part I, 'advertisement', p. v.

133 Darwin, *The Botanic Garden*, Part I, Third Canto, IX, ll. 321–44 (p. 140–1)

134 Darwin, *The Botanic Garden*, Part I, Addition to Note XXIII.----COAL, p. 113; Part I, Additional notes, p. 66.

135 Darwin, *The Botanic Garden*, Part I, Third Canto, II, ll. 65–6 (p. 120)

136 Hunt, *The Radical Potter*, p. 140.

137 Part I, Second Canto, VI, ll. 311–20 (pp. 87–8).

138 'First Fleet' appears in inverted commas because it suggests a primacy that the European settlers assumed but, clearly, did not actually hold.

139 For an account of the medallions see Hunt, *The Radical Potter*, p. xv.

140 'Account of the Vignette', *The Voyage of Governor Phillip to Botany Bay* (London: Stockdale, 1789).

141 'Paint up – Aboriginal Dance', *Australian Museum* (2018), *https://australianmuseum.net.au/about/history/exhibitions/body-art/paint-up-aboriginal-dance/* (accessed 1 August 2022).

142 For the ongoing dispossession of Aboriginal peoples in Australia see Emma Fitch and Patricia Easteal, 'Proposed Closures of Remote Australian Aboriginal Communities: Dispossession without Free and Informed Consent and Legal Remedies for Appealing Government Budget Decisions', *Australian Journal of Human Rights* 22/1 (2016), 85–110; Siiri A. Wilson, 'Entitled as Against None: How the Wrongly Decided Croker Island Case Perpetuates Aboriginal Dispossession', *Pacific Rim Law and Policy Journal* 18/1 (2009), 249; Amy Quayle, Christopher C. Sonn and Julie van den Eynde, 'Narrating the Accumulation of Dispossession: Stories of Aboriginal Elders', *Community Psychology in Global Perspective* 2/2 (2016), 79; and Barry Morris, *Protests, Land Rights and Riots: Postcolonial Struggles in Australia in the 1980s* (Oxford: berghahn, 2015).

143 Bruce Pascoe, *Dark Emu: Black Seeds, Agriculture or Accident* (Broome: Magabala, 2014), pp. 21–3, 39; 53–4; 105; 12–13.

144 Erasmus Darwin, 'Visit of "Hope" to Sydney Cove, Near Botany Bay', *Poems of Lichfield and Derby*, ed. Desmond King-Hele and Stuart Harris (Sheffield: Stuart Harris, 2011), p. 32, ll. 4, 5, 7.

145 A. N. Wilson, *The Potter's Hand* (London: Atlantic, 2012), p. 474.

Notes to Chapter 3

1 John Hassell, *Tour of the Grand Junction* (London: n. pub., 1819); Charles Dickens, *Dombey and Son* (London: Bradbury and Evans, 1848), p. 200.

2 Richard Cobden, *England, Ireland, and America* (London: Ridgway, 1835), 3rd edn; Alfred Russel Wallace, *The Wonderful Century* (New York: Dodd, Mead and Company, 1898), p. 3.

3 In fact, even the Duke of Bridgewater was a 'keen promoter' of leisure boating on the canal. See Hugh Malet, *Bridgewater: The Canal Duke, 1736–1803* (Manchester University Press, 1977), p. 111. See Brian Dolan, *Josiah Wedgwood: Entrepreneur to the Enlightenment* (London: HarperCollins, 2004), p. 316 for Wedgwood's trip on Bridgewater's passenger boat.

4 Max Satchell, 'Navigable waterways and the economy of England and Wales: 1600–1835', *Online Historical Atlas of Transport, Urbanization and Economic Development in England and Wales c.1680–1911*, ed. L. Shaw-Taylor, D. Bogart and M. Satchell (2017) *https://www.campop.geog.cam.ac.uk/research/projects/transport/onlineatlas/* (accessed 1 August 2022), p. 35.

5 'Canals And Railways', *The Times*, 12 May 1888, 8, *Times Digital Archive*.

6 'The Destruction of our Canals', *Reynolds's Newspaper*, 4 November 1894. *British Library Newspapers*.

7 'On the Canal', *Household Words*, 11 September 1858, 289–93.

8 Anthony Trollope, *The Kellys and the O'Kellys* (Oxford University Press, 1978), pp. 95–7. I am grateful to Claire Connolly for pointing me towards this reference.

9 George Eliot, *Felix Holt: The Radical*, ed. Lynda Mugglestone (London: Penguin, 1995), p. 3. For more detailed readings of these Victorian canal representations, see my 'Canals in nineteenth-century literary history', in David Turner (ed.), *Transport and its Place in History* (London: Routledge, 2020).

10 Vincent Hughes, 'Through Canal-land in a Canadian Canoe', *Boy's Own Paper*, 7 October 1899, 8.

11 David Ker, 'A Bold Climber or, For an Empire', 7 October 1899, 1–3.

12 For instance, Thomas Collings, 'A B. O. P. Chat with Clement Hill, Australia's Champion Batsman', 14 October 1899, 31–2.

13 Frank Feller, 'Alligator-Shooting in Florida', 14 October 1899, 25; Isabel Suart-Robson, 'A Thousand Days in the Arctic, 21 October 1899, 41–3; 'An Indian Conjuror', 4 November 1899, 78 9; Isabel Suart Robson, 'The Longest Bicycle Ride Ever Attempted', 11 November 1899, 90–1.

14 'Tenting as a Holiday for Boys', 28 October 1899, 61–3.

15 Henry C. Devine, 'Roughing it on the Thames', 11 November 1899, 87–8.

16 Justin D. Livingstone, 'Travels in Fiction: Baker, Stanley, Cameron and the Adventure of African Exploration', *Journal of Victorian Culture* 23/1 (2018), 64–85, pp. 64; 67.

17 Bernard Porter, *The Absent-Minded Imperialists: Empire, Society and Culture in Britain* (Oxford University Press, 2004), p. xii.

18 Ivan Broadhead, 'When things go bump . . . the Tunnel Ghost', *Northamptonshire and Bedfordshire Life*, January 1980. Reproduced at *http://www.blisworth.org.uk/images/Tunnel1982/Ghost/ghost-stories.htm* (accessed 1 August 2022).

19 Hughes, 'Through Canal-land in a Canadian Canoe', *Boy's Own Paper*, 7 October 1899, 10.

20 Dane Kennedy, *The Last Blank Spaces: Exploring Africa and Australia* (Cambridge, MA and London: Harvard University Press, 2013), p. 60.

21 Kennedy, *Last Blank Spaces*, p. 85.

22 The Royal Museums Greenwich have recently drawn attention to the MacGregor items in their collection, including his canoe, the *Rob Roy*, and travel journals. See Katherine Oxley, 'The archive collection of John "Rob Roy" MacGregor', *Royal Museums Greenwich* (2022), *https://www.rmg.co.uk/stories/blog/archive-collection-john-rob-roy-macgregor* (accessed 1 August 2022).

23 Edwin Hodder, *John MacGregor ("Rob Roy")* (London: Hodder, 1894), pp. 209–11; preface; p. 38. In a letter from the Red Sea in November 1868, MacGregor also recounts meeting 'a Mr. Stanley at the Suez Hotel', who was very enthusiastic about the Rob Roy. MacGregor wrote Stanley a letter of introduction to Livingstone – and the rest is history (Hodder, *John MacGregor*, pp. 317–18). Incidentally, Stanley was one of the very few 'contemporary examples of self-made men' to make it into *Boy's Own Magazine*, and even then with a highly censored version of his early life. Elizabeth Penner, 'Masculinity, Morality, and National Identity in the *Boy's Own Paper*, 1879–1913' (unpublished PhD thesis, De Montfort University, 2016), p. 113.

24 Hodder, *John MacGregor*, p. 278.

25 John MacGregor, *A Thousand Miles in the Rob Roy Canoe on Rivers and Lakes of Europe*, 7th edn (Boston, MA: Roberts, 1871), p. 17.

26 Hodder, *John MacGregor*, pp. 309–10.
27 Glen Balfour-Paul, 'Britain's Informal Empire in the Middle East' in Judith Brown (ed.), *The Oxford History of the British Empire* (Oxford University Press, 2001), pp. 490–514.
28 'A Stirring Life-Story', *Boy's Own Paper*, 25 January 1879.
29 Penner, 'Masculinity, Morality, and National Identity', p. 185.
30 Robert Louis Stevenson, *An Inland Voyage* (London: Chatto and Windus, 1913), pp. 16–23; 73.
31 [A. T. Schofield], *The Waterway to London, as explored in the "Wanderer" and "Ranger," with Sail, Paddle, and Oar, in a voyage on the Mersey, Perry, Severn, and Thames, and several canals* (London: Simkin Marshall, 1869), preface, pp. 19; 45.
32 Richard Fairhurst, 'Pioneer Paddlers', *Waterways World*, December 2016, 48–51.
33 James Stephen Jeans, *Waterways and Water Transport in Different Countries* (London: Spon, 1890), p. viii.
34 I have taken this phrasing from Graham Greene's *Journey Without Maps* (London: Vintage, 2006), first published in 1936 and which detailed his journey across Liberia the previous year.
35 Hughes, 'Through Canal-land in a Canadian Canoe', *Boy's Own Paper*, 7 October 1899, 10.
36 [Sara Jeannette Duncan]/V. Cecil Cotes, *Two Girls on a Barge* (London: Chatto and Windus, 1891), pp. 83–8.
37 Hughes, 'Through Canal-land in a Canadian Canoe', *Boy's Own Paper*, 7 October 1899, 8.
38 Hughes, 'Through Canal-land in a Canadian Canoe', *Boy's Own Paper*, 7 October 1899, 10; 14 October 1899, 28; 21 October 1899, 40.
39 Shino Konishi, Maria Nugent, Tiffany Shellam, 'Exploration archives and indigenous histories: an introduction', *Indigenous Intermediaries: New Perspectives on Exploration Archives* (Canberra: ANU Press, 2015), pp. 1–10.
40 John MacGregor, *The Rob Roy on the Jordan* (London: Murray, 1869), p. 179.
41 7 October 1899, p. 10.
42 Cited by Tobias Menely and Jesse Oak Taylor in *Anthropocene Reading: Literary History in Geologic Times* (University Park, PA: Pennsylvania State University Press, 2017), p. 5.
43 Elizabeth Carolyn Miller, *Extraction Ecologies and the Literature of the Long Exhaustion* (Princeton and Oxford: Princeton University Press, 2021), p. 2.
44 From W. E. B. Du Bois, 'The Place, The People', reflecting on a visit to Liberia. Cited in Walter Gordon, 'International Powers: Energy and

Progress in *Dark Princess* and *Black Empire*', *American Quarterly* 72/3 (2020), 581–602.

45   21 October 1899, 39–40.

46   David Livingstone, *Missionary Travels and Researches in South Africa* (London: Murray, 1857), p. 271.

47   Miller, *Extraction Ecologies*, p. 56.

48   Hughes is not alone in producing this type of imperialist vision on British waterways. B. P. Stockman, author of *A Trip Through the Caledonian Canal* (1861), hoped to admire 'romantic' Scottish scenery with friends and relations aboard a rather different craft than the canoe: the cutter, *Whipper*, accompanied by another vessel, the *Snapper*. Locals 'filled with wonder' waited at a pierhead to see the party land: 'little urchins with heads like mops, ragged and short kilts and bare legs, standing with their mouths as well as their eyes wide open. . . . There were many of the children of larger growth in almost aboriginal coverings'. The narrator adds that these figures demonstrated an attractive guilelessness. They are presented as innocent, amazed natives. Stockman thus continues a long tradition of representing Scottish Highlanders as non-white others, the kind of discourse that had legitimised the Highland Clearances, often seen from a postcolonial perspective in parallel with colonial policies beyond the British Isles. *A Trip Through the Caledonian Canal* (London: n. pub., 1861), p. 97. For the authorship of this work see Mick Vedmore, 'A Rare Early Voyage', *Old Waterway Books*, 13 December 2016, *http://canalbookcollector.blogspot.com/2016/12/a-rare-early-voyage.html* (accessed 1 August 2022). On the link between the representation of Highlanders and Clearances see Colin Calloway's *White People, Indians and Highlanders: Tribal Peoples and Colonial Encounters in Scotland and America* (Oxford University Press, 2008).

49   Alan Davies, *The Wigan Coalfield* (Stroud: Tempus, 2000), p. 7.

50   John Hannavy, *Wigan: History and Guide* (Stroud: Tempus, 2003), pp. 61–4.

51   Davies, *The Wigan Coalfield*, p. 116.

52   Davies, *The Wigan Coalfield*, p. 9.

53   'The Crisis in the Coal Trade', *Leeds Mercury*, 5 March 1890.

54   Davies, *The Wigan Coalfield*, p. 19. National Archives, *Currency Converter: 1270–2017*, *https://www.nationalarchives.gov.uk/currency-converter/* (accessed 1 August 2022).

55   'Sending Coal to Wigan', *Hull Daily Mail*, 1 November 1893.

56   'Miners' Strike Near Wigan', *Sheffield Daily Telegraph*, 23 August 1895, 2.

57   'Foreign Intelligence', *John Bull*, 13 November 1886, 735.

58   'Another Great African Waterway', *The Times*, 20 July 1885, 8.

59 MacGregor, *The Rob Roy on the Jordan*, p. 254.

60 Andrew Ure, *The Cotton Manufacture of Great Britain* (London: Charles Knight, 1836), 2 vols, II, p. 397.

61 Colin Luke (dir.), *The Black Safari* (BBC, 1972).

62 Andy Tidy, 'John Corbett the Salt Tycoon', *NarrowBoat*, Autumn 2019.

63 [Sara Jeannette Duncan], *Two Girls on a Barge* (London: Chatto and Windus), p. 21.

64 7 October 1899, p. 10.

65 The attribution of the authorship of *Two Girls on a Barge* is contested (see Karyn Huenemann, 'The Authorship of *Two Girls on a Barge* (1891), Reassessed', *Papers of the Bibliographical Society of Canada* 58 (2021), 145–53) but my reading assumes that Duncan was, indeed, the author. Chatto and Windus were clearly keen, via their marketing, for purchasers to assume that they would hear the same authorial voice and experience the same kind of story in Duncan's *An American Girl in London*, in *A Social Departure* and in *Two Girls on a Barge*. In addition, there are numerous examples of near-identical phrasing and recurring themes across these works. All three focus not just on strong-willed women but on female friendship as a source of strength when departing from the expected role of their sex in nineteenth-century British and imperial society. If Duncan did *not* write *Two Girls*, then whoever did accomplished a very successful pastiche.

66 Germaine Warkentin, 'Duncan [married name Cotes], Sara Jeannette (1861–1922), novelist and journalist', in *Oxford Dictionary of National Biography* (Oxford University Press, 2004).

67 Marian Fowler, *Redney: A Life of Sara Jeannette Duncan* (Toronto: Anansi, 1983), p. 32.

68 Fowler, *Redney*, pp. 84–5.

69 See Faye Hammill, 'Round the World without a Man: Feminism and Decadence in Sara Jeannette Duncan's *A Social Departure*', *The Yearbook of English Studies* 34 (2004), 112–26 for discussion of this latter work. The 'S. D.' of the title's initials, as well as the 'S.J.D.' in the novel indicate a very deliberate autobiographical connection.

70 Andy Tidy, 'John Corbett the Salt Tycoon'.

71 Information provided by email by Chris M. Jones (History Editor of *NarrowBoat* magazine) and Cath Turpin, former editor of *Waterways Journal*.

72 Misao Dean, *A Different Point of View: Sara Jeannette Duncan* (Montreal: McGill-Queen's University Press, 1991), p. 66.

73 Lena Wånggren, *Gender, Technology and the New Woman* (Edinburgh: Edinburgh University Press, 2017), p. 2.

74 Wånggren, *Gender, Technology and the New Woman*, p. 2.

75 Duncan did go on to write more explicitly New Woman fiction, such as *A Daughter of To-Day* (1894).

76 Sara Jeannette Duncan/Mrs Everard Cotes, *The Imperialist* (London: Archibald Constable, 1904), p. 375.

77 'On the Canal: First Stage', *Household Words*, September 25, 1858, 354–60.

78 See my *The Gypsy Woman: Representation in Literature and Visual Culture* (London: I. B. Tauris, 2018) and 'Mobilising the Imperial Uncanny: Nineteenth-Century Textual Attitudes to Travelling Romani People, Canal-Boat People, Showpeople and Hop-Pickers in Britain', *Nineteenth-Century Contexts*, 37/4 (2015), 359–75 for a further exploration of Romani people framed by ideologies of Empire. At this time, the recognised spelling was 'Gypsy' (and the capital G is important today because the word denotes a legally recognised ethnic group) but George Smith, discussed in detail shortly, insisted on using the older spelling 'gipsy', and Duncan seems to follow his lead. When I am referring to the figure in the texts I replicate their spelling; when I refer to the actual group of people with a long history in Britain I refer to 'Romani people'. Many Romani people today consider 'Gypsy' to be a racial slur.

79 Duncan, *The Imperialist*, p. 37.

80 As Duncan wrote, the framing of bargees as 'water gipsies' was also broadly available as a trope in fiction of the period. See, for instance, L. T. Meade, *Water Gipsies: A Story of Canal Life in England* (London: Shaw, 1883).

81 Amos Reade, *Life in the Cut* (London: Swann, Sonnenschein, Lowry, 1888).

82 George Smith, *Canal Adventures by Moonlight* (London: Hodder and Stoughton, 1881), pp. 57; 111; 62; 74; 97–9.

83 There was already a tradition of visiting Romani camps, either for research by members of the Gypsy Lore Society, or for entertainment. For more detail on the latter, see Jodie Matthews and Ken Lee, 'Romani Rebel Writing: George "Lazzy" Smith's Entrepreneurial Auto-Exoticism', in Lauren O'Hagan (ed.), *Rebellious Writing: Contesting Marginalisation in Edwardian Britain* (Peter Lang, 2020).

84 Huenemann, 'The Authorship of *Two Girls on a Barge* Reassessed'.

85 See Deborah Epstein Nord, *Gypsies and the British Imagination, 1807–1930* (New York: Columbia University Press, 2006), pp. 126–7.

86 L. T. C Rolt, *Narrow Boat* (Stroud: The History Press, 2014), p. 54.

87 Jules Gehrke, 'Countryside, Recreation, and the Transformation of Canals in Britain in the Mid-Twentieth Century', *Journal of Tourism History* 11/2 (2019), 167–86 (p. 177).

88 Rolt, *Narrow Boat*, p. 11. Thurston's *The Flower of Gloster* (1911) is one of the most well-known examples of canal literature – and is famous

for a particular generation because of its loose Granada TV adaptation in 1967.

89 Patrick Brantlinger, *Dark Vanishings: Discourse on the Extinction of Primitive Races, 1800–1930* (Ithaca, NY and London: Cornell University Press, 2003), pp. 1–3. Brantlinger's elaboration of extinction discourse builds on James Clifford's work on 'salvage' ethnography.

90 On the origin, elaboration and political deployment of the 'noble savage', see Stelio Cro, *Noble savage: Allegory of Freedom* (Waterloo, ON: Wilfrid Laurier University Press, 1990).

91 Today, in public policy, the term 'Traveller' includes 'Bargees' or itinerant boat dwellers. There is ongoing tension between the state's desire to regulate travelling life out of existence, a broader need to recognise and outlaw racism, and the social imperative to protect the rights of various minorities. These minorities may find political expediency in being grouped together for certain purposes, but blunt definitions used in law and official policy often fail to respect cultural distinctiveness.

92 Brantlinger, *Dark Vanishings*, p. 191.

93 Regenia Gagnier, 'Cultural Philanthropy, Gypsies, and Interdisciplinary Scholars: Dream of a Common Language', *19: Interdisciplinary Studies in the Long Nineteenth Century*, 1 (2005), p. 9.

94 Gagnier, p. 12.

Notes to Chapter 4

1 Emma Smith, *Maidens' Trip* (London: Bloomsbury, 2011), p. 73.

2 Smith, *Maidens' Trip*, pp. 146–7.

3 'Women want canal work', *Hull Daily Mail*, 2 April 1941. *British Library Newspapers*.

4 Imperial War Museum sound collection, Lyn E. Smith interviewing Margaret Cornish Ridout, 18 April 2002. Catalogue number 23089, reel 7. *https://www.iwm.org.uk/collections/item/object/80021875* (accessed 1 August 2022).

5 Eily Gayford, *The Amateur Boatwomen* (Harrow: Belmont, 2008), p. 115.

6 Margaret Mayhew, *The Boat Girls* (London: Bantam, 2007).

7 Milly Adams, *The Waterways Girls* (London: Arrow, 2017), p. 103.

8 Kim Wilkins, Beth Driscoll and Lisa Fletcher, *Genre Worlds: Popular Fiction and Twenty-first Century Book Culture* (Amherst and Boston: University of Massachusetts Press, 2022), pp. 167–9.

9 United Nations, 'Water and Gender', *https://www.unwater.org/water-facts/gender/* (accessed 23 March 2021).

10 Barbara Hately-Broad and Bob Moore, 'Idle Women: Challenging Gender Stereotypes on Britain's Inland Waterways During the Second World War', in Maggie Andrews and Janis Lomas (eds), *The Home Front in Britain: Images, Myths and Forgotten Experiences since 1914* (Houndmills: Palgrave, 2014), pp. 201–16 (p. 203).

11 'Canals and the War Effort', *Tamworth Herald*, 2 August 1941. *British Library Newspapers.*

12 Phil Goodman, '"Patriotic Femininity": Women's Morals and Men's Morale During the Second World War', *Gender and History* 10/2 (1998), 278–93.

13 Nancy Ridgway, *Memories of a Wartime Canal Boatwoman*, ed. Mike Clarke and Timothy Peters (Ellesmere Port: National Waterways Museum, 2014), p. 11; Emma Smith, *As Green as Grass* (London: Bloomsbury, 2014), p. 154.

14 Susan Woolfitt, *Idle Women* (Harrow: Belmont, 2001), p. 9.

15 Margaret Cornish, *Troubled Waters: Memoirs of a Canal Boatwoman* (London: Robert Hale, 1987), p. 13; Imperial War Museum sound collection, Lyn E. Smith interviewing Margaret Cornish Ridout, 18 April 2002. Catalogue number 23089, reel 2. *https://www.iwm.org.uk/collections/item/object/80021875* (accessed 1 August 2022).

16 Molly Green, *A Sister's War* (London: Avon, 2021).

17 Ridgway, *Memories of a Canal Boatwoman*, p. 37.

18 Smith, *As Green as Grass*, p. 267.

19 Cornish, *Troubled Waters*, p. 85.

20 Emma Smith, *Maidens' Trip*, p. 66.

21 Lauren Berlant, *The Female Complaint: The Unfinished Business of Sentimentality in American Culture* (Durham, NC: Duke University Press, 2008) *ProQuest Ebook*, pp. vii, x, 2.

22 Smith, *Maidens' Trip*, p. 66.

23 Imperial War Museum sound collection, Lyn E. Smith interviewing Margaret Cornish Ridout, 18 April 2002. Catalogue number 23089, reel 7. *https://www.iwm.org.uk/collections/item/object/80021875* (accessed 1 August 2022).

24 Smith, *As Green as Grass*, p. 172.

25 Gayford, *Amateur Boatwomen*, p. 52.

26 Milly Adams, *Hope on the Waterways* (London: Arrow, 2018), p. 22; *Waterways Girls*, p. 115.

27 Gayford, *Amateur Boatwomen*, pp. 106; 22.

28 Woolfitt, *Idle Women*, p. 50.

29 Gayford, *Amateur Boatwomen*, p. 44; 111.

30 Veronica Horwell, 'Sonia Rolt obituary', *Guardian*, 31 October 2014.

31 Cornish, *Troubled Waters*, p. 179.

32 Tim Coghlan, 'The Canal Adonis and the Idle Woman', *Canals, Rivers +
    Boats* (April 2013), pp. 40–51. The lavishly illustrated microhistories in
    this publication are, unfortunately, hard to find in sequence. This one is
    at *https://braunstonmarina.co.uk/wp-content/uploads/Geroge-S-Part-1.
    pdf* (accessed 1 August 2022).
33 Gayford, *Amateur Boatwomen*, p. 59.
34 Smith, *Maidens' Trip*, p. 2; *As Green as Grass*, p. 159.
35 Adams, *Waterways Girls*, p. 167.
36 Christine V. Wood, 'Tender Heroes and Twilight Lovers: Re-Reading the
    Romance in Mass-Market Pulp Novels, 1950–1965', *Journal of Lesbian
    Studies* 18/4 (2014), 372–92; Rosie Archer, *The Narrowboat Girls* (Lon-
    don: Quercus, 2018), p. 104; Mayhew, *Boat Girls*, p. 424.
37 Adams, *Hope on the Waterways*, pp. 447; 479.
38 Smith, *Maidens' Trip*, pp. 97; 193; 219.
39 Smith, *As Green as Grass*, p. 191; *Maidens' Trip*, p. 108; Adams, *Water-
    ways Girls*, p. 296.
40 Archer, *The Narrowboat Girls*, pp. 33; 364.
41 '1 Girl in 3 Fits a Barge: The Hatchway Decides', *The Daily Mail*, 15 April
    1944, 3. *Daily Mail Historical Archive*, Gale.
42 Ridgway, *Memories of a Wartime Canal Boatwoman*, p. 37.
43 Adams, *Waterways Girls*, p. 453; *Hope on the Waterways*, p. 475.
44 Kate McNicholas Smith and Imogen Tyler, 'Lesbian Brides: Post-queer
    Popular Culture', *Feminist Media Studies*, 17/3 (2017), 315–31 (pp. 316–
    18; 323; 326).
45 Adams, *Waterways Girls*, pp. 315; 362.
46 Woolfitt, *Idle Women*, p. 82
47 Milly Adams, *Love on the Waterways* (London: Arrow, 2018), pp. 208–9.
48 Smith, *Maidens' Trip*, pp. 128–9.
49 Woolfitt, *Idle Women*, p. 204.
50 Gayford, *Amateur Boatwomen*, pp. 75; 107; Smith, *Maidens' Trip*,
    p. 97.
51 Woolfitt, *Idle Women*, p. 78.
52 Jamie Linton, *What is Water? The History of a Modern Abstraction* (Van-
    couver and Toronto: UBC Press, 2010), p. 77.
53 Smith, *Maidens' Trip*, p. 2. In another intriguing historical loop, Erasmus
    Darwin, discussed in Chapter 2, invented a flushing toilet, as detailed in
    his Commonplace Book.
54 Adams, *Waterways Girls*, p. 22.
55 Adams, *Waterways Girls*, p. 210.
56 Smith, *Maidens' Trip*, p. 130.
57 Rahul Bhattacharya, *The Sly Company of People Who Care* (London:
    Picador, 2011), p. 6.

58 Adams, *Waterways Girls*, p. 111.

59 Adams, *Love on the Waterways*, pp. 3–4.

60 Adams, *Hope on the Waterways*, p. 84.

61 Cornish, *Troubled Waters*, pp. 46; 155.

62 Antarmike, Canalworld Discussion Forum, 11 August 2012.

63 J. Hurstfield, *The Control of Raw Materials* (London: HMSO, 1953), p. 106.

64 Adams, *Hope on the Waterways*, p. 309.

65 Other cargoes can be explored for their historical connections and contemporary resonance. For instance Woolfitt and her crewmates deliver a load to the Celotex factory at Alperton. This name calls out to the reader in the twenty-first century because the firm made insulation material that contributed to the deadliest fire in the UK since the Second World War, at Grenfall Tower in London.

66 Matthew Evenden, 'Aluminum, Commodity Chains, and the Environmental History of the Second World War', *Environmental History* 16/1 (2011), 69–93 (p. 72).

67 Robin S. Gendron, Mats Ingulstad, Espen Storli (eds), *Aluminum Ore: The Political Economy of the Global Bauxite Industry* (Vancouver and Toronto: UBC Press, 2013).

68 Alvin O. Thompson, 'Symbolic Legacies of Slavery in Guyana', *New West Indian Guide* 80/3–4 (2006), 191–220 (pp. 194–5).

69 Ruzbeh Babaee, 'An Interview with David Dabydeen on Literature and Politics', *International Journal of Comparative Literature and Translation Studies* 4/3 (2016), 73–5.

70 Andrew Perchard, '"Of the Highest Imperial Importance": British Strategic Priorities and the Politics of Colonial Bauxite, ca. 1916–1958', in Gendron et al. (eds), *Aluminum Ore*, pp. 53–78 (p. 54).

71 Cornish, *Troubled Waters*, p. 127.

72 Gayford, *The Amateur Boatwomen*, p. 45.

73 Evenden, 'Aluminum, Commodity Chains and the Environmental History of the Second World War', p. 73.

74 Perchard, 'Of the Highest Imperial Importance', pp. 60–3.

75 Raymond Dumett, 'Africa's Strategic Minerals During the Second World War', *Journal of African History* 26 (1985), 381–408.

76 Martin Gutmann, 'The Nature of Total War: Grasping the Global Environmental Dimensions of World War II', *History Compass* 13/5 (2015), 251–61 (p. 251).

77 Evenden, 'Aluminum, Commodity Chains and the Environmental History of the Second World War', p. 84.

78 Perchard, 'Of the Highest Imperial Importance', p. 65.

79 Hurstfield, *The Control of Raw Materials*, p. 243.

80 Evenden, 'Aluminum, Commodity Chains and the Environmental History of the Second World War', p. 73.

81 Maurice St Pierre, 'Race, the Political Factor and the Nationalization of the Demerara Bauxite Company, Guyana', *Social and Economic Studies* 24/4 (1975), 481–503 (p. 498).

82 Gendron et al., *Aluminum Ore*, p. 13.

83 Á. D. Anton et al., 'Geochemical recovery of the Torna-Marcal river system after the Ajka red mud spill, Hungary', *Environmental Science: Processes and Impacts* 16 (2014), 2677–85.

84 Gendron et al., *Aluminum Ore*, p. 14.

85 Evenden, 'Aluminum, Commodity Chains and the Environmental History of the Second World War', p. 83.

86 Gayford, *Amateur Boatwomen*, p. 67.

87 Smith, *Maidens' Trip*, pp. 52; 70.

88 Smith, *Maidens' Trip*, p. 96.

89 Beyond the *landscape* of other places, one might examine the texts' representation of *people* from beyond Britain, especially at a time when Britain was becoming more ethnically diverse than it ever had been before, as Wendy Webster points out in *Mixing It* (Oxford University Press, 2018). The treatment of race is clumsy to the twenty-first-century reader in some of the autobiographical works, with racist epithets left unedited even in recent editions.

90 Smith, *Maidens' Trip*, p. 160.

91 David Dabydeen, *Our Lady of Demerara* (Leeds: Peepal Tree, 2008), p. 7.

92 Shivani Sivagurunathan, 'A "Coolitudian" Caribbean Text: The Trajectory of Renewal in David Dabydeen's *Our Lady of Demerara*', in D. A. Dunkley (ed.), *Readings in Caribbean History and Culture* (Lanham, ML: Lexington, 2011), pp. 167–82 (p. 169).

93 Elizabeth Jackson, 'Voyeurism or Social Criticism? Women and Sexuality in David Dabydeen's *The Intended, The Counting House* and *Our Lady of Demerara*', *Women: A Cultural Review* 26/4 (2015), 427–42 (pp. 428; 432).

94 Smith, *As Green as Grass*, p. 174.

95 Smith, *As Green as Grass*, p. 174.

96 Smith, *Maidens' Trip*, p. 56.

Notes to Chapter 5

1 John Thorpe, 'Ice – Just a Memory?' *Waterways World*, January 2003, 52–3.

2 Jos Smith, 'An Archipelagic Literature: Re-Framing "The New Nature Writing"', *Green Letters* 17/1 (2013), 5–15.

3 Joe Moran, 'A Cultural History of the New Nature Writing', *Literature and History* 23/1 (2014), 49–63 (p. 50).

4 Phil Hubbard and Eleanor Wilkinson, 'Walking a Lonely Path: Gender, Landscape and "New Nature Writing"', *Cultural Geographies* 26/2 (2019), 253–61 (pp. 254; 258); Kathleen Jamie, 'A Lone Enraptured Male', *London Review of Books* 30/5 (2008).

5 Alys Fowler, *Hidden Nature: A Voyage of Discovery* (London: Hodder and Stoughton, 2017), p. 24.

6 Kate Oakley, Jonathan Ward and Ian Christie, 'Engaging the Imagination: "New Nature Writing", Collective Politics and the Environmental Crisis', *Environmental Values* 27/6 (2018), 687–705, online with different pagination at *https://eprints.whiterose.ac.uk/121524* (accessed 1 August 2022) (p. 8).

7 Oakley, Ward and Christie, 'Engaging the imagination', p. 10.

8 Tim Edensor, *Industrial Ruins: Space, Aesthetics and Materiality* (Oxford: Berg, 2005), p. 14.

9 Lee Horsley, *The Noir Thriller* (Houndmills: Palgrave, 2001), p. 8.

10 Timothy Morton, *Dark Ecology: For a Logic of Future Coexistence* (New York: Columbia University Press, 2016). *ProQuest Ebook*, p. 9.

11 See, for instance, Jo Lindsay Walton and Samantha Walton 'Introduction to *Green Letters*: Crime Fiction and Ecology', *Green Letters* 22/1 (2018), 2–6.

12 Lucas Hollister, 'The Green and the Black: Ecological Awareness and the Darkness of Noir', *PMLA* 134/5 (2019), 1012–27 (p. 1013).

13 Harry Pitt Scott, 'Offshore Mysteries, Narrative Infrastructure: Oil, Noir, and the World-Ocean', *Humanities* 9/3 (2020), p. 4.

14 Laura Roberts, 'Taking up space: Community, belonging and gender among itinerant boat-dwellers on London's waterways', *Anthropological Notebooks* 25/2 (2019), 57–69 (p. 61); Fowler, *Hidden Nature*, p. 27.

15 Fowler, *Hidden Nature*, pp. 29; 137–8.

16 Danie Couchman, *Afloat* (London: Quadrille, 2019), Kindle Edition, p. 93.

17 Helen Babbs, *Adrift: A Secret Life of London's Waterways* (London: Icon, 2016), p. 151.

18 Margaret Mayhew, *The Boat Girls* (London: Bantam, 2007), pp. 66–9.

19 Julian Dutton, *The Water Gypsies: A History of Life on Britain's Rivers and Canals* (Cheltenham: The History Press, 2021). Couchman, too, makes much of the Gypsy ancestry of her boat's previous owner's partner, and says she feels an affinity with 'gypsies and travellers' (Couchman, *Afloat*, p. 16).

20 Fowler, *Hidden Nature*, p. 139.
21 Richard Mabey, *The Unofficial Countryside* (Toller Fratrum: Little Toller Books, 2010), p. 78.
22 Iain Sinclair, 'Introduction' to Mabey, *The Unofficial Countryside*, pp. 9–10.
23 Graham Huggan, 'Back to the future: the "new nature writing", ecological boredom, and the recall of the wild', *Prose Studies* 38/2 (2016), 152–71 (p. 157).
24 Joe Minihane, 'Anatomy of a green riverbank', *Waterfront* 10 (2019), p. 8.
25 Paul Farley and Michael Symmons Roberts, *Edgelands: Journeys into England's True Wilderness* (London: Vintage, 2012), pp. 5; 118.
26 Babbs, *Adrift*, p. 243.
27 Benjamin O. L. Bowles, Maarja Kaaristo, Nataša Rogelja Caf, 'Dwelling on and with water – materialities, (im)mobilities and meanings', *Anthropological Notebooks* 25/2 (2019), 5–12.
28 Babbs, *Adrift*, p. 22. Babbs refers frequently to Mabey, but I would argue that her poetic images owe more to Ted Hughes.
29 Babbs, *Adrift*, p. 266. Couchman makes the opposite decision: when a permanent mooring becomes available she 'grabbed it' (*Afloat*, p. 148).
30 Benjamin O. L. Bowles, 'Dwelling, Pollution and the Rhetorical Creation of "Nature" on Inland Waterways', in Chryssanthi Papadopoulou (ed.), *The Culture of Ships and Maritime Narratives* (Routledge, 2019), pp. 77–93 (p. 83).
31 Bowles, Kaaristo and Caf, 'Dwelling on and with Water', pp. 5–12.
32 Babbs, *Adrift*, p. 70. See R. Scerbo et al., 'Lichen (Xanthoria parietina) biomonitoring of trace element contamination and air quality assessment in Pisa Province (Tuscany, Italy)', *Science of The Total Environment* 286/1–3 (2002), 27–40.
33 British Lichen Society, *Lichenicolous fungi occurring on* Xanthoria parietina *in the United Kingdom* (London, 2020), *https://www.britishlichensociety.org.uk/sites/www.britishlichensociety.org.uk/files/Guide%20-%20Xanthoria%20parietina.pdf* (accessed 1 August 2022).
34 Babbs, *Adrift*, p. 75.
35 Anthony Carter, 'Dwale: an anaesthetic from old England', *BMJ* 319/1623 (1999), doi:10.1136/bmj.319.7225.1623.
36 Ryan J. Huxtable, 'On the nature of Shakespeare's cursed hebona', *Perspectives in Biology and Medicine* 36/2 (1993), 262–80.
37 Fowler, *Hidden Nature*, p. 223.
38 Hollister, 'The Green and the Black', p. 1021.
39 Fowler, *Hidden Nature*, p. 154.
40 Kerry Hadley-Pryce, *Gamble* (Cromer: Salt, 2018), p. 34.
41 Hadley-Pryce, *Gamble*, p. 35.

42 Elizabeth Jane Howard, *Three Miles Up and Other Strange Stories* (Leyburn: Tartarus, 2003).

43 Stephen Booth, *Drowned Lives* (London: Sphere, 2020), p. 393.

44 Isabel Costello, 'Writers on Location – Kerry Hadley-Pryce on the Black Country', *The Literary Sofa*, 19 June 2018, *https://literarysofa.com/2018/06/19/5924/* (accessed 1 August 2022).

45 Barrie Trinder, *The Making of the Industrial Landscape* (London: Dent, 1982), pp. 4; 103.

46 Hadley-Pryce, *Gamble*, p. 4.

47 Andy Griffee, *Canal Pushers* (Leominster: Orphans, 2019), p. 336.

48 William Engdahl, *Century of War: Anglo-American Oil Politics and the New World Order* (London: Pluto Press, 2004) *ProQuest Ebook*, p. 248.

49 'Corporations, national security and war profiteering – the great game: Oil and Afghanistan', *Multinational Monitor, 22* (2001), 20–21; Bülent Gökay, 'Oil, war and geopolitics from Kosovo to Afghanistan', *Journal of Southern Europe and the Balkans*, 4/1 (2002), 5–13.

50 Engdahl, *Century of War*, p. 253.

51 Faith Martin, *Murder on the Oxford Canal* (London: Joffe, 2020), p. 5.

52 Maanvi Singh, 'American west stuck in cycle of "heat, drought and fire", experts warn', *The Guardian*, 13 July 2021.

53 Oliver Milman, 'Severe drought threatens Hoover dam reservoir – and water for US west', *The Guardian*, 13 July 2021.

54 Hadley-Pryce, *Gamble*, p. 5.

Notes to Chapter 6

1 Imre Szeman, 'Conjectures on world energy literature: Or, what is petroculture?', *Journal of Postcolonial Writing* 53/3 (2017), 277–88 (p. 277).

2 Graeme Macdonald, 'Research Note: The Resources of Fiction', *Reviews in Cultural Theory* 4/2 (2013), 1–24 (p. 6).

3 Donald R. Prothero, *The Story of the Earth in 25 Rocks: Tales of Important Geological Puzzles and the People Who Solved Them* (New York: Columbia University Press, 2018), p. 57.

4 Macdonald, 'Research Note', p. 4.

5 Darwin, *The Botanic Garden* (Menston: Scholar Press, 1973), part 1, Additional notes, p. 60.

6 Emma Smith, 'Foreword', to Eily Gayford, *The Amateur Boatwomen* (Harrow: Belmont, 2008).

7 Szeman, 'Conjectures on world energy literature', p. 279.

8 Ralph O'Connor, 'Hyena-Hunting And Byron-Bashing In The Old North: William Buckland, Geological Verse And The Radical Threat', in Ben

Marsden, Hazel Hutchison, Ralph O'Connor (eds), *Uncommon Contexts: Encounters between Science and Literature, 1800–1914* (Pittsburgh: University of Pittsburgh Press, 2016), pp. 55–82 (p. 72).

9 Prothero, *Story of the Earth in 25 Rocks*, p. 62.

10 Jasper Winn, *Water Ways: A Thousand Miles Along Britain's Canals* (London: Profile, 2018), p. 266.

11 Gideon Mantell, *The Wonders of Geology* (London: Relfe and Fletcher, 1838), 2 vols, I, p. 201. Digitised at *https://www.biodiversitylibrary.org/item/257307* (accessed 1 August 2022).

12 Letter from Josiah Wedgwood to Thomas Bentley, 1 November 1779, *Letters of Josiah Wedgwood* (transcribed), vol. XIII, p. 146.

13 Derek Gregory cited in Jamie Linton, *What is Water? The History of a Modern Abstraction* (Vancouver and Toronto: UBC Press, 2010), p. 14.

14 Jane Costlow, Yrjö Haila and Arja Rosenholm (eds), *Water in Social Imagination: from Technological Optimism to Contemporary Environmentalism* (Leiden and Boston: Brill Rodopi, 2017).

15 Nancy Campbell, 'The Short Story of a Long Paddle on the Leeds and Liverpool Canal', *Navigations* (Glenrothes: Happenstance, 2020), p. 6.

16 A. N. Wilson, *The Potter's Hand* (London: Atlantic, 2012), pp. 125; 140; 297.

17 Bruno Latour, *Reassembling the Social: An Introduction to Actor-Network-Theory* (Oxford University Press, 2005), pp. 128–33.

18 Margaret Cornish, *Troubled Waters: Memoirs of a Canal Boatwoman* (London: Robert Hale, 1987), p. 191.

BIBLIOGRAPHY

'1 Girl in 3 Fits a Barge: The Hatchway Decides', *The Daily Mail*, 15 April 1944.

'About Minster Pool and Walk', *Lichfield Historic Parks*, [n. d.], *http://lichfieldhistoricparks.co.uk/minster-pool-walk/about-minster-pool-and-walk/* (accessed 1 August 2022).

'Account of the Duke of Bridgewater's Navigation across the Irwell', *The Oxford Magazine*, June 1771.

'Account of the Vignette', *The Voyage of Governor Phillip to Botany Bay* (London: Stockdale, 1789).

'Another Great African Waterway', *The Times*, 20 July 1885.

'Canals And Railways', *The Times*, 12 May 1888.

'Canals and the War Effort', *Tamworth Herald*, 2 August 1941.

'Coalbrookdale Museum of Iron', Ironbridge Gorge Museum Trust (2022), *https://www.ironbridge.org.uk/visit/coalbrookdale-museum-of-iron/* (accessed 1 August 2022).

'Corporations, national security and war profiteering–the great game: Oil and Afghanistan', *Multinational Monitor, 22* (2001), 20–21.

'The Crisis in the Coal Trade', *Leeds Mercury*, 5 March 1890.

The Destruction of our Canals', *Reynolds's Newspaper*, 4 November 1894.

'Flood Damage on Calder and Hebble Canal', *Examiner* Live, 4 January 2016, *https://www.examinerlive.co.uk/incoming/gallery/flood-damage-calder-hebble-canal-10685492* (accessed 1 August 2022).

'Five terminals, limitless solutions', Manchester Ship Canal (2022), *https://www.peelports.com/our-ports/manchester-ship-canal* (accessed 1 August 2022).

'Foreign Intelligence', *John Bull*, 13 November 1886.

'History of the Sankey Canal', *Pennine Waterways, http://www.pennine waterways.co.uk/sankey/sa2.htm* (accessed 1 August 2022).

'An Indian Conjuror', *The Boy's Own Paper*, 4 November 1899.

'The Longest Bicycle Ride Ever Attempted', *The Boy's Own Paper*, 11 November 1899.

'Miners' Strike Near Wigan', *Sheffield Daily Telegraph*, 23 August 1895.

'On the Canal', *Household Words*, 11–25 September 1858.

'Paint up – Aboriginal Dance', *Australian Museum* (2018), *https://australianmuseum.net.au/about/history/exhibitions/body-art/paint-up-aboriginal-dance/* (accessed 1 August 2022).

'Sending Coal to Wigan', *Hull Daily Mail*, 1 November 1893.

'A Stirring Life-Story', *Boy's Own Paper*, 25 January 1879.

'Tenting as a Holiday for Boys', *Boy's Own Paper*, 28 October 1899.

'Women want canal work', *Hull Daily Mail*, 2 April 1941.

Adams, M., *The Waterways Girls* (London: Arrow, 2017).

Adams, M., *Love on the Waterways* (London: Arrow, 2018).

Adams, M., *Hope on the Waterways* (London: Arrow, 2018).

Aikin, J. and A. L., *Miscellaneous Pieces in Prose* (London: Johnson, 1773).

Aikin, J., *Essay on the Application of Natural History to Poetry* (Warrington: Eyres, 1777).

Aikin, J., *A Description of the Country from Thirty to Forty Miles round Manchester* (London: John Stockdale, 1795).

Anderson, B., 'Affective Materialism', *Dialogues in Human Geography* 8/2 (2018), 229–31.

Anderson, B., *Encountering Affect: Capacities, Apparatuses, Conditions* (London: Routledge, 2017).

Anton, Á. D. et al., 'Geochemical recovery of the Torna-Marcal river system after the Ajka red mud spill, Hungary', *Environmental Science: Processes and Impacts* 16 (2014), 2677–85.

Archer, R., *The Narrowboat Girls* (London: Quercus, 2018).

Austen, J., *Persuasion*, ed. Patricia Meyer Spacks (London and New York: Norton, 1995).

Babaee, R., 'An Interview with David Dabydeen on Literature and Politics', *International Journal of Comparative Literature and Translation Studies* 4/3 (2016), 73–5.

Babbs, H., *Adrift: A Secret Life of London's Waterways* (London: Icon, 2016).

Bagwell, P., *The Transport Revolution 1770–1985* (London: Routledge, 1988).

Balfour-Paul, G., 'Britain's Informal Empire in the Middle East', in Judith Brown (ed.), *The Oxford History of the British Empire* (Oxford University Press, 2001), pp. 490–514.

Barbauld, A. L., *Poems* (London: Joseph Johnson, 1773).

Barbauld, A. L., *Eighteen Hundred and Eleven, A Poem* (London: Johnson, 1812).

Barnard, T., *Anna Seward: A Constructed Life, A Critical Biography* (Farnham: Ashgate, 2009).

Bell, J., 'Working Pair', *Waterlines: Canal and River Poetry, https://waterlines. org.uk/poems* (accessed 1 August 2022).

Berlant, L., *The Female Complaint: The Unfinished Business of Sentimentality in American Culture* (Durham, NC: Duke University Press, 2008).

Bhattacharya, R., *The Sly Company of People Who Care* (London: Picador, 2011).

Black, W., *The Strange Adventures of a House-Boat* (London: Sampson Low, 1893).

Blair, J., *Waterways and Canal-Building in Medieval England* (Oxford University Press, 2008).

Booth, S., *Drowned Lives* (London: Sphere, 2020).

Borlik, T., 'Iron Age as Renaissance Anthropocene: Periodization and the Ecology of War in Shakespearean History', *Early Modern Culture* 13 (2018), 115–26.

Boucher, C. T. G., *James Brindley, Engineer 1716–1772* (Norwich: Goose, 1968).

Boughey, J., 'From Transport's Golden Ages to an Age of Tourism: L.T.C. Rolt, Waterway Revival and Railway Preservation in Britain, 1944–54', *The Journal of Transport History* 34/1 (2013), 22–38.

Bowerbank, S., 'Seward, Anna [*called* the Swan of Lichfield] (1742– 1809)', *Oxford Dictionary of National Biography* (Oxford University Press, 2004).

Bowles, B. O. L., Kaaristo, M. and Rogelja Caf, N., 'Dwelling on and with water – materialities, (im)mobilities and meanings', *Anthropological Notebooks* 25/2 (2019), 5–12.

Bowles, B. O. L., 'Dwelling, Pollution and the Rhetorical Creation of "Nature" on Inland Waterways', in Chryssanthi Papadopoulou, *The Culture of Ships and Maritime Narratives* (London: Routledge, 2019), pp. 77–93.

Bradley, S., *The Railways: Nation, Network and People* (London: Profile, 2015).

Brantlinger, P., *Dark Vanishings: Discourse on the Extinction of Primitive Races, 1800–1930* (Ithaca, NY and London: Cornell University Press, 2003).

British Lichen Society, *Lichenicolous fungi occurring on* Xanthoria pari- etina *in the United Kingdom* (London, 2020).

Broadhead, I., 'When things go bump . . . the Tunnel Ghost', *North- amptonshire and Bedfordshire Life*, January 1980. Reproduced at *http://www.blisworth.org.uk/images/Tunnel1982/Ghost/ghost-stories. htm* (accessed 1 August 2022).

Broglio, R., *Technologies of the Picturesque: British Art, Poetry and Instruments, 1750–1830* (Lewisburg: Bucknell University Press, 2008).

Brown, C. M., *Aquinas and the Ship of Theseus: Solving Puzzles About Material Objects* (London and New York: Continuum, 2005).

Burton, A., *The Canal Builders* (Stroud: Tempus, 2005).

Burroughs, R., 'Travel Writing and Rivers', in Nandini Das and Tim Youngs (eds), *The Cambridge History of Travel Writing* (Cambridge University Press, 2019), pp. 330–44.

Calloway, C., *White People, Indians and Highlanders: Tribal Peoples and Colonial Encounters in Scotland and America* (Oxford University Press, 2008).

Campbell, N., *Navigations* (Glenrothes: Happenstance, 2020).

Carter, A., 'Dwale: an anaesthetic from old England', *BMJ* 319/1623 (1999).

Cartwright, A., *The Cut* (London: Peirene, 2017).

Chakrabarty, D., 'The Climate of History: Four Theses', *Critical Inquiry* 35/2 (2009), 197–222.

Chen, C., MacLeod, J. and Neimanis, A. (eds), *Thinking With Water* (Montreal and Kingston: McGill-Queen's University Press, 2013).

Clement, A. et al., 'The Environmental and Geomorphological Impacts of Historical Gold Mining in the Ohinemuri and Waihou River Catchments, Coromandel, New Zealand', *Geomorphology*, 295 (2017), 159–75.

Clough, P. T. with Halley, J. (eds), *The Affective Turn: Theorizing the Social* (Durham, NC: Duke University Press).

Cobden, R., *England, Ireland, and America* (London: Ridgway, 1835), 3rd edn.

Coffey, D., 'Protecting the Botanic Garden: Seward, Darwin, and Coalbrookdale', *Women's Studies* 31/2 (2002), 141–64.

Coghlan, T., 'The Canal Adonis and the Idle Woman', *Canals, Rivers + Boats* (April 2013).

Cohn, E., 'Affect', *Victorian Literature and Culture* 46/3–4 (2018), 563–7.

Cole, S., 'Space into Time: English Canals and English Landscape Painting 1760–1835' (unpublished PhD thesis, Columbia, 2013).

Collings, T. C., 'A B. O. P. Chat with Clement Hill, Australia's Champion Batsman', *Boy's Own Paper*, 14 October 1899.

Copeland, R., *Wedgwood Ware* (Botley: Shire, 1995).

Corble, N., *James Brindley: The First Canal Builder* (Stroud: Tempus, 2005).

Cornish, M., *Troubled Waters: Memoirs of a Canal Boatwoman* (London: Robert Hale, 1987).

Costello, I., 'Writers on Location – Kerry Hadley-Pryce on the Black Country', *The Literary Sofa*, 19 June 2018, *https://literarysofa.com/2018/06/19/5924/* (accessed 1 August 2022).

Costlow, J., Haila, Y., and Rosenholm, A. (eds), *Water in Social Imagination: from Technological Optimism to Contemporary Environmentalism* (Leiden and Boston: Brill Rodopi, 2017).

Couchman, D., *Afloat* (London: Quadrille, 2019).

Cro, S., *Noble Savage: Allegory of Freedom* (Waterloo, ON: Wilfrid Laurier University Press, 1990).

Crocco, F., 'The Colonial Subtext of Anna Letitia Barbauld's "Eighteen Hundred and Eleven"', *The Wordsworth Circle* 42/2 (2010), 91–4.

Crompton, G. W., 'Canals and the Industrial Revolution', *The Journal of Transport History* 14.2 (1993): 93–110.

Dabydeen, D., *Our Lady of Demerara* (Leeds: Peepal Tree, 2008).

Darwin, E., *The Botanic Garden* (Menston: Scholar Press, 1973).

Darwin, E., *The Temple of Nature*, ed. Martin Priestman, *Romantic Circles* electronic edition (2006), *https://www.rc.umd.edu/editions/darwin_temple* (accessed 1 August 2022).

Darwin, E., *Poems of Lichfield and Derby*, ed. Desmond King-Hele and Stuart Harris (Sheffield: Stuart Harris, 2011)

Davies, A., *The Wigan Coalfield* (Stroud: Tempus, 2000).

Davies, R. H., *Canal Crimes* (Stroud: Amberley, 2010).

Dean, M., *A Different Point of View: Sara Jeannette Duncan* (Montreal: McGill-Queen's University Press, 1991).

Deane-Drummond, C., 'Rivers at the End of Nature: Ethical Trajectories of the Anthropocene Grand Narrative', in Jason M. Kelly et al. (eds), *Rivers of the Anthropocene* (Oakland, CA: University of California Press), pp. 55–62.

Derrida, J., *Writing and Difference*, trans. Alan Bass (London and New York: Routledge, 2003).

Devine, H. C., 'Roughing it on the Thames', *Boy's Own Paper*, 11 November 1899.

Dick, M. M., 'Discourses for the new industrial world: industrialisation and the education of the public in late eighteenth–century Britain', *History of Education* 37/4 (2008), 567–84.

Dickens, C., *Dombey and Son* (London: Bradbury and Evans, 1848).

Dolan, B., *Josiah Wedgwood: Entrepreneur to the Enlightenment* (London: HarperCollins, 2004).

Dolphijn R. and van der Tuin, I., *New Materialism: Interviews and Cartographies* (Ann Arbor, MI: Open Humanities Press, 2012).

Drury, J., 'Literature and Science in Enlightenment Britain: New Directions', *Literature Compass* 14 (2017).

Dumett, R., 'Africa's Strategic Minerals During the Second World War', *Journal of African History* 26 (1985), 381–408.

Duncan, S. J./Cotes, V. C., *Two Girls on a Barge* (London: Chatto and Windus, 1891).

Duncan, S. J., *An American Girl in London* (London: Chatto and Windus, 1891).

Duncan, S. J., *The Imperialist* (London: Archibald Constable, 1904).

Dutton, J., *The Water Gypsies: A History of Life on Britain's Rivers and Canals: A History of Life on Britain's Rivers and Canals* (Cheltenham: The History Press, 2021).

Eden, E., *Up the Country: Letters Written to her Sister from the Upper Provinces of India*, new edn (London: Bentley, 1867).

Edensor, T., *Industrial Ruins: Space, Aesthetics and Materiality* (Oxford: Berg, 2005).

Eklund, H. (ed.), *Ground-Work: English Renaissance Literature and Soil Science* (Pittsburgh, PA: Duquesne University Press, 2017).

Eliot, G., *Felix Holt: The Radical*, ed. Lynda Mugglestone (London: Penguin, 1995).

Engdahl, W., *Century of War: Anglo-American Oil Politics and the New World Order* (London: Pluto Press, 2004).

Evenden, M., 'Aluminum, Commodity Chains, and the Environmental History of the Second World War', *Environmental History* 16/1 (2011), 69–93.

Eyre, F. and Hadfield, C., *English Rivers and Canals* (London: Collins, 1945).

Fairey, F. C. B., 'The Voyage of the Evangelist Canoe', *The Boy's Own Paper*, 29 July 1882–16 September 1882.

Fairhurst, R., 'Pioneer Paddlers', *Waterways World*, December 2016, 48–51.

Fairhurst, R. 'Two Girls on a Barge', *Waterways World*, March 2017, 62–5.

Farley, P. and Symmons Roberts, M., *Edgelands: Journeys into England's True Wilderness* (London: Vintage, 2012).

Feller, F., 'Alligator-Shooting in Florida', *Boy's Own Paper*, 14 October 1899.

Ferber, M., *A Dictionary of Literary Symbols*, 2nd edn (Cambridge University Press, 2007).

Ferguson, M., *First Feminists: British Women Writers, 1578–1799* (Bloomington, IN: Indiana University Press, 1985).

Fielding, P., '"Usurpt by Cyclops": Rivers, Industry, and Environment in Eighteenth-Century Poetry', in Evan Gottlieb and Juliet Shields (eds), *Representing Place in British Literature and Culture, 1660–1830: From Local to Global* (Farnham and Burlington, VT: Ashgate, 2013), pp. 139–54.

Fitch, E. and Easteal, P., 'Proposed Closures of Remote Australian Aboriginal Communities: Dispossession without Free and Informed Consent and Legal Remedies for Appealing Government Budget Decisions', *Australian Journal of Human Rights* 22/1 (2016), 85–110.

Fletcher, L., *Historical Romance Fiction: Heterosexuality and Performativity* (London: Routledge, 2016).

Fowler, A., *Hidden Nature: A Voyage of Discovery* (London: Hodder and Stoughton, 2017).

Fowler, M., *Redney: A Life of Sara Jeannette Duncan* (Toronto: Anansi, 1983).

Freeth, J., *The Political Songster* (Birmingham: Baskerville, 1771).

Gagnier, R., 'Cultural Philanthropy, Gypsies, and Interdisciplinary Scholars: Dream of a Common Language'. *19: Interdisciplinary Studies in the Long Nineteenth Century*, 1 (2005).

Gayford, E., *The Amateur Boatwomen* (Harrow: Belmont, 2008).

Gavin, A. and Humphries, A., *Transport in British Fiction: Technologies of Movement, 1840–1940* (Houndmills: Palgrave, 2015).

Gendron, R. S., Ingulstad, M. and Storli, E. (eds), *Aluminum Ore: The Political Economy of the Global Bauxite Industry* (Vancouver and Toronto: UBC Press, 2013).

Giles, M., 'Making Metal and Forging Relations: Ironworking in the British Iron Age', *Oxford Journal of Archaeology* 26/4 (2007), pp. 395–413.

Gilroy, P., *The Black Atlantic: Modernity and Double Consciousness* (Cambridge, MA: Harvard University Press, 1993).

Gehrke, J., 'Countryside, Recreation, and the Transformation of Canals in Britain in the Mid-Twentieth Century', *Journal of Tourism History* 11/2 (2019), 167–86.

Gökay, B., 'Oil, war and geopolitics from Kosovo to Afghanistan', *Journal of Southern Europe and the Balkans*, 4/1 (2002), 5–13.

Goodman, P., '"Patriotic Femininity": Women's Morals and Men's Morale During the Second World War', *Gender and History* 10/2 (1998), 278–93.

Goodridge, J., 'Hell, Hull, and Halifax: John Dyer Visits the Workhouse', *Literature & History* 21/2 (2012), 1–15.

Gooley, T., *How to Read Water: Clues and Patterns from Puddles to the Sea* (London: Sceptre, 2017).

Gordon, W., 'International Powers: Energy and Progress in *Dark Princess* and *Black Empire*', *American Quarterly* 72/3 (2020), 581–602.

Green, M., *A Sister's War* (London: Avon, 2021).

Greene, G., *Journey Without Maps* (London: Vintage, 2006).

Griffee, A., *Canal Pushers* (Leominster: Orphans, 2019).

Gutmann, M., 'The Nature of Total War: Grasping the Global Environmental Dimensions of World War II', *History Compass* 13/5 (2015), 251–61.

Hadfield, C., *British Canals: An Illustrated History* (London: Phoenix, 1950).

Hadfield, C., *The Canal Age* (Newton Abbott: David and Charles, 1968).

Hadfield, C., *World Canals: Inland Navigation Past and Present* (Newton Abbott: David and Charles, 1986).

Hadley-Pryce, K., *Gamble* (Cromer: Salt, 2018).

Hammill, F., 'Round the World without a Man: Feminism and Decadence in Sara Jeannette Duncan's *A Social Departure*', *The Yearbook of English Studies* 34 (2004), 112–26.

Hanlon, H. M., Bernie, D., Carigi, G. and Lowe, J. A., 'Future Changes to High Impact Weather in the UK', *Climatic Change* 166/50 (2021).

Hannavy, J., *Wigan: History and Guide* (Stroud: Tempus, 2003).

Harvey-Fishenden, A., Macdonald, N. and Bowen, J. P. 'Dry weather fears of Britain's early "industrial" canal network', *Regional Environmental Change* 19 (2019), 2325–37.

Hassell, J., *Tour of the Grand Junction* (London: n. pub., 1819).

Hately-Broad, B., and Moore, B., 'Idle Women: Challenging Gender Stereotypes on Britain's Inland Waterways During the Second World War', in Maggie Andrews and Janis Lomas (eds), *The Home Front in Britain: Images, Myths and Forgotten Experiences since 1914* (Houndmills: Palgrave, 2014), pp. 201–16.

Hayman, R., 'The Shropshire Wrought-Iron Industry *c.*1600–1900: A Study of Technological Change' (unpublished PhD thesis, University of Birmingham, 2003).

Heringman, N., *Romantic Rocks, Aesthetic Geology* (Ithaca, NY and London: Cornell University Press, 2004).

Hill, T., 'From Packhorse to Railway: Changing Transport Systems from the Seventeenth to the Nineteenth Centuries and their Impact upon

Trade and Industry in the Shropshire Area' (unpublished PhD thesis, University of Leicester, 1998).

Hodder, E., *John MacGregor ("Rob Roy")* (London: Hodder, 1894).

Hoegh-Guldberg, O. et al., 'Impacts of 1.5°C global warming on natural and human systems' in *Global warming of 1.5°C. An IPCC Special Report on the impacts of global warming of 1.5°C above pre-industrial levels and related global greenhouse gas emission pathways, in the context of strengthening the global response to the threat of climate change, sustainable development, and efforts to eradicate poverty.* 2018. *https:// www.ipcc.ch/sr15/* (accessed 1 August 2022).

Hofkosh, S., 'Materiality, Affect, Event: Barbauld's Poetics of the Everyday', in William McCarthy and Olivia Murphy (eds), *Anna Letitia Barbauld: New Perspectives* (Lewisburg: Bucknell University Press, 2013), pp. 80–102.

Hoffman, P. T., 'The Great Divergence: Why Britain Industrialised First', *Australian Economic History Review* 60/2 (2020), 126–47.

Hollister, L., 'The Green and the Black: Ecological Awareness and the Darkness of Noir', *PMLA* 134/5 (2019), 1012–27.

Holmes, R., *The Age of Wonder: How the Romantic Generation Discovered the Beauty and Terror of Science* (London: HarperCollins, 2008).

Horsley, L., *The Noir Thriller* (Houndmills: Palgrave, 2001).

Horwell, V., 'Sonia Rolt obituary', *Guardian*, 31 October 2014.

Howard, E. J., *Three Miles Up and Other Strange Stories* (Leyburn: Tartarus, 2003).

Hubbard, P. and Wilkinson, E., 'Walking a Lonely Path: Gender, Landscape and "New Nature Writing"', *Cultural Geographies* 26/2 (2019), 253–61.

Huenemann, K., 'The Authorship of *Two Girls on a Barge* (1891), Reassessed', *Papers of the Bibliographical Society of Canada* 58 (2021), 145–53.

Huggan, G., 'Back to the future: the "new nature writing", ecological boredom, and the recall of the wild', *Prose Studies* 38/2 (2016), 152–71.

Hughes, V., 'Through Canal-land in a Canadian Canoe', *Boy's Own Paper*, October 1899.

Hunt, T., *The Radical Potter: Josiah Wedgwood and the Transformation of Britain* (London: Allen Lane, 2021).

Hurley, R., Rothwell, J. and Woodward, J., 'Metal contamination of bed sediments in the Irwell and upper Mersey catchments, northwest England: exploring the legacy of industry and urban growth', *Journal of Soils and Sediments*, 17/11 (2017), 2648–65.

Hurstfield, J., *The Control of Raw Materials* (London: HMSO, 1953).

Huxtable, R. J., 'On the nature of Shakespeare's cursed hebona', *Perspectives in Biology and Medicine* 36/2 (1993), 262–80.

Imperial War Museum sound collection. Lyn E. Smith interviewing Margaret Cornish Ridout, 18 April 2002. Catalogue number 23089.

Jackson, E., 'Voyeurism or Social Criticism? Women and Sexuality in David Dabydeen's *The Intended, The Counting House* and *Our Lady of Demerara*', *Women: A Cultural Review* 26/4 (2015), 427–42.

Jagoda, P., *Network Aesthetics* (Chicago University Press, 2016).

Jamie, K., 'A Lone Enraptured Male', *London Review of Books* 30/5 (2008).

Jardine, L., *Ingenious Pursuits: Building the Scientific Revolution* (London: Abacus, 2000).

Jeans, J. S., *Waterways and Water Transport in Different Countries* (London: Spon, 1890).

Jones, P., *Industrial Enlightenment: Science, Technology and Culture in Birmingham and the West Midlands, 1760–1820* (Manchester University Press, 2008).

Kennedy, D., *The Last Blank Spaces: Exploring Africa and Australia* (Cambridge, MA and London: Harvard University Press, 2013).

Ker, D., 'A Bold Climber or, For an Empire', *Boy's Own Paper*, 7 October 1899.

King-Hele, D., *Erasmus Darwin and Evolution* (Sheffield: Stuart Harris, 2014).

Konishi, S., Nugent, M and Shellam, T., 'Exploration archives and indigenous histories: an introduction', *Indigenous Intermediaries: New Perspectives on Exploration Archives* (Canberra: ANU Press, 2015), pp. 1–10.

Kovacevich, I., 'The Mechanical Muse: The Impact of Technical Inventions on Eighteenth-Century Neoclassical Poetry', *Huntingdon Library Quarterly* 28/3 (1965), 263–81.

Latour, B., *Reassembling the Social: An Introduction to Actor-Network-Theory* (Oxford University Press, 2005).

Lawrence, L., Davies, P., and Turnbull, J., 'The Archaeology of Anthropocene Rivers: Water Management and Landscape Change in "Gold Rush" Australia', *Antiquity* 90/353 (2016), 1348–62.

Lee, K. and Matthews, J., 'Romani Rebel Writing: George "Lazzy" Smith's Entrepreneurial Auto-Exoticism', in Lauren O'Hagan (ed.), *Rebellious Writing: Contesting Marginalisation in Edwardian Britain* (Bern: Peter Lang, 2020).

Levine, C., *Forms: Whole, Rhythm, Hierarchy, Network* (Princeton University Press, 2015).

Levitt, D. and Kommenda, N., 'Is Climate Change Making Hurricanes Worse?', *The Guardian*, 10 October 2018, *https://www.theguardian.com/weather/ng-interactive/2018/sep/11/atlantic-hurricanes-are-storms-getting-worse* (accessed 1 August 2022).

Linton, J., *What is Water? The History of a Modern Abstraction* (Vancouver and Toronto: UBC Press, 2010).

Livingstone, D., *Missionary Travels and Researches in South Africa* (London: Murray, 1857).

Livingstone, J. D., 'Travels in Fiction: Baker, Stanley, Cameron and the Adventure of African Exploration', *Journal of Victorian Culture* 23/1 (2018), 64–85.

Liu, A., English 238: Critical Infrastructure Studies (Fall 2018), *https://alanyliu.org/course/english-238-critical-infrastructure-studies-fall-2018/* (accessed 1 August 2022).

Luke, C. (dir.), *The Black Safari* (BBC, 1972).

McCarthy, W., *Anna Letitia Barbauld: Voice of the Enlightenment* (Baltimore: Johns Hopkins University Press, 2008).

McCutcheon, W. A., 'The Newry Navigation: The Earliest Inland Canal in the British Isles', *The Geographical Journal*, 129/4 (1963), 466–80.

Macdonald, G., 'Research Note: The Resources of Fiction', *Reviews in Cultural Theory* 4/2 (2013), 1–24.

MacGregor, J., *A Thousand Miles in the Rob Roy Canoe on Rivers and Lakes of Europe*, 7th edn (Boston, MA: Roberts, 1871).

MacGregor, J., *The Rob Roy on the Jordan* (London: Murray, 1869).

McGeorge, Chris, *Now You See Me* (London: Orion, 2019).

McIvor, L. *Canals: The Making of a Nation* (London: BBC Books, 2015).

McMillin, T. S., *The Meaning of Rivers: Flow and Reflection in American Literature* (Iowa City: University of Iowa Press, 2011).

McNeir, L., *Getaway with Murder* (2000).

McNicholas Smith, K., and Tyler, I., 'Lesbian brides: post-queer popular culture', *Feminist Media Studies*, 17/3 (2017).

Mabey, R., *The Unofficial Countryside* (Toller Fratrum: Little Toller Books, 2010).

Malet, H., *Bridgewater: The Canal Duke, 1736–1803* (Manchester University Press, 1977).

Malm, A., *Fossil Capital: The Rise of Steam Power and the Roots of Global Warming* (London and New York: Verso, 2016).

Mantell, G., *The Wonders of Geology* (London: Relfe and Fletcher, 1838).

Marrs, C., 'Dickinson in the Anthropocene', *ESQ: A Journal of Nineteenth-Century American Literature and Culture* 63/2 (2017), 201–25.

Martin, F., *Murder on the Oxford Canal* (London: Joffe, 2020).

Marzec, R., 'Reflections on the Anthropocene Dossier', *MFS Modern Fiction Studies* 64/4 (2018), 585–616.

Mathias, P., *The First Industrial Nation: An Economic History of Britain, 1700–1914* (London: Methuen, 1969).

Mathieson, C., *Mobility in the Victorian Novel: Placing the Nation* (Houndmills: Palgrave, 2015).

Matthews, J., 'Canals in nineteenth-century literary history', in David Turner (ed.), *Transport and its Place in History* (London: Routledge, 2020).

Matthews, J., *The Gypsy Woman: Representation in Literature and Visual Culture* (London: I. B. Tauris, 2018).

Matthews, J., 'Mobilising the Imperial Uncanny: Nineteenth-Century Textual Attitudes to Travelling Romani People, Canal-Boat People, Showpeople and Hop-Pickers in Britain', *Nineteenth-Century Contexts* 37/4 (2015), 359–75.

Matthews, J., 'Thousands of these floating hovels: Picturing Bargees in Image and Text', *Nineteenth-Century Contexts* 35/2 (2013), 121–42.

Maw, P., Wyke, T. and Kidd, A., 'Canals, Rivers, and the Industrial City: Manchester's Industrial Waterfront, 1790–1850', *Economic History Review* 65/4 (2012), 1495–523.

Mayhew, M., *The Boat Girls* (London: Bantam, 2007).

Meade, L. T., *Water Gipsies: A Story of Canal Life in England* (London: Shaw, 1883).

Menely T. and Taylor, J. O., *Anthropocene Reading: Literary History in Geologic Times* (University Park: Pennsylvania State University Press, 2017).

Mentz, S., *Shipwreck Modernity: Ecologies of Globalization, 1550–1719* (Minneapolis: University of Minnesota Press, 2015).

Middleton, N., *Rivers: A Very Short Introduction* (Oxford University Press, 2012).

Miller, E. C., *Extraction Ecologies and the Literature of the Long Exhaustion* (Princeton University Press, 2021).

Milman, O., Severe drought threatens Hoover dam reservoir – and water for US west', *The Guardian*, 13 July 2021.

Minihane, J., 'Anatomy of a green riverbank', *Waterfront* 10 (2019).

Mitchell, B. R., *British Historical Statistics* (Cambridge University Press, 1988).

Moens, W. J. C., *The Voyage of the Steam-yacht 'Ytene' through France and Belgium by River and Canal* (London: n.p., 1876).

Moers, E., *Literary Women* (London: W. H. Allen, 1977).

Moran, J., 'A Cultural History of the New Nature Writing', *Literature & History* 23/1 (2014), 49–63.

Morris, B., *Protests, Land Rights and Riots: Postcolonial Struggles in Australia in the 1980s* (Oxford: berghahn, 2015).

Morton, T., *Dark Ecology: For a Logic of Future Coexistence* (New York: Columbia University Press, 2016).

Neimanis, A., *Bodies of Water: Posthuman Feminist Phenomenology* (London and Oxford: Bloomsbury, 2017).

Norbury, K., *The Fish Ladder* (London: Bloomsbury Circus, 2015).

Norbury, K., 'The Top 10 Books about Rivers', *The Guardian*, 18 February 2015. *https://www.theguardian.com/books/2015/feb/18/top-10-books-about-rivers-katharine-norbury* (accessed 1 August 2022).

Nord, D. E., *Gypsies and the British Imagination, 1807–1930* (New York: Columbia University Press, 2006).

O'Connor, R., 'Hyena-Hunting And Byron-Bashing In The Old North: William Buckland, Geological Verse And The Radical Threat', in Ben Marsden, Hazel Hutchison, Ralph O'Connor (eds), *Uncommon Contexts: Encounters between Science and Literature, 1800–1914* (University of Pittsburgh Press, 2016), pp. 55–82.

Oakley, K., Ward, J. and Christie, I., 'Engaging the Imagination: "New Nature Writing", Collective Politics and the Environmental Crisis', *Environmental Values* 27/6 (2018), 687–705.

Orr, B., '"Maui and Orphic Blood": Cook's Death in Contemporary Maori Poetry', *The Eighteenth Century* 49/2 (2008), 165–79.

Otter, C. et al., 'Roundtable: The Anthropocene in British History', *Journal of British Studies* 57 (2018), 568–96.

Oxley, K., 'The archive collection of John "Rob Roy" MacGregor', *Royal Museums Greenwich* (2022), *https://www.rmg.co.uk/stories/blog/archive-collection-john-rob-roy-macgregor* (accessed 1 August 2022).

Pascoe, B., *Dark Emu: Black Seeds, Agriculture or Accident* (Broome: Magabala, 2014).

Pearse, M. G., *Rob Rat: A Story of Barge Life* (London: Wesleyan Conference Office, 1879).

Penner, E., 'Masculinity, Morality, and National Identity in the *Boy's Own Paper*, 1879–1913' (unpublished PhD thesis, De Montfort University, 2016).

Perchard, A., "'Of the Highest Imperial Importance": British Strategic Priorities and the Politics of Colonial Bauxite, ca. 1916–1958', in Gendron et al. (eds), *Aluminum Ore*, pp. 53–78.

Philips, D., *Women's Fiction: From 1945 to Today* (London: Bloomsbury, 2006).

Phillips, J., *A General History of Inland Navigation*, 4th edn (London: Baldwin, 1803).

Pitt Scott, H., 'Offshore Mysteries, Narrative Infrastructure: Oil, Noir, and the World-Ocean', *Humanities* 9/3 (2020).

Pomeranz, K., *The Great Divergence: China, Europe, and the Making of the Modern World Economy* (Princeton University Press, 2000).

Porter, B., *The Absent-Minded Imperialists: Empire, Society and Culture in Britain* (Oxford University Press, 2004).

Prothero, D. R., *The Story of the Earth in 25 Rocks: Tales of Important Geological Puzzles and the People Who Solved Them* (New York: Columbia University Press, 2018).

Pye, H. J., *Faringdon Hill: A Poem in Two Books*, 2nd edn. (Oxford: Daniel Prince, 1778).

Quayle, A., Sonn, C. C. and van den Eynde, J., 'Narrating the Accumulation of Dispossession: Stories of Aboriginal Elders', *Community Psychology in Global Perspective* 2/2 (2016), 79–96.

Radcliffe, F., *Union Clues* (2020).

Reade, A., *Life in the Cut* (London: Swann, Sonnenschein, Lowry, 1888).

Ridgway, N., *Memories of a Wartime Canal Boatwoman*, ed. Mike Clarke and Timothy Peters (Ellesmere Port: National Waterways Museum, 2014).

Roberts, L., 'Taking up space: Community, belonging and gender among itinerant boat-dwellers on London's waterways', *Anthropological Notebooks* 25/2 (2019), 57–69.

Rocha, M., et al., Historical Responsibility for Climate Change – from countries emissions to contribution to temperature increase, *Climate Analytics* (2015), *https://climateanalytics.org/media/historical_responsibility_report_nov_2015.pdf* (accessed 1 August 2022).

Rogers, A., 'Water and the Urban Fabric: A Study of Towns and Waterscapes in the Roman Period in Britain', *International Journal of Nautical Archaeology* 41/2 (2012), 327–39.

Rogers, N., Castree, N. and Kitchin, R., 'Anthropocene', in *A Dictionary of Human Geography* (Oxford University Press, 2013).

Rolt, L. T. C., *Narrow Boat* (Stroud: The History Press, 2014).

Rourke, L., *The Canal* (New York and London: Melville House, 2010).

St Pierre, M., 'Race, the Political Factor and the Nationalization of the Demerara Bauxite Company, Guyana', *Social and Economic Studies* 24/4 (1975), 481–503.

Sargent, J., *The Mine: A Dramatic Poem*, 2nd edn (London: Cadell, 1788).

Satchell, M., 'Navigable waterways and the economy of England and Wales: 1600–1835', *Online Historical Atlas of Transport, Urbanization and Economic Development in England and Wales c.1680–1911*, ed. L. Shaw-Taylor, D. Bogart and M. Satchell (2017), *www.campop.geog. cam.ac.uk/research/projects/transport/onlineatlas.*

Saunders, J., '"The Mouse's Petition": Anna Laetitia Barbauld and the Scientific Revolution', *The Review of English Studies* 53/212 (2002), 500–16.

Scerbo, R., et al., 'Lichen (Xanthoria parietina) biomonitoring of trace element contamination and air quality assessment in Pisa Province (Tuscany, Italy)', *Science of The Total Environment* 286/1–3 (2002), 27–40.

[Schofield, A. T.], *The Waterway to London, as explored in the "Wanderer" and "Ranger," with Sail, Paddle, and Oar, in a voyage on the Mersey, Perry, Severn, and Thames, and several canals* (London: Simkin Marshall, 1869).

Schweighofer, J., 'The Impact of Extreme Weather and Climate Change on Inland Waterway Transport', *Natural Hazards* 72/1 (2014).

Scott-Davies, A., *Death on the Waterways* (Stroud: The History Press, 2011).

Seshan, R., 'Representing Water: Travel Accounts, Water and the Constructions of Difference', *Water History* 7, 151–8.

Setzer, S., '"Pond'rous Engines" in "Outraged Groves": The Environmental Argument of Anna Seward's "Colebrook Dale"', *European Romantic Review* 18/1 (2007), 69–82.

Seward, A., 'Elegy on Captain Cook', *Digital Archives and Pacific Cultures, http://pacific.obdurodon.org/CookElegy1780.html* (accessed 1 August 2022).

Seward, A., *Original Sonnets on Various Subjects; and Odes Paraphrased from Horace* (London: Sael, 1799).

Seward, A., *The Poetical Works of Anna Seward*, ed. Walter Scott, 3 vols (Edinburgh: Ballantyne: 1810).

Singh, M., 'American west stuck in cycle of "heat, drought and fire", experts warn', *The Guardian*, 13 July 2021.

Sivagurunathan, S., 'A "Coolitudian" Caribbean Text: The Trajectory of Renewal in David Dabydeen's *Our Lady of Demerara*', in

D. A. Dunkley (ed.), *Readings in Caribbean History and Culture* (Lanham, ML: Lexington, 2011), pp. 167–82.

Smiles, S., *James Brindley and the Early Engineers* (London: Murray, 1864).

Smith, E., *Maidens' Trip* (London: Bloomsbury, 2011).

Smith, E., *As Green as Grass* (London: Bloomsbury, 2014).

Smith, G., *Canal Adventures by Moonlight* (London: Hodder and Stoughton, 1881).

Smith, J., 'An Archipelagic Literature: Re-Framing "The New Nature Writing"', *Green Letters* 17/1 (2013), 5–15.

Smith, J., *The New Nature Writing: Rethinking the Literature of Place* (London: Bloomsbury, 2018).

Spenser, E., 'The Shepheardes Calendar', *Renascence Editions* (1996; based on facsimile of the first edition, 1579). *http://www.luminarium.org/renascence-editions/shepheard.html* (accessed 1 August 2022).

Stephens, W. B., 'The Exeter Lighter Canal, 1566–1698', *Journal of Transport History* 3/1 (1957), 1–11.

Stevenson, R. L., *An Inland Voyage* (London: Chatto and Windus, 1913).

[Stockman, B. P.], *A Trip Through the Caledonian Canal* (London: n. pub., 1861).

Strang, V., 'Forum: What to do about "Flow"?', *Suomen Antropologi: Journal of the Finnish Anthropological Society* 2 (2014), 92–6.

Suart-Robson, I., 'A Thousand Days in the Arctic', *Boy's Own Paper*, 21 October 1899.

Suart-Robson, I., 'The Longest Bicycle Ride Ever Attempted', *Boy's Own Paper*, 11 November 1899.

Szeman, I., 'Conjectures on world energy literature: Or, what is petroculture?', *Journal of Postcolonial Writing* 53/3 (2017), 277–88.

Szerszynski, B., 'The Anthropocene Monument: On Relating Geological and Human Time', *European Journal of Social Theory* 20/1 (2017): 111–31.

Tann, J., 'James Watt (1736–1819)', *Oxford Dictionary of Literary Biography* (2014), *https://doi.org/10.1093/ref:odnb/28880* (accessed 1 August 2022).

Tann, J., 'Matthew Boulton (1728–1809)', *Oxford Dictionary of Literary Biography* (2013), *https://doi.org/10.1093/ref:odnb/2983* (accessed 1 August 2022).

Taylor, J. O., 'Anthropocene', *Journal of Victorian Literature and Culture* 46/3–4 (2018).

Thomson, J., *The Castle of Indolence: An Allegorical Poem Written in Imitation of Spenser* (London: Millar, 1747).

Thompson, A. O., 'Symbolic Legacies of Slavery in Guyana', *New West Indian Guide* 80/3–4 (2006), 191–220.

Thorpe, J., 'Ice – Just a Memory?' *Waterways World*, January 2003, 52–3.

Tidy, A., 'John Corbett the Salt Tycoon', *NarrowBoat*, Autumn 2019.

Tonna, C. E., *Helen Fleetwood* (London: Seeley and Burnside, 1841).

Trethewey, R. H., The Progressive Ideas of Anna Letitia Barbauld (unpublished PhD thesis, University of Exeter, 2013).

Trinder, B., *The Making of the Industrial Landscape* (London: Dent, 1982).

Trollope, A., *The Kellys and the O'Kellys* (Oxford University Press, 1978).

United Nations, 'Water and Gender', *https://www.unwater.org/water-facts/gender/* (accessed 1 August 2022).

Uglow, J., *The Lunar Men: The Friends who Made the Future* (London: Faber, 2002).

Ure, A., *The Cotton Manufacture of Great Britain* (London: Charles Knight, 1836), 2 vols.

Vedmore, M., 'A Rare Early Voyage', *Old Waterway Books*, 13 December 2016, *http://canalbookcollector.blogspot.com/2016/12/a-rare-early-voyage.html* (accessed 1 August 2022).

Wånggren, L., *Gender, Technology and the New Woman* (Edinburgh University Press, 2017).

Wallace, A. R., *The Wonderful Century* (New York: Dodd, Mead and Company, 1898).

Wallace-Wells, D., *The Uninhabitable Earth: A Story of the Future* (London: Allen Lane, 2019).

Walton, J. L. and Walton, S., 'Introduction to *Green Letters*: Crime Fiction and Ecology', *Green Letters* 22/1 (2018), 2–6.

Warkentin, G., 'Duncan [married name Cotes], Sara Jeannette (1861–1922), novelist and journalist', in *Oxford Dictionary of National Biography* (Oxford University Press, 2004).

Webster, W., *Mixing It* (Oxford University Press, 2018).

Wedgwood, J., *Letters of Josiah Wedgwood* (transcribed), Wedgwood Museum and Archive.

Wedgwood, J., 'Some experiments upon the ochra friabilis nigro susca of Da Costa, Hist. Foss. p. 102;. and called by the miners of Derbyshire, Black Wadd', *Philosophical Transactions of the Royal Society of London* 73, January 1783.

Weisman, A., 'Earth Without People', *Discover Magazine*, 6 February 2005, *https://www.discovermagazine.com/planet-earth/earth-without-people* (accessed 1 August 2022).

Whately, T., *Observations on Modern Gardening*. Fourth edn (London: Payne, 1777).

White, D. E., 'The "Joineriana": Anna Barbauld, the Aikin Family Circle, and the Dissenting Public Sphere', *Eighteenth-Century Studies* 32/4 (1999), 511–33.

White, W., *History, Gazetteer, and Directory of Leicestershire* (Sheffield: Robert Leader, 1846).

Wilkins, K., Driscoll, B. and Fletcher, L., *Genre Worlds: Popular Fiction and Twenty-first Century Book Culture* (Amherst and Boston: University of Massachusetts Press, 2022).

Wilson, A. N., *The Potter's Hand* (London: Atlantic, 2012).

Wilson, P. K., Dolan, E. A. and Dick, M. (eds), *Anna Seward's Life of Erasmus Darwin* (Studley: Brewin, 2010).

Wilson, S. A., 'Entitled as Against None: How the Wrongly Decided Croker Island Case Perpetuates Aboriginal Dispossession', *Pacific Rim Law and Policy Journal* 18/1 (2009), 249.

Winn, J., *Water Ways: A Thousand Miles Along Britain's Canals* (London: Profile, 2018).

Wolfe, S. E., 'Fear, Anger and Responsibility: The Emotional Content of Historical Speeches about Water and Water Policy', *Water History* 9/3 (2017), 317–36.

Wood, C. J., *The Duke's Cut: The Bridgewater Canal* (Stroud: Tempus, 2002).

Wood, C. V., 'Tender Heroes and Twilight Lovers: Re-Reading the Romance in Mass-Market Pulp Novels, 1950–1965', *Journal of Lesbian Studies* 18/4 (2014), 372–92

Woolf, V., *Orlando* (London: Penguin, 2016).

Woolfitt, S., *Idle Women* (Harrow: Belmont, 2001).

INDEX